MERCH AND THE WORLD OF PRINT ON DEMAND

By: Jacob Topping

First Print Edition (302 pages!!!)

This page is Intentionally left blank.

Legal Disclosures:

RISK WARNING: Attempting anything mentioned in this book may involve risk, both of TIME and MONEY. Attempting any of the strategies in the book are done at your own risk, and the authors cannot be held liable or responsible in any way for the resulting losses of any kind which may result. (For example: you decided to spend $10,000 on Facebook ads, and you get no sales... this is a risk you take). All strategies in this book carry a level of risk, so please know your own risk tolerance and use good judgement.

SLEEP WARNING: Many of the concepts and ideas contained in this book may cause you to become more excited than you can imagine, and may result in severe sleep loss. Exercise caution, and consult your health professionals as needed. ... personally I had to take sleeping aids in order to fall asleep, because I was so excited writing this book... but everyone's different. So be safe, and enjoy the book. ... and don't forget to sleep!

This book is an educational resource guide, and as such will connect you with many links to outside resources for additional information, and clarity. All of the outside links from this book are independently owned by their respective creators and rights owners, and a link from this book to any outside website, service, blog, newsletter, group, service, video, image, or any other form of content is not an endorsement of the outside source. Each of them can be found using an internet search engine, and they are not protected or otherwise secret information. Some of the links require application to view contents to, for example a closed Facebook group, requires entry to see some features. All of the permissions are the right of their respective rights owners, and a link to them does not grant users access, in the cases that access is needed.

This page is Intentionally left blank.

Table of Contents:

// Acknowledgements: People without whom this book would not likely become a reality...

Acknowledgements:

People without whom this book would not likely become a reality...

Thank you to the following people who have helped me along in my journey to this point, and provided insights and inspiration to me and others along the way:

Tara Topping
Jono Topping
Oliver Topping
Alexis Topping
Chris Green
Chris Wilkey
Stephen Harrison
Sean Zent
Jewel Tolentino
Venny Zhurkova
Mike Peterson
Marcy Mo
Monte Werle & Jacob Bates
Shawn Mayo
Alex Moss
Nate McCallister
Jason Brink
Travis Renn
Adam Black
Christopher Grant
Joshua Adams
Wayne and Katie Friesen

Preface:

What is this book?

Although this book is intended to provide a broad overview, there is in depth information included to be able to expand your business to new heights and areas you may have not previously considered. This book focuses on the multiple parts of ***Merch and the World of Print On Demand*** (henceforth referred to as **POD**).

Different people will use it in different ways. Some people might use it to add another layer to their existing POD business. For others, POD might be a new concept all together, and they might find it useful as a learning tool, as an option for additional business venture. Still others may use this book as a reference guide to solve specific questions, or possibly to clarify how or why to do something that they have heard about elsewhere, but never understood how it works, or why someone would do it that way. This book can be used in many ways, and is written for multiple audiences. For advanced POD sellers, some parts might seem very basic, and for other newer sellers, some parts might be absolutely mind blowing.

I sincerely hope that you enjoy this material, and that it provides you with great value. It was my intention when assembling this information, to provide maximum value, AND to put many aspects of the business in one convenient place. This will go beyond basic speaking points, or education, and be used as a resource as well that should save you *hours and hours* of reading and listening to gather. At the same time, you will notice that this book is filled with many many links outward. I have typed these out so that they are useful to those who have bought the book in print form, as well as "hot linked" the links, so that people who have this book in electronic form are able to click the links (or touch if you're on a touch based device), and be taken to more information (websites, videos, blogs, podcasts, and more!). This book does not cover everything, as "everything" is constantly changing. As time passes, so will some of the things described in this book (currently Q1 2018). I've done my best to provide a good snapshot of where things are at now, and I hope that the principles and strategies will be applicable far past the initial print runs of this book.
This book contains information which can be used to earn additional income, and outlines methods and services, some of which have costs, and some of which are free. Unless otherwise stated, all prices are in US dollars. I cannot *guarantee* that this book will make you money, should you attempt any of the ideas, processes, or strategies contained within.

However, I do very much hope that it adds tremendous value to you, and that you are able to greatly improve your earning potential as a result of the information provided (even if you're just getting started with Merch and the World of POD, or if you've a seasoned veteran of POD). I think there is a little bit of something for everyone.

Again, I really hope you enjoy this book, and that it provides you with the information you were looking for, and if I've done my job right, you may find even more than you expected, and you may even want to buy or gift copies for friends, family, coworkers, and/or clients.
If you bought this via Gumroad, the bonus files are part of your Gumroad purchase are located in your Gumroad account, in the library section.

Updates to both the book, the files, and additional treats will be pushed up into your Gumroad account, so check back periodically to see newer better versions, and content. These updates are all included with your purchase, and are my FREE gift to you. I hope you ***LOVE*** them ;-)

CHAPTER 1 - Introduction

What's in this book, and how it will help you.

Welcome to training for the world of Print On Demand, also called Merch (short for Merchandise). Within this book, you will find information about how the process works, a giant list of websites you can get started with today, people and places to find out more information from, and even tips and tricks to optimize platforms you might already be using.

That's right, you could make actual sales **TODAY!**

I will cover additional information about multiple aspects of Print On Demand. After learning the basics, we will delve into different ways people utilize and leverage this awesome opportunity. Included within: many websites which offer Print On Demand products (and information about them, to help you decide which to use or not use), how to drive different types of traffic, multiple methods on coming up with new design ideas, strategies for growing your POD business, resources to learn more, and communities of people to connect with. This book will definitely assist you in nearly every stage of selling online via Print On Demand. From getting you started, improving your current Print On Demand processes and workflow, to expanding your reach and options to consider in the future.

Be sure to notice that throughout the book there are notes (**NOTE:**...), and tips (**PRO TIP:**...). These are intended to draw your attention to things that might not be as obvious as they would seem. You may know many of these items already, but many more will be totally new to you.

After the main chapters, there are some other helpful sections, such as the glossary (great for learning more about the jargon used in this crazy POD world), appendixes (each designed to give you specific benefits, and can be used separate from the book itself), and files (links will be provided, in case the files were not provided via the method which you bought this book).

Now that you're one chapter in, you have a better idea of what's coming next ;-) Hold onto your SHIRTS, it's about to get crazy!

END OF CHAPTER 1

NOTE: The chapters are designed to accommodate people from all levels, from beginning to advanced, so the further into the book you go, the more complex it gets.

CHAPTER 2 - Overview of Print On Demand (POD)

POD - What is it, and how does it work?

The process we are about to unwrap is broadly called Print On Demand (POD), and it works like this:

HIGH LEVEL:
You have some art and/or design(s) you want people to see, buy and own it in a physical form. Print On Demand platforms allows you to show your art or designs to buyers online. When your buyers purchase your items, the Print On Demand platform(s) you've listed on creates the physical item and ships it to the customer.

Here's HOW Print On Demand makes it happen:
Step 1: MAKE AND UPLOAD YOUR DESIGN(S)
Step 2: PEOPLE BUY YOUR THINGS
Step 3: THE MAGIC HAPPENS
Step 4: YOU GET PAID

Step 1: MAKE AND UPLOAD YOUR DESIGN(S)
1. You create artwork and/or designs, and create a digital file for each item you wish to make available online.
2. You upload your digital artwork via an image file (usually a .png, but other file types can be used on many PODs) to the POD website, where you would like to offer it for sale.
NOTE: Each site has specifications about what file type and sort of minimum and maximum file size they accept, more on that later.
3. Once your image file is uploaded to the POD platform, you can choose the items you would like to make available to your buyers, for that design. Each site has different items and services available (T-shirts, hoodies, pillows, mugs, paper products, etc. more about these later). Each site also offers different options on each item (colors, variations, etc. also listed in more detail later).
4. Once your image file is uploaded, and your options and preferences are all setup, your item is now either A: available for sale, or B:sent for review. In situation B, after successful manual or automated review, the item becomes available for sale (different sites work slightly differently, more on this later).

BAM! Like that, your artwork is available for buyers to purchase!

Here's where it gets interesting...

Step 2: PEOPLE BUY YOUR THINGS
1. Buyers will find your items through a number of different ways (marketing, search, social media, and more).
2. From the items you have listed, your buyer will pick what they want, and how they want it.
3. The buyer purchases the item(s) that they like, using the site they're on, and wait for it to arrive on their doorstep.

Step 3: THE MAGIC HAPPENS
Once a buyer has completed their purchase, they're done and the magic begins...
1. First, the platform will likely send your buyer a confirmation email, to let them know they just bought something from you. Many will also send you an e-mail to let you know you made a sale. Exciting right?! YOU just made a sale!
2. The Print On Demand site BUILDS THE STUFF! *(From here on in, the item(s) your buyer bought will be called 'the stuff'.)* Yes, they make it! Your artwork, which YOU uploaded in Step1: MAKE AND UPLOAD YOUR DESIGN(S) up above... is turned into real physical goods. Another way to put it... before this point, the item you just sold DID NOT exist, now IT DOES exist.
3. Once the stuff the buyer just purchased is manufactured (made), the Print On Demand platform prepares the stuff for shipping, packs it up, and ships it to your buyer. Each service does this in it's own way (for example: some wait for a few days, and send out many items at once, some send them daily, they use different modes of shipping from courier to local postal services). Some POD platforms even outsource the manufacturing, depending on where in the world the order is being shipped to.

Step 4: YOU GET PAID

1. Each time a buyer buys your stuff, their money is split into the following:
    1. **MATERIALS and MANUFACTURING:**
       The base cost of the item they have bought.
       For example: when a t-shirt is bought: a t-shirt, the ink on the t-shirt, the packaging to pack the t-shirt, the wages to pay the people to operate the machines that are used to manufacture the t-shirt, and all the other costs associated with producing the item which was purchased.
    2. **LOGISTICS AND LISTING:**
       The warehousing of the factory your t-shirt is being made in, the

people running the platform you sold your item though (including their website, customer support service, security, payment processing, etc), the cost of the platform to market themselves and/or your product, the logistics of the platform getting all the items, etc.

3. **SHIPPING TO YOUR BUYER:**
   The cost to ship your stuff from the platform's manufacturing location, to your buyers (or to wherever the item is going, in the case of a gift / purchase for someone else).
4. **YOUR PIECE: aka - 'THE ROYALTIES' OR 'THE PROFITS' OR 'THE COMMISSIONS' OR 'THE DIFFERENCE IN RETAIL PRICE VS. WHOLESALE COST'**
   You receive a portion of the proceeds your buyer spent to buy the stuff. This could be either a fixed amount, a fixed percentage, or a variable amount, depending the platform. For Example: in Q4 2017, via the **Merch By Amazon** platform; the royalty paid on a 'one sided', 'front printed' design, 'Anvil t-shirt' which sold for $19.99USD to your buyer, paid you a royalty of $7.19USD (which happens to work out to 35.9% of the sale price), (minus any withholding tax, depending on how your account and business is setup with Amazon, and your jurisdiction, the withholding tax could be up to 30%, and is withheld from your royalty payment). Please note, in the example just given, although the total percentage paid is 35.9%, it is not calculated as a fixed percentage, so for example if the same shirt was listed for MORE - or LESS - you would not receive 35.9%, you would get MORE - or LESS - percentage; depending on the price of the shirt. More about these numbers later.
   NOTE: Merch By Amazon is well known for changing it's payout amount, this is typically communicated prior to price changes, however know that it can change at any time, see the terms of service of the platform you're using for more info.

2. As your stuff sells to buyers through each platform, your platform account balance grows. With each sale it goes up, and up!

3. Once your balance crosses a threshold OR after a certain period of time OR when you request a payout (depending on the platform), you are paid. Typically the payment is made to you either via Paypal (or Payoneer), OR via direct deposit to your bank account, OR by check. In the cases where the platform offers multiple payment choices, the choice is yours to make, and can often be changed if or as needed.

At this point in the book, hopefully you now have a great foundation of the basic processes of Print On Demand, also called Merch.

In the next chapter, we will cover what you need to get started. Followed by chapters on the various platforms which offer POD services.

END OF CHAPTER 2

CHAPTER 3 - Getting Started

The tools, and things you will need to get started

Now that we have a basic overview of the POD process from creating your designs, to uploading them to the POD platforms, to buyers purchasing your stuff, to you getting paid; lets talk about what is needed to get started.

The Basics:

1: SOMETHING TO MAKE YOUR ART / DESIGN
2: A WAY TO GET YOUR ART / DESIGN INTO AN IMAGE FILE
3: AN INTERNET CONNECTION

1: SOMETHING TO MAKE YOUR ART / DESIGN:
This can be a pencil and paper, a digital camera, art and canvas, pen and paper, a computer program, a smartphone app, your finger and beach sand, a stick and soft snow, a bottle of glitter and a glue-stick... whatever you want! Simply make the design that you want to upload and sell on the platform(s) of your choice. In fact you could even just use plain text (called a 'text based design')

2: A WAY TO GET YOUR ART / DESIGN INTO AN IMAGE FILE:
Typically this is done on a computer program, or app on your smartphone or tablet. Depending on how or what your design or artwork is, you might also need to take a picture, or capture the art or design first, before creating your image file.

3: AN INTERNET CONNECTION:
You will need access to an internet connection. This can be a home computer, smartphone, library computer, work computer, Wi-Fi enabled tablet, any device which allows you to connect to the POD platform.

With these basics above, you have everything you NEED to start making money with Merch, or Print On Demand!

Beyond the Basics:

Although you could make your design out of nearly any material, given that your design will be applied to various items for sale, typically through a printing method (multiple manufacturing types and processes discussed later), I recommend making your designs on either a computer, tablet, or smartphone. Here's why: you will be uploading your design to the POD platform(s) in an image file, so by starting with an image file, you reduce the number of steps between what you create, and the image file you upload. Print On Demand tends to work best with volume. So the more designs you have uploaded, the more likely it is that you will see sales.

Here are some of my favorite programs/apps/ websites:

On a desktop Computer

<u>Vector Art Programs:</u>

Adobe Illustrator

($19.99USD or more per month, depending on your plan)
Link here: <u>http://www.adobe.com/ca/products/illustrator/free-trial-download.html</u>

Adobe Illustrator is the absolute industry leader in vector graphics design software. Used across all levels of serious design teams, Adobe Illustrator allows for the creation and customization of complex and simple vector graphics. Used in partner with Adobe's Photoshop, Adobe Illustrator is a great program to use, and has affordable monthly subscription pricing plans, for most budgets. When outsourcing or working with a VA Designer, one good question might be: "How comfortable are you with using Adobe Illustrator? "

From a -design for commercial use- perspective, vector graphics are really the golden goose, as they can be scaled to almost any size, with minimal to no pixilation, unlike Photoshop images, which are rasterized graphics, and will tend to pixilate when scaled too far either larger or smaller. Although Illustrator is the industry standard, it also has great competition vying for the position of top spot in vector graphics - such as Affinity Design! Which we discuss next.

One of the most beloved features in Adobe Illustrator is live trace, as it allows you to take an image, and turn it into a vector. Just one of thousands of things you could do with Adobe Illustrator.

HOW TO LIVE TRACE: To trace the image using the default tracing options, click Live Trace in the Control panel, or choose Object > Live Trace > Make.

Link to **FREE** training on how to use Adobe Illustrator - Directly from Adobe: https://helpx.adobe.com/illustrator/tutorials.html

NOTE: There's lots more later in the book on finding resources, like how to design.

Affinity Design

($49.99USD ONE TIME FEE)
Link here: https://affinity.serif.com/en-us/designer/
Affinity Designer, like Adobe Illustrator is a fully featured plasma vector format application. Affinity Designer is a ONE TIME payment, with NO MONTHLY FEES, and FREE UPGRADES FOR LIFE. It is compatible with most .ai and .psd file formats. Features I like in Affinity Designer include: infinity zoom - zoom to 1,000,000% if you want to; Typography path mapping and editing functionality (adjust typography leading, kerning, baseline shift, and tab stops).

Plus you can apply style modifications across your whole document. With live adjustments and live blend modes - you can fully render your adjustments or blends as you hover over each one - no need to select and wait for rendering one at a time like Adobe Illustrator or Photoshop. It is very powerful, very affordable, full vector control. Oh, and the ONE TIME price, includes FREE updates for life... never pay another monthly fee for this pro level vector application again!

Link to FREE tutorial training on how to use Affinity Design available here: https://vimeo.com/channels/affinitydesigner (over 90+ FREE Training videos)

Here's what the Affinity Designer buy screen looks like - shown in Canadian dollars - **NOTE:** the free trial! :

Inkscape
(FREE)
Link Here: https://inkscape.org/en/
In the same way that GIMP is often referred to as the FREE version of Photoshop, Inkscape is like a free version of Illustrator. A full featured professional vector design application, for FREE. Because some people would rather invest monthly fees into marketing their listings, not paying for their vector art tools…

Link to FREE training tutorials (written and video) for Inkscape: https://inkscape.org/en/learn/

About Vector Images:

What's a vector image, and why would you want a vector image?

Vector images allow you to scale with limited to no pixilation. This is useful especially when re-sizing an image to fit your use. Vector images can be scaled both larger, and smaller without pixilation (Pixilation - jagged square rough edges that make images look awful). Another way to say this, is that Vector images use lines or curves, while Raster images use pixels. See the difference:

Can Non-vector images be made into Vector images?

YES! By using lines or paths to trace the pixels of a non-vector image, a vector version can be made.

How to *MAKE YOUR OWN* vector image?

There are several ways. Here are a few:

Do It Yourself

(FREE if you have Adobe Illustrator)

1. OPTIONAL: Prepare your image by desaturating it in Photoshop or Illustrator (image->adjustments->desaturate). This creates a black and white (aka grayscale) image.
2. Open it in Adobe Illustrator.
3. Trace the image: Object -> Image Trace -> Make
4. Expand the image: Object -> Image Trace -> Expand

Now you have the image in vector form. You can copy the traced lines and paste into Photoshop, or wherever you would like to use your vector image. From there, as you apply Transform, to make larger or smaller, without the pixilation :-)

VIDEO: For a more detailed explanation, with additional steps on transforming a pen and paper artwork into a fully vectorized piece of digital art, watch this 10 min YouTube clip: https://youtu.be/pyLzazEpKrQ

Vectorizer
https://www.vectorizer.io
(Free or 24.99EUR/year)
Vectorizer is a great web-based service where you can convert your images to .png or .svg (vector). Service starts for free for up to 3 images per hour, or their basic plan which allows up to 10 per hour.

Looking for more than 10 per hour? check this out:

Vector Magic
https://vectormagic.com/
($7.95 monthly, or one time $295)
Like Vectorizer above, Vector Magic lets you easily convert existing images into vector images, quick and simply. This is a good option, especially if you would like a standalone desktop option, however, keep in mind, $295 can get you quite a few months of Adobe Illustrator, which of course has an auto tracer function built in. The choice is yours. I like the option to have a one time fee vs. monthly subscription, but both options can work. Vector Magic also works with a large number of file formats. They have a complete breakdown of them here: https://vectormagic.com/support/file_formats

Note: there are some feature differences between the web-based option, and the standalone desktop version, below is a handy comparison.

Vector Magic DESKTOP vs. WEB BASED Comparison:

Which option should I choose?

To help you choose between the Online and the Desktop Editions, here is the feature matrix:

Feature	Online	Desktop
Fully automatic vectorization	Yes	Yes
Basic vectorization mode, with easy-to-choose settings	Yes	Yes
Advanced vectorization mode, with fine-grained control		Yes
EPS, SVG and PDF vector output	Yes	Yes
AI, DXF vector output		Yes
PNG, GIF, BMP bitmap output		Yes
JPG, TIFF bitmap output		PC
Powerful preview to inspect the result in detail	Yes	Yes
Segmentation editing capabilities	Yes	Yes
Super-convenient copy-paste input	Yes	Yes
Super-convenient drag-and-drop input	Yes	Yes
Super-convenient drag-and-drop output		Yes
Vectorize very large images		Yes
Group shapes by color		Yes
Transparency support		Yes
Batch processing		Yes

Fiverr
($5USD)
Link Here: http://track.fiverr.com/visit/?bta=18240&nci=5490
Paying a freelancer on a one off basis for each file conversion. This is good for individual files, or if you don't have the time or tools to do it yourself, and you don't like the idea of paying an ongoing fee for something like Vector Magic above.

You can also convert images into vectors using Adobe Capture on your mobile device. More about that in the mobile apps section ;-)

Desktop Digital Photo Programs:

Adobe Photoshop

($9.99USD or more per month, depending on your plan, check with Adobe for current pricing, for the version and iteration that you want to use.)
Link Here: https://creative.adobe.com/products/download/photoshop (FREE TRIAL)

Photoshop is really the gold standard for digitally editing photos on your desktop. With features like layers, masking, adjustments, filters, and more, it can be used to adjust your image(s) just about any way you like. One big drawback from a design perspective is that the images are raster images, meaning that scaling them up or down in size can lead to pixilation. To avoid this, consider using one of the vector graphic programs mentioned above.

FREE TUTORIALS: What better source to learn basic to advanced Photoshop than by using Adobe's training by video? Link Here: https://helpx.adobe.com/photoshop/tutorials.html

QUICK TIP: LEARN DESIGN
One thing that I highly recommend whether you choose to make your own designs, or outsource them, is to familiarize yourself with whichever software you choose to use, or your designers use. This is not only a great skill to have in your tool belt, but it can ALSO give you additional options in the area of inspiration, AND gives you the advantage of being able to sell your owns designs. Here's an example of a quick free online tutorial online via YouTube (on creating clipping masks, and using custom brushes for stylized effects): https://youtu.be/P62XWCpAZDA If you

enjoyed that quick tutorial, as much as I did... here is more from the same designer: https://www.youtube.com/user/DhruvalModi/videos?view=0&flow=grid&sort=p

There are literally hundreds or thousands of similar quick training tutorials for Photoshop, Illustrator, and many other design tools. So, if you need to learn a quick skill, or you need to show your outsourced designer an example of what you're looking for, I recommend using free YouTube tutorials, and video examples as a way to improve yourself and your design team(s) :-)

Affinity Photo

($49.99 ONE TIME FEE)
Link Here: https://affinity.serif.com/en-us/photo/

Similar to Affinity Design (mentioned above), Affinity Photo is a ONE TIME payment, with NO MONTHLY FEES, and FREE UPGRADES FOR LIFE. It is an award winning, widely used professional image editing program, and it is compatible with most types of .ai and .psd file types. One of my favorite features, is the AMAZINGLY FAST selection tool. Difficulty selecting fine hairs, and details is a thing of the past, as Affinity Photo's advances selection tools can identify individual hairs. Other great features I love about Affinity Photo, are it's advanced image mapping to textured objects, 360 degree image edits, and it's dynamic custom brushes. Speaking of dynamic, it also allows for dynamic LIVE filters and LIVE previewing (see what you get as your move your mouse over filter options), something Photoshop still doesn't do yet!

Affinity Photo, and Affinity Design also come with world class FREE training videos, on hundreds things you can do in Affinity, watch these here: https://vimeo.com/channels/affinityphoto (229 videos!!!!)

PRO TIP: If you're a Photoshop guru, and you've never tried Affinity Photo, check out its features here: https://affinity.serif.com/en-gb/photo/full-feature-list/

GIMP

(FREE)

Link Here: https://www.gimp.org/

Often described as the free version of photoshop. I agree, it is like a free version of photoshop. It has some unique features of it's own, and it doesn't do 100% of the things that photoshop does... but basically, it's like photoshop, without the monthly cost... or the up front costs either... it's totally FREE. Updates and version enhancements... also FREE. Works on multiple OS's Mac/PC/Linux....

FREE TUTORIALS on how to use GIMP, Link Here: https://www.gimp.org/tutorials/

Signlab

($500USD)

Link Here: https://www.cadlink.com/index.php/en/signlab-version-10

Signlab is mainly a program for setting up your vinyl cuts for vinyl heat press, or sign making. Also used for vehicle wraps. Since I'm sure some of you have experience with making vinyl heat press T-shirts, or if you didn't know, some of the POD platforms use vinyl heat press, among other POD technologies. Here is a list of additional benefits for using Signlab over Adobe Illustrator: https://www.cadlink.com/images/top-ten/WEB_Top_10_Reasons_Data_Sheets_Illustrator.pdf

TUTORIALS: Here is a stack of tutorials about how to use Signlab for your design work:
https://www.cadlink.com/index.php/en/infosource-forum-tutorials-tips-tricks/tutorials/signlab-tutorials

Corel PaintShop Pro X9 + Corel ParticleShop
($99 ONE TIME FEE) (Not Mac Friendly)

Link Here: http://www.paintshoppro.com/en/ ***AND*** http://www.painterartist.com/en/product/particleshop/

Described as an affordable alternative to Adobe Photoshop, Corel has been playing Adobe's second fiddle for years, but with their amazing graphics suites like CorelDraw , and PaintShop Pro, it's a wonder why more people aren't using these amazingly powerful tools. One nice bonus is that they are available with NO MONTHLY SUBSCRIPTION, meaning that you buy them ONCE, and own them FOREVER. Plus, Corel has plenty of 'sales', and 'bonus offers' happening. To save beyond the list pricing, I encourage you to join their newsletter/mailing list. Their drip email marketing has plenty of sale pricing. It's pretty insane what kinds of things you can do in Corel products, that you just can't do elsewhere.

Mobile Design Options:

Apps for designing on iOS: (iPhone / iPad / iPod)

Over:
Link Here: https://itunes.apple.com/ca/app/over-edit-photos-add-text-captions-to-pictures/id535811906?mt=8
Over allows you to choose custom images sizes or presets (think 4500x5400 for Merch By Amazon), save transparent .png image files (be sure to click save to .png, not save image - as doing so would save it as a .jpg). Enables import of custom fonts, which you buy (for commercial use). To add these, you want to email a .zip folder containing your fonts, and then open them on your device, when you do, select ***copy to Over*** to add the fonts into Over. One reason you want to import your own commercial use custom fonts, is that the fonts included with Over app are not all authorized for commercial use. Be careful with licensing.

Over also connects to cloud storage (Google Drive, iCloud, and more). Images can be layered easily, and each layer has options such as duplicate, re-order and delete. Almost everything in Over can be colored to your liking, including a color picker, to match any colors. Resize anything in any layer, move with guides for centre, left, right, and align to multiple elements on the layer. AND MORE! Everything described above is in the FREE version of Over!

For even more functionality such as mask layers, shadows, blur effects, blending images, and more - buy Over Pro (it's just $7.99 per month or $39.99 per year - well worth the investment, if you would like to create a lot on your mobile device).

QUICK VIDEO: Joe Clay from Merch University has put together a great overview of using the Over App here: https://www.youtube.com/watch?v=hUtFVXrRCg0

LONGER VIDEO: Chris Green put together an outstanding overview video about the Over App, link here: https://youtu.be/aeysnXdjIpc

Assembly (by Pixite Apps)
Link Here: https://itunes.apple.com/ca/app/assembly-design-graphics-stickers-and-logos/id1024210402?mt=8
Build custom images using vector shapes and designs! In the app for iOS, you can resize, stretch, color, rotate, add text (with great text features like *stroke*), and more!...

See the assembly promo short video here: https://vimeo.com/141464427

If you want to really take your designs for Merch and POD to the next level, also check out these other award winning apps from Pixie Apps: Fragment, LoryStripes, Union, Pigment, Tangent, Shift and more! ... Link to more info on all their apps here: http://pixiteapps.com/

NEXT LEVEL TIP: If you want to add some "grunge" or texture to your fonts from your Over .png export... bring in the exported font .png saved file to the Shift App (https://itunes.apple.com/us/app/shift/id939767518?pt=14691&ct=shift_website&at=11l4HQ&mt=8). Here you can apply a wide variety of textures to your font, adding both depth and complexity to it. Once you have something you're really happy with, re-save it, and bring it back into Over, and add it as a photo layer, just where you want it. Complexity of this mobile move: HIGH

ADDITIONAL MOBILE APPS JACOB TOPPING USES:

Here are more Mobile apps, which I personally have used, and continue use to make designs for use on Merch and over 21 additional POD platforms:

LetterFX:

Link here: https://itunes.apple.com/ca/app/letterfx-word-frames-for-photos-instagram-edition/id571745670?mt=8

Word Dream:

Link Here: https://itunes.apple.com/ca/app/word-dream-cool-fonts-typography-generator/id992296710?mt=8

Vintage Design

Link Here: https://itunes.apple.com/ca/app/vintage-design-logo-maker-poster-creator-diy/id878042995?mt=8

FotoRus
Link Here: https://itunes.apple.com/ca/app/vintage-design-logo-maker-poster-creator-diy/id878042995?mt=8

Tangled FX
Link Here: https://itunes.apple.com/ca/app/tangled-fx/id588126769?mt=8

Font Candy
Link Here: https://itunes.apple.com/ca/app/tangled-fx/id588126769?mt=8

Customize Monogram lite
Link Here: https://itunes.apple.com/ca/app/customize-monogram-background-maker/id988353494?mt=8
Create beautiful single letter Monograms, and use beautiful patterns and/or backgrounds.

Eraser
Link Here: https://itunes.apple.com/ca/app/background-eraser-superimpose-photo-editor-cut-out/id815072622?mt=8
Erase image backgrounds, save as transparent background .png files. There are many eraser apps, but this is the one that I prefer. It allows you to magically select an area, as well as precisely select or de-select as needed.

WordSalad
Link Here: https://itunes.apple.com/ca/app/wordsalad-beautiful-word-clouds-lite-edition/id545164778?mt=8
Creates a word cloud using a set of words that you provide.

PicMonkey
Link Here: https://itunes.apple.com/ca/app/picmonkey-photo-editor-add-text-filters-draw/id1105556534?mt=8

LunaPic
Link Here: https://itunes.apple.com/ca/app/lunapic-best-collage-layout-creator-to-stitch-multiple/id1005044992?mt=8

So, you have all these wonderful creations created on your iPad or iPhone, or iPod touch… how are you going to get them into Merch By Amazon, they can't be loaded directly from your mobile device right? WRONG! They CAN be uploaded directly onto Merch By Amazon! Use Safari or Chrome, or whatever browser you like best to submit the 4500x5400 .png file into Merch By Amazon (just like you would from your desktop).

HISTORY LESSON: At one time, you used to then have to use the Puffin Mobile browser for iOS to open your saved draft design, and you will be able to complete the live submission to Merch, fully via mobile. <— — this step is no longer needed.

Apps for Designing on an Android Smartphone or Tablet

Simplector Pro:

Link Here: https://play.google.com/store/apps/details?id=plasma.vector.editor.app.pro&hl=en

This is a full featured mobile vector image application for Android. You can save as either .svg, or .png, includes loads of fonts, layers, exporting of custom file dimensions (including the coveted 4500x5400 size that Merch By Amazon requires). You can save your images to your local Android file folders, or to the cloud. This is one of the best plasma vector editors I've ever seen running on Android, and in many ways, it gives Over (even the iOS version), a run for it's money. Great value for under $10 for the pro version!

PicMonkey:

Link Here: https://play.google.com/store/apps/details?id=com.picmonkey.picmonkey

Over Pro:

Link Here: https://play.google.com/store/apps/details?id=com.overllc.over&hl=en

Note: The Android version of Over, is very similar to the iOS version, however at the time of writing, the iOS version is measurably better than it's Android counterpart. Looking forward to the continuous improvements to both version over time.

Online Image editing tools and services

Make-Merch:

(packages from $19.99 / $29.99 / $39.99 billed monthly)
Link Here: http://make-merch.com/
New in 2017, Make-Merch is a wonderful tool for helping you to very quickly create Merch ready designs ready for upload into Merch By Amazon, and other platforms. Make-Merch gives you access to hundreds of images, and fonts that you can arrange to develop just the design you're looking to publish. In addition to the graphics and fonts available, it gives you options to filter and mask your images with a variety of effects and patterns. Curved text, vintage filter effects, even promotion ready images, featuring your designs. See how your design looks across the full variety of Merch By Amazon shirt colors, Make-Merch is a great solution for anyone who enjoys building their own designs, and wants an alternative way to scale many designs, without employing a team of VA's or design services to do design for you.

TUTORIAL: Here is a full tutorial about how to use Make-Merch from it's creator Dan Ostroff https://player.vimeo.com/video/231882193

Canva:

Link Here: canva.com
(FREE or $12.95/user/month , Plus Additional add on buys starting at $1 each)
Canva is a great way to quickly design for Merch or any POD, using online templates, fonts, images and styles. Canva is free to join, and offers a paid membership as well. Layouts and templates are also a mix of free and paid designs and services (many of the paid templates are $1, so the cost barrier is very low). In addition to creating Merch designs, Canva has a number of form fitting designs you can use to promote your designs for ads you may use in marketing. They have broad categories for: Social Media Graphics, Presentations, Blog Graphics, Banners, Cards, Book Covers, Infographics, Photo Collages, Flyers, Business cards and more!

FREE CANVA TUTORIALS: https://www.canva.com/learn/design/tutorials/

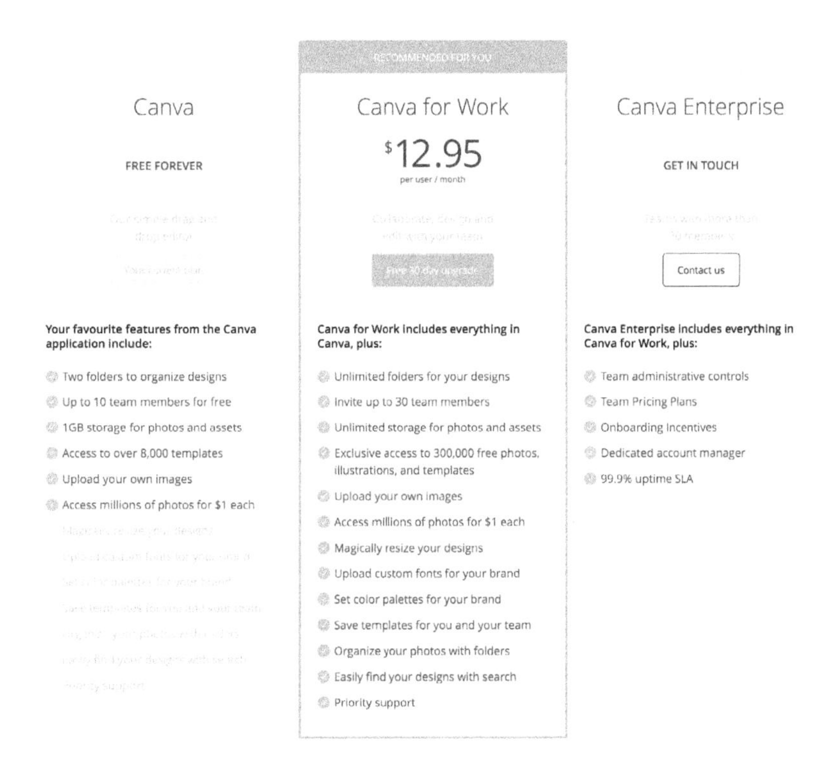

For more on pricing Canva, link here: https://about.canva.com/pricing/

Canva for work gives you access to more images, Collaboration with up to 30 team members, Priority support, and more (see comparison below):

SumoPaint:
(FREE or Pro version starts as low as $4/Month)
Link Here: https://www.sumopaint.com/home/
Sumo Paint can be downloaded and run stand alone, or run in your browser (Flash plugin required). It is a fully featured digital image editor, similar in features to something like Adobe Photoshop. Some interesting features I like about SumoPaint are: trailing, symmetry (mirroring), and its advanced brush tool. To see some artwork made by Sumo Paint users, or connect with other users, they have an image gallery here: https://www.sumoware.com/images/#featured/
Here's a quick video from their youtube channel showing the program in action: https://www.youtube.com/watch?v=NAEoeWnYYvI

PicMonkey:
Link here: https://www.picmonkey.com/
(Premium $7.99/month CND billed monthly, less when billed Annually, OR $8.99CND Supremium)
Online image editor. Full of fonts, and images. Has a free trial, Premium or Supremium fee based option. Great place to put Merch designs together, plus it's on the web, so you can pull it up anywhere as needed. This is also available as a mobile app on iOS and Google Play store.

BONUS TIP: There's even a chrome extension here: https://chrome.google.com/webstore/detail/picmonkey-extension/dhipmoghimfdldnocmopeoanjmoolofl

Premium

$5.99 CAD/mo
$71.88 billed annually

$7.99 CAD/mo
Billed monthly

Start 7-day free trial

Hub storage for 50 images
Sort Hub images
Save, Export, Share
Advanced touch up tools
Primo effects, overlays, fonts
Re-editable images, in Hub
Top-shelf templates
No ads

Supremium

$8.99 CAD/mo
$107.88 billed annually

Buy Supremium

Unlimited Hub storage
Organize Hub with Collections
Save, Export, Share
Advanced touch up tools
Primo effects, overlays, fonts
Re-editable images, in Hub
Top-shelf templates
No ads

Lunapic:
Link here: www.lunapic.com/
Upload your images, and edit them online. Loads of features for an online editor including borders, adjustments, effects and filters, cropping, blending, and more. Also available as an app on iOS, which includes all these things:

Editing Tools	Effects and Filters	Video Tutorials
Crop Image	Black and White	Adding Text Effects
Transparent	Color Change	Blending Images
Paste / Blend	Add Borders	Create Video Gifs
Add Text	Country Flags	Creating Collages
Drawing Tools	200+ more effects	More Tutorials..

Picsplosion:
http://www.picsplosion.com/
(FREE)
This is a very fast, very thinly features web based design tool that can be used to crank out thousands of text baed designs. Great for designing for mugs, phone cases, and other items where text based designs sell really well. Type in your text, choose a font, color and layout. You can save with transparent background, as well as add image layers if you like. Simply change words for scaled text based designs, and you can make hundreds of designs a day for free.

Inspiration For New Font Uses

Fonts in Use:

Link Here: https://fontsinuse.com/

Fonts in Use is a great way to see how other people and designers are using many fonts for many different kinds of projects. From books, to posters, apparel, to website, fonts (text) is everywhere! This is a great one-stop location to see loads of fonts in use in real world situations.

Industries ▾

Activism (172)
Architecture (282)
Art (875)
Automotive (104)
Business/Finance (152)
Education (458)
Entertainment (422)
Event (539)
Fashion/Apparel (351)
Film/TV (428)
Food/Beverage (767)
Governmental/Civic (174)
Graphic Design (966)
Health/Fitness (180)
Home/Interior (238)
Industrial Design (116)
Institutional (196)
Kids (187)
Lifestyle (279)
Literature (802)
Local (200)
Men (81)
Music (598)
News (264)
Performing Arts (174)
Politics (199)
Product (329)
Religion/Spirituality (81)
Retail/Shopping (284)
Science/Nature (178)
Services (301)
Social Media (96)
Sports (183)
Technology (374)
Transportation (101)
Travel (305)
Women (101)

Formats ▾

Advertising (613)
Album Art (549)
Art/Illustration (194)
Booklets/Pamphlets (464)
Books (1543)
Branding/Identity (1673)
Ephemera (183)
Exhibition/Installation (174)
Film/Video (187)
Infographics/Maps (176)
Magazines (640)
Mobile (104)
Newspapers (119)
Object/Product (216)
Packaging (519)
Posters/Flyers (1095)
Signs (555)
Software (92)
Tablet/iPad (87)
Web (1256)

Typefaces ▾

Abril Text (16)
Adelle (26)
Adelle Sans (19)
Adobe Caslon (32)
Akkurat (35)
Akzidenz-Grotesk (
Albertus (32)
Alright Sans (28)
Alternate Gothic (5
ITC American Type
Antenna (34)
Antique Olive (34)
Aperçu (23)
Archer (27)
Arial (57)
ITC Avant Garde Gc
Avenir (37)
Avenir Next (18)
Baskerville (32)
FF Bau (23)
Bello (23)
Benton Sans (65)
Bickham Script (23
Block (25)
Bodoni (62)
Bookman (20)
Brandon Grotesque
Brothers (25)
Bureau Grot (34)
Calibre (70)

Century Expanded
Chronicle (19)
Clarendon (58)
Compacta (29)
Cooper Black (56)
Copperplate Gothic
Dala Floda (21)
Davida (35)
FF DIN (57)
Eagle (19)
Elephant (Alias) (3
Euclid Flex (34)
Eurostile (47)
FB Titling Gothic (
Flama (18)
Folio (23)
Founders Grotesk (
ITC Franklin Gothic
Franklin Gothic (94
Freight Sans (21)
Freight Text (19)
Frutiger (21)
Futura (411)
Futura Black (42)
Futura Display (20)
Garage Gothic (29)
Geogrotesque (26)
Georgia (56)
Gill Kayo (54)
Gill Sans (105)

Gotham (118)
Graphik (34)
Grotesque No. 9 (1
GT Sectra (21)
GT Walsheim (34)
Harbour (39)
Harriet Series (19)
Hellenic Wide (18)
Helvetica (270)
Helvetica Condens
Hobo (20)
Interstate (70)
Kabel (36)
Kabel Black (31)
Knockout (71)
LL Brown (35)
LL Circular (33)
Lydian (26)
Lyon (27)
FF Mark (18)
Mercury (19)
FF Meta (28)
FF Meta Serif (22)
Miller (37)
Minion (27)
Mistral (22)
Monotype Grotesq
Mrs Eaves (18)
National (22)
Neue Helvetica (79

Neutraface (53)
Neuzeit S (19)
News Gothic (52)
Open Sans (21)
Optima (33)
Palatino (19)
Plantin (20)
Platform (19)
Proxima Nova (59)
Replica (22)
Rockwell (19)
Sentinel (H&Co) (1
ITC Serif Gothic (4
Skolar (18)
ITC Souvenir (29)
Suisse Int'l (25)
Telefon (26)
Tempo (22)
Tiempos (40)
Times (28)
Times New Roman
Trade Gothic (81)
Tungsten (24)
unidentified typefa
Univers (131)
Univers Ultra Cond
Venus (21)
Verlag (30)
Whitney (26)
Windsor (32)

These are the most common typefaces in the database, but there are many more. **Try a search!**

Images for Inspiration, or use on / with POD:

Below is a fairly large list of places where you can find images for inspiration on your POD designs. However, what sets most of this list apart, is that beyond just inspiration, many of these images are also available for use. As POD designers, you may have days where you wish to use images directly as your POD designs, or maybe use an image as a starting point to create your amazing original artwork/designs. However you use these images, its VERY IMPORTANT that you both understand the license under which you can use these images, and where. You MUST have the IP (Intellectual Property) rights in order to use, and or sell your designs, so be sure that you are allowed to use whatever you're thinking of using.

One great invention in the last few decades is the license organization known as Creative Commons (this is not some kind of legal license, it's a group that has been pushing the concept of artists being clearer about how their work can be used). It has multiple layers of rights use indicators, with the most popular, and more versatile being CC0 - Creative Commons Zero. This level of license allows you to use images for personal and/or commercial use, without attribution as permission is granted by the creator/license holder.

As designer, this is fantastic, as it gives you the assurance that you can use the image(s) under this license as components, or even directly in your designs. For a full overview, and explanation of CC0, go to the source here: https://creativecommons.org/publicdomain/zero/1.0/

Pexels:

Link here: pexels.com

There are a few image resources now offering full CC0 license on ALL images on their sites, and Pexels is one of them. What does this mean to you? It means under the site's license, permission has been granted to use all images for both personal and commercial license, under CC0 (more info about CC0 above). Pexels has over 30,000 images for use, with thousands more being added monthly.

For full license policy from Pexels, click here: https://www.pexels.com/photo-license/

One of the nice thing about Pexels, is that in addition to it's website full of images you can use in your artwork and designs, is their chrome plugin - located here: https://chrome.google.com/webstore/detail/pexels/fdnpgodccdfgofepkclnopmbnacjkbnj With the plugin, you can open new tabs showing you stunning new CC0 images for you use, and more!

But wait, there's more! They also have mobile app for Apple's MacOS, and Windows, located here: https://www.pexels.com/pro/mac-and-windows-app/ This desktop app allows you to copy images, and paste them into your documents all from your desktop, no browser required.

Plus, for Adobe Photoshop users, there is a direct Pexels Photoshop plugin, allowing you to find and use images directly from within Photoshop, as you need them. Link here: https://www.pexels.com/pro/photoshop-plugin/

There's also a Pexels add-on for MS Office, and an IFTTT recipe for Android :-)
See all the Pexels tools here: https://www.pexels.com/pro/

Pixabay:
Link here: https://pixabay.com/
Pixabay offers both images and videos you could use for Merch. Or, as they proudly display on their site: All images and videos on Pixabay are released free of copyrights under Creative Commons CC0. You may download, modify, distribute, and use them royalty free for anything you like, even in commercial applications. Attribution is not required.

That being said, use this service with CAUTION.... As the platform has become more popular, some people have abused it, and are loading in images that they don't own the rights to, so that they can download them, and when they get caught, claim that they were from Pixabay and are free to use. This is ridiculous. However, since it's happening, be very cautious when using Pixabay, or any service that offers similar free use claims.

Below, is an example of the kind of high quality images that Pixabay offers. To get such an image, you can use their search bar on their website, browse through the images that come up and click the one you're interested in. You'll be provided with a button called "Free Download", and you can select the quality level that you desire. Some of the larger quality levels require you to login, but most have a "no-login" option as well. They do make you answer a quick "are you human" test (typically type in some street names, or check a box), and BAM! There you have it, you have a new fresh image to use on your Merch or POD platform(s).

PRO TIP: To access Pixabay from your mobile phone, open the website, select the icon to save to your smartphone, and you'll now have a direct link to the site from your smartphone! Images on mobile download into you're photo library, for easy access on your mobile, or e-mail or push to your desktop.

Sample image on next page ;-)

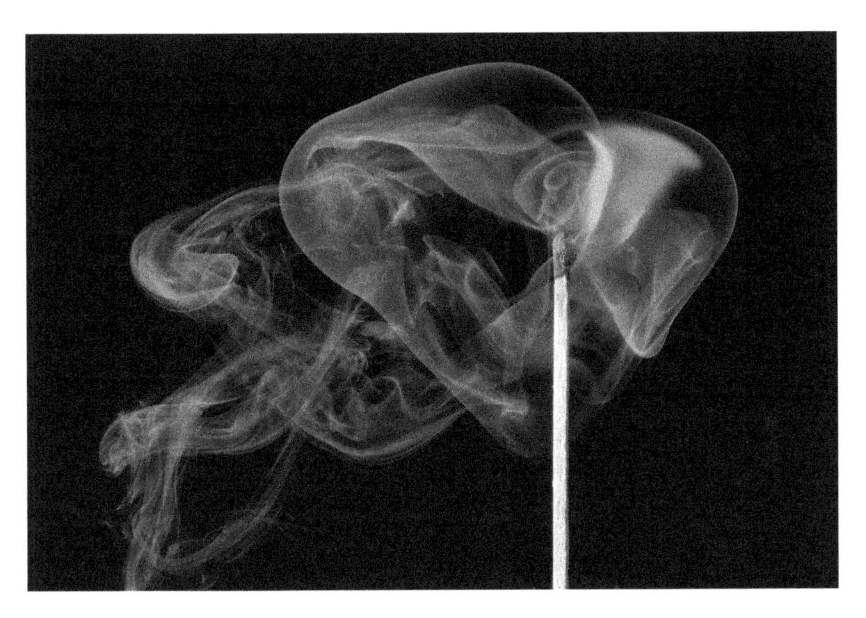

Here is a sample image from Pixabay - a match to light your fire of creativity!

Unsplash:

Link here: unsplash.com

Like Pixabay above, Unsplash is a wealth of images, offered for use. The things that is really interesting about their licence policy is what it says:

"License All photos published on Unsplash can be used for free. You can use them for commercial and noncommercial purposes. You do not need to ask permission from or provide credit to the photographer or Unsplash, although it is appreciated when possible.

More precisely, Unsplash grants you an irrevocable, nonexclusive copyright license to download, copy, modify, distribute, perform, and use photos from Unsplash for free, including for commercial purposes, without permission from or attributing the photographer or Unsplash. This license does not include the right to compile photos from Unsplash to replicate a similar or competing service."

Now, I'm not a lawyer or an attorney, but it seems to me that they are granting licence that cannot always be granted. For example: does the original uploader of the file have all the rights to grant that kind of access to Unsplash? Do they have waivers from all the people used in images with people? What about images of the Eiffel Tower, or other landmarked and notable buildings. Etc. ... So, it's a great site to use as inspiration, and according to it's licence page, all the images can be used for commercial purposes, but like Pixabay, I would recommend using with CAUTION. Theoretically the uploaders to the site have agreed to comply with the rules of use for the site, so you technically should be safe, but just be careful and use common sense.

Here is a great response that they give to the issue of licence: https://medium.com/unsplash/can-i-use-photos-of-landmarks-and-notable-buildings-b10bf0703134

Negative Space:

Link here: negativespace.co

Negative space images are full Creative Commons Zero (CC0) licence. So they can all be used for bother commercial and personal use, without attribution. Like Unsplash and Pixabay above, do take precaution to ensure that the images you are using do not infringe on any copyright. Note: Negative Space does vet it's images, and make it easy to report infringement. For it's full license details, click here: https://negativespace.co/license

Burst By Shopify:

Link Here: burst.shopify.com

Another great source for CC0 images service created by Shopify to help support Shopify's over 500,000 customers who use Shopify to sell things online. A great service both for POD design inspiration, but also for using on your website if you use Shopify, BigCommerce, or any commerce enabled website :-) (lots more about options and ways to do multiple integrations to Shopify, and multiple PODs later in the book). Burst has done a great job at outlining in great detail their license and uses policy, located here: https://burst.shopify.com/legal/terms

Google Images:
Link Here: https://www.google.com/imghp
If you want to see more fonts in use in different types of places, try Google Images. YES! It's a great place to browse through, and see lots of inspiration on many types of things, from posters, to tattoos, T-shirts to mugs, billboards, wherever you see marketing or font used. With Google images, just type in what you're looking to browse through, and you will find hundreds or sometimes thousands of examples of things other people have made, and ways that fonts and images have been used to generate many emotions.

Looking for something big and bold? Type in big and bold! Looking for something feminine, or masculine? Just type in what you would like to see more of, and then have a peek at what images are out there. Once you've jotted down some overall concepts, and ideas for ways your designs could look, send your ideas to your designer, and have them make a one of a kind original custom design for you... or make one yourself, using some or all of the tools we discussed earlier (desktop, mobile, web - see above).

Google Images does have the option to search for images labeled for re-use. This can be found by clicking on **TOOLS -> USAGE RIGHTS -> LABELED FOR REUSE**

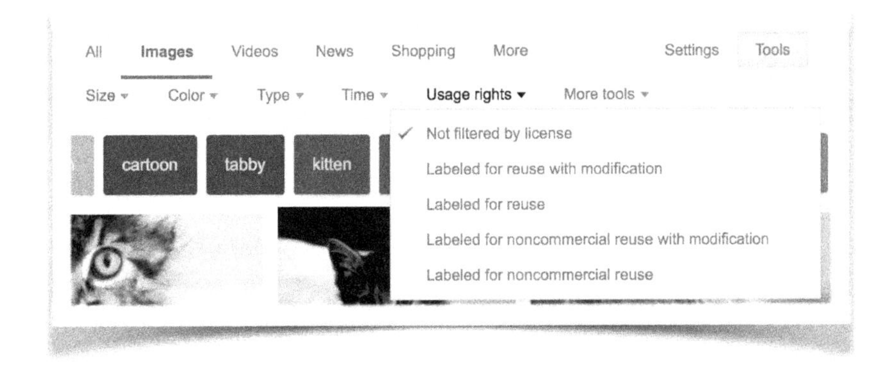

Here's an example: https://www.google.ca/search?q=amazing+text+based+designs&num=50&espv=2&source=lnms&tbm=isch&sa=X&ved=0ahUKEwiSjpPBibfSAhXlxYMKHduzCaYQ_AUICCgB&biw=2131&bih=1316

PRO TIP:

You can also use Google images to find Copycats, hint hint

Want to take Google images to the next level? Try providing Google images with an image you have, and running a reverse Google image search! YES!! This is great to identify where an image originated from. OR to make sure your new designer VA is creating original images, and not copying from elsewhere (NEVER COPY!!). OR to see what kinds of other designs are similar visually to something you like, which you could browse through for more inspiration.

To do a reverse Google image search, go to Google Images: https://www.google.com/imghp

Search by image

Search Google with an image instead of text. Try dragging an image here.

Paste image URL Upload an image

Choose File No file chosen

Now, either drag an image you want to reverse search into the search bar (above)...

OR

Click the little camera icon, and enter a URL for the image.

OR... pick your image from your device! (YES, THIS WORKS ON MOBILE TOO!)

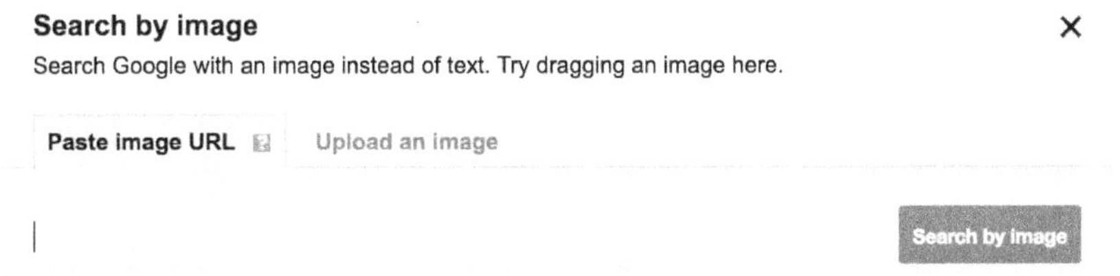

Search by image

Search Google with an image instead of text. Try dragging an image here.

Paste image URL | Upload an image

Search by image

Alternatives to Google Images for Reverse Image Search:

TinEye

(Free)

Link Here: https://www.tineye.com/

Tin Eye searched over 24 Billion images and shows you matches for designs that are the same or similar to the one(s) you show it. You can use either a URL, or a file upload to search by. It's fast, accurate, and will give you different results than the Google Image's reverse search. Great tool for VA's (Virtual Assistant) to use to authenticate the authenticity of designers in the case that you're outsourcing your design creation.

NooBox

(Free)

Link Here: https://chrome.google.com/webstore/detail/noobox/kidibbfcblfbbafhnlanccjjdehoahep?hl=en

NooBox is a chrome extension that allows you to search across multiple reverse image search services (including both Google Images, and TinEye above). It also allows you to perform the search by right clicking an image you see on your chrome browser, or by uploading your own images to be searched. Here is a full video explaining the service in more detail: https://youtu.be/NjqLmWdQ9Fg

Bulk Resize Photos:

Link here: https://bulkresizephotos.com/

Drag or upload your images one at a time, or in bulk, and you can have them resized as needed by exact height and width (4500 X 5400 is used for Merch By Amazon, of course!). This includes for any specific platform, or need. If you have an image that you need re-sized, this is a quick way to get the job done, and have a folder full of images resized in seconds, sitting in your downloads folder, ready to use where you need them. Fast. Convenient. Web based.

NOTE: This is a great option for re-sizing for hoodies on Merch By Amazon, which have a different dimension for a hoodie *front side design* of 4500 x 4050 (note as well, that the option to print on the back of hoodies on Merch By Amazon is still 4500 x 5400 like all of their other options at the moment).

SPECIAL DESIGN CASES:

1: UGLY CHRISTMAS SWEATER DESIGNS:

One trend that seems to be popular year after year in the Q4 season (October-November-December), is "Ugly Christmas Sweaters", or at least ugly Christmas sweater designs. These are designs that appear as a knitted pattern, and/or are pixilated to a large degree. Although you can buy these designs (theres a whole section later in the book about how to buy pre-made designs, hire designers, or request designs from design services - see chapter 7), you can also make your own. Here is a great article via Redbubble's blog on how to create an ugly Christmas sweater design (complete with template files): https://blog.redbubble.com/2017/12/create-ugly-christmas-sweater-design/

CREATING REPEAT DESIGNS FOR ALL-OVER PRINTS:

Print-All-Over designs are available on some POD platforms. Certain items are best served with a repeating design. Why? Simple, a repeating design can go right to the edge, and over it, thus covering all of the item. This is in contrast to many front or back designs which would fit within a designated printable area of an item (T-Shirts on Merch By Amazon being a great example). So, how do you create a repeating design suitable for print-all-over patterns/designs? Here's a great Blog post from Society6 on how to create a repeating pattern via Photoshop: https://blog.society6.com/design-repeating-pattern-using-photoshop/

NOTE: the blog post also includes 3 short videos showing where exactly to click to make it happen.

Fonts:

Fonts are the letters and numbers that you use in your designs. Using a variety of fonts can create a different look and feel to your designs. Different fonts also take up space differently, so you can really change the spacing of a design with different fonts.

When using fonts for your designs, be SURE that you own the Intellectual Property (IP) rights to use the fonts for commercial use, including print, and print on clothing!

How do you know if you have the rights to use the font? Read the terms and conditions of the source of the fonts. Often they will outline if the fonts can be used in various ways, and how they cannot be used. Also, just because you are using a program or app (especially mobile apps), DO NOT assume that you have the rights to use it for commercial print on clothing. Always check the terms of use.

For example: Over (possibly the greatest POD design creator program of all time for mobile), includes several fonts for use in the app. However, they DO NOT allow those fonts to be used for commercial purposes. So, how the heck do you make a text based design in Over, if the included fonts are not allowed? Simple: YOU BUY RIGHTS to use fonts commercially, then you import those fonts into the app. In the app font manager, you can deselect the fonts that come with Over, and you can select the fonts that you've added, ones which you have the commercial rights to use. Now you can use these fonts to create your designs, knowing that you have the rights to use them.

HOW TO INSTALL PURCHASED FONTS ON YOUR COMPUTER:

Not sure how to install downloaded fonts? Here's a quick guide, covering how to for both Windows and Mac: https://www.fontspring.com/support/installing

This brings us to an interesting question, where can you find or buy fonts for commercial use? Here are some places that offer fonts, which people have used in designs for Print On Demand:

Creative Market:
(variable costs: both FREE and paid)
Link here: https://creativemarket.com/?u=jacobtopping
Creative Market is an online marketplace offering a variety of both fonts and vector files for purchase. Again, like any source, be sure to check the licensing rights prior to using in your designs. Again, why bother paying for some of these premium fonts, when you can easily find some free fonts here and there? Here's a good example of some of the capabilities of premium fonts that you won't typically find in many free fonts: https://www.youtube.com/watch?time_continue=143&v=t4Rb6_qC5tk

PRO TIP: Want to save right off the bat, instead of buying the fonts directly, buy font credits, and save 10% or more, depending on which bundle you choose, discounts start at $100 credit level. Link Here: https://creativemarket.com/account/credits/?u=jacobtopping

Font Bundles:
(variable costs both FREE and paid)
Link Here: https://fontbundles.net/free-fonts/rel=lnahsb
Font Bundles offers bundles of fonts for purchase, as well as some for FREE! They offer multiple license options, so check out a pile of new fonts, and buy bundles and save. Why pay for fonts where you can get them for free? Because, there are different fonts, and the paid ones are often outstanding! Brush fonts, overlapping fonts, color fonts, and more! Check out the world of fonts, and use the best ones that you own right to, in your designs :-) The link above takes you to a FREE rotating font bundle, and typically they are available for commercial use, which includes use on T-Shirts.

Font Squirrel:
(FREE)
Link Here: https://www.fontsquirrel.com/
100% free fonts for commercial use! Just what you're looking for to get started in the text based design game. Simply download the fonts that you intend to use in your designs, and you're off to a great start, no costs, no hassles, no having to check for permissions or worry about if you can use it or not. Font Squirrel calls themselves a "free font utopia", and they may be right.

In addition to having loads of free for commercial use free fonts, **Font Squirrel** also allows you to sort and filter fonts to find exactly the fonts that you need for your designs. choose from:

CLASSIFICATIONS	
Sans Serif	385
Display	336
Serif	181
Script	86
Slab Serif	70
Handdrawn	62
Dingbat	40
Retro	36
Monospaced	36
Novelty	33

TAGS	
Paragraph	915
Display	465
Oblique	147
Headings	126
Bold	120
Sans Serif	113
Casual	100
Contemporary	84
All Caps	81
Calligraphic	78
Retro	78
Distressed	77
Grunge	73
Elegant	72
Rough	71
Decorative	69
Heavy	67
Serif	66
Comic	28
Stencil	24
Calligraphic	20
Blackletter	17
Typewriter	14
Pixel	6
Grunge	3
Programming	2

Show More Tags

Google Fonts:

(FREE)

Link Here: https://fonts.google.com/

Google Fonts give you access to over 800+ fonts. You can search by font type (serif, san-serif, handwritten, monotype, etc). You will see multiple styles of the font, and preview your own phrases with adjustable sizing to see how each font you're looking at works with the phrase(s) you're thinking of using in your design. You can also download many of the fonts to your computer for later use, and give you a breakdown of where in the world the font is used (by country).

Even more powerful, on the left hand side menu, you can see a list of fonts that are often paired with the one that you are looking at. This can be a great way to see and or learn about how to pair fonts.

Be sure to check the license type to ensure you can use it for your designs, though many of them are open font license. Google fonts also gives you information about the author of the fonts, so if you really like a font and want to see if the creator has more like it, you can often track down the creator of the font, and see if they have more that you would enjoy. I've also noticed that there is definitely a lean towards web fonts within Google Fonts, as opposed to Artistic, or print fonts (generally speaking).

Da Font:
(FREE)
Link here: http://www.dafont.com/
Da Font offers many fonts, some of which offer full commercial use. Be sure to check the details of any font you're interested in, as some of the fonts have rules about how they are used. Others do not.
(from the DaFont FAQ: Are all the fonts free of charge?
The fonts presented on this website are their authors' property, and are either freeware, shareware, demo versions or public domain. The licence mentioned above the download button is just an indication. Please look at the readme-files in the archives or check the indicated author's website for details, and contact him if in doubt. If no author/licence is indicated that's because we don't have information, that doesn't mean it's free.)

What Font is that??
Like a font, and want to know what it is? Find out using:

MyFont:
Link here: https://www.myfonts.com/WhatTheFont/
Upload an image containing the font that you would like to discover, and using character isolation, and some other indicators, it will usually do a good job at telling you what font is being used, as well as very similar fonts based on the characteristics of the font in the image you load up. This is great if you see a font out in the wild, and you would like to find it so you can purchase it to use in your designs. Just take a picture of it on your smartphone, and use MyFont to look it up later.

Wordmark:
(FREE)
Link here: http://wordmark.it/
What if you are making a design on your computer, and you want to see the words you want to put into your design, using fonts you have installed on your computer (all on one screen). Wouldn't that be magical? Well, it's possible! Use Wordmark to do just this! See the words you type, in every installed font on your computer. It's also web based, so you can use it on multiple computers or devices.
NOTE: uses adobe Flash, which might not work on ALL devices…

FONT EXAMPLE:

TypeSlab:

(FREE)

Link Here: http://typeslab.com/

Typeslab is a great place to experiment with a few font combinations, where the site takes care of word spacing, as per your simple inputs in the message section. Simply type in a message that you would like to see, pick a font pairing and color type, and boom, Typeslab will generate a useable image. Great on it's own for generating headlines for social media, or quick projects. Even better, it can be used to very quickly help you visualize a text only design layout. Once you find a combination you like, you can re-create it using fonts you have IP rights to use, using your favorite graphics software. BONUS: It works in browser, including on your mobile device!

EXAMPLE:

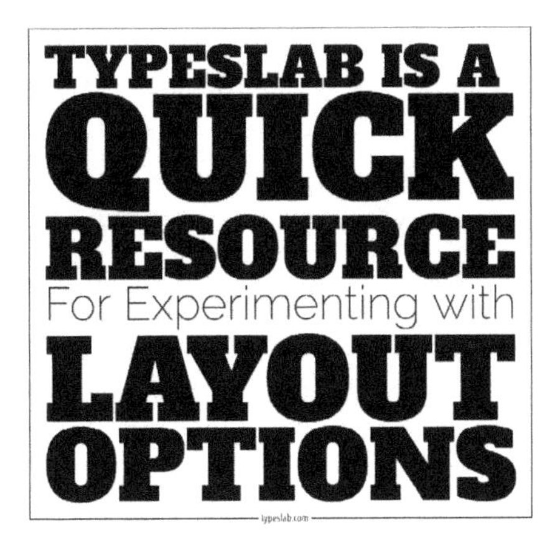

END OF CHAPTER 3

CHAPTER 4 - ONLINE PLATFORMS - THE POD WEBSITES

Print On Demand platforms you want to know about!

Here is a list of platforms that offer Print On Demand: the first 10 are ordered in order of amount of user traffic, according to alexa.com/siteinfo (an Amazon owned company, which offers detailed information about websites, including traffic, and ranking globally, and by country - among other services). The Alexa rank is calculated using a combination of average daily visitors to this site and page views on this site over the past 3 months. The site with the highest combination of visitors and page views is ranked #1 (lower is better). Ranks listed below are as of mid February 2017 and December 2017, and change daily. Looking for rankings today add your favorite URL here: alexa.com/siteinfo If you're looking for even more in depth traffic and additional data on any POD or marketplace, or website, you should also check out Similar Web, link here: https://www.similarweb.com/ it has most of what Amazon provides with site info, plus a few extras like downloadable .PDF reports, more on traffic sources, estimated revenue #'s, and more (and that's just the free parts).

Why are there so many?

OK OK ... So there's clearly a lot of places to do Print On Demand, why so many? Well, each one is a little different. Some ship only in the USA (like Merch by Amazon), some have time limited campaigns, some attract organic traffic, some attract affiliate marketers who bring you traffic, some you send traffic to, some ship fast, some offer low prices, some have special perks for buyers or sellers, each one offers a different combination of items for sale (different types of t-shirts, mugs, totes, canvas, clocks, cell phone cases, stickers, cards, and more) .... you get the picture. They're all different.

merch.amazon.com

Merch By Amazon is by a large margin, the most heavily trafficked POD option, and generally yields the best ratio of most buyers per design. If you can only choose 1 POD site, this is the thousand pound gorilla in the room, and it's growing every day.

How to join?

Merch By Amazon is by application only, be sure to apply for the invite asap, as it can take a while to get accepted. Estimated wait times are always changing. In 2017 they were around three to six months, but it could change at any time, and varies throughout the year. Changes to the Application process in 2018, reduced the waiting time, although they still vary widely.

Designs uploaded to Merch By Amazon are currently only available on the amazon.com platform, and only ship within the USA. They carry 2 brands of T-shirts (Standard [now Port and Co. (was previously Anvil)] and Premium [now Bella+Canvas was formerly American Apparel]). Long Sleeve T-Shirts, Sweatshirts, and Hoodies for some select sellers. Lower tiers may have limited access to some items offered. At this time, they carry over 3,000,000 live designs (this number was over 2,400,000 in November 2016, but changes to how they show Merch By Amazon listings apart from other listings in the category make it nearly impossible to know exactly how many are via Merch By Amazon, and how many are other listings in the category). One of the newest POD options, Merch By Amazon launched Sept 30th 2015, and has been undergoing rapid growth, and constant change since that time. Here is a partial list of some of the most notable changes:

- initially open to all, now it is invitation only
- initially no tiers. Currently the tier levels are: 10, 25, 100, 500, PRO (1000, 2000, 4000, 6000(NEW), 8000, 10,000 and there are sellers with over 18,000+ listings). 10 tier is new as of mid Dec 2016. Generally, Merch by Amazon has allowed a seller to move to the next tier once their number of sold designs equals their current tier (for example, if you are at tier 25, once you have 25 sales, you are levelled up to tier 100... at tier 100, after 100 sales, you are tiered up to 500 tier level, and so on). However, tier ups are currently semi-frozen, meaning some sellers are being tiered up, while others are not. In Q4 of both 2016 and 2017, Merch By Amazon has limited the number of designs which sellers can access, regardless of their tier level. In December of both 2016 and 2017, no additional live uploads were available, however sellers could load new designs into draft during the Dec 2017 freeze.

- 60 day rule added Nov 15th 2016 (if a design does not have any sales after 60 days, it is automatically removed. As long as it has at least 1 sale during that time, it remains live). This has been modified to become the 90 day rule, up from 60. Prior to the 60 day rule, a seller could upload as many designs as they wanted to up to their total tier maximum.
- throttled uploads per day (currently many sellers are limited to a partial number of uploads per day. This is related to tier levels, but not always. Common throttles were 2 per day at tiers 10 and 25, 3-4 uploads per day at tier 100 and 500, ... up to 40 uploads per day at higher tiers. Sometimes, throttled sales are sporadic, as some sellers are not able to upload at all, while others are throttled, and the throttled amounts are not exactly applied evenly across tier levels or sellers. This is likely to continue to change as the program changes and improves over time.

For more info on Merch By Amazon significant events, check out the "messages" section, on the dashboard tab (https://merch.amazon.com/dashboard) available for those who are accepted into the program. Additional information about the Merch by Amazon program can be found on the resources page here: https://merch.amazon.com/resource which is open to the public, and should be reviewed thoroughly if you ever intend to apply or use the program. Within the resources available you will find information such as Merch By Amazon policies, best practices, sizing, royalty calculations, and more!

Since you might be interested in how they calculate royalties, here's a direct link to their page about how they are calculated: https://merch.amazon.com/resource/201858580 Announced November 17, 2017, pricing changed for royalty calculations from January 15th 2018. Payments generally are direct to your bank account, and are paid in the currency of the bank account (for example: US based accounts are paid in $USD, Canadian based accounts are converted by Amazon to $CAD, etc.). Payments generally occur near the end of the month following the month the sale was made in (for example: December payments would generally be paid out near the end of January). Many sellers see payment in their accounts on or around the 29th of each month. Some sellers from outside of the USA, will also see a 30% withholding Tax on royalties earned. Check with tax professional/accountant on how to recoup those withheld payments when you file your taxes.

T-Shirts:
Merch by Amazon offers T-shirts in the following size options:
Male: S - M - L - XL - 2XL - 3XL
Female: S - M - L - XL
Youth: 4 - 6 - 8 - 10 - 12

Sizing charts available on the items' buy page. At this time, their sizing guide covers far more options than do their buy options. Sizing Link: https://www.amazon.com/gp/product/ajax-handlers/apparel-sizing-chart.html/ref=dp_sizechart?ie=UTF8&asin=B01N15L5IN&isUDP=1

Amazon offers Standard T-Shirts in 21 colors (up from 15): Dark Heather, Heather Grey, Heather Blue, Black, Navy, Silver, Royal Blue, Brown, Slate, Red, Asphalt, Grass, Olive, Kelly Green, Baby Blue, White, Lemon, Cranberry, Pink, Orange, Purple, which look like this:

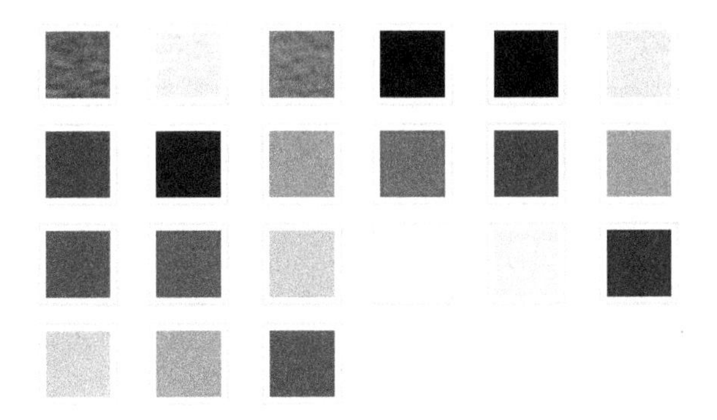

T-Shirt Design File Requirements:
Designs for both the Standard and Premium and Long Sleeve T-shirts on Merch By Amazon should be:
.png file format at 4500X5400 size (front or back), 300DPI resolution (recommended), 25MB or smaller in file size. Physically, this size works out to 15 inches by 18 inches, although it can be cropped by Merch By Amazon, as outlined in the FAQ section of it's Resources: https://merch.amazon.com/resource/201846470

Merch By Amazon T-Shirt Pricing:

Below is a summary of Merch By Amazon Royalties as of Q4 2017, including pricing before and after the Jan 15 2018 pricing change: https://merch.amazon.com/resource/201858580

Royalties

You earn a royalty on every product sold. Your royalty is based on the list price you set less Amazon's costs. Amazon costs include materials, production, fulfillment, customer service, returns, exchanges, and resources required to detect and prevent fraud. Fulfillment costs include picking and packing your product when a customer orders it and shipping your product to the customer—including shipping for Amazon Prime and Free Shipping eligible orders.

11/17/17: We have seen an increase in the costs to support Merch, including storage, fulfillment, transportation, raw materials, customer service, and the resources required to detect and prevent fraud. As a result, we will be adjusting the royalty on Merch by Amazon products. This change will take effect for sales of all new and existing products starting January 15th, 2018. If your product is priced below the new minimum price, it will be automatically updated to the minimum price.

Standard T-Shirt Examples

Currently

List price	$15.99	$17.99	$19.99	$21.99	$23.99	$25.99
Royalty	$3.79	$5.49	$7.19	$8.89	$10.59	$12.29

As of January 15, 2018

List price	$15.99	$17.99	$19.99	$21.99	$23.99	$25.99
Royalty	$2.36	$3.87	$5.38	$6.89	$8.40	$9.92

Long Sleeve T-Shirt Examples

Currently

List price	$22.99	$24.99	$26.99	$28.99	$30.99	$32.99
Royalty	$2.04	$3.74	$5.44	$7.14	$8.84	$10.54

As of January 15, 2018

List price	$22.99	$24.99	$26.99	$28.99	$30.99	$32.99
Royalty	$2.50	$3.75	$5.00	$6.25	$7.50	$8.75

Additional costs will be incurred for 2-sided printing as well as using a premium brand t-shirt

2-sided printing	+$4.00
Using premium brand t-shirts	+$1.50

Promote your products through Amazon Associates and earn an additional 7% for each Merch apparel purchase. It's easy and free to join. Learn more.

Hoodies:
Hoodies are available for some sellers, and come in the following sizes (all unisex):
Unisex: S-M-L-XL-2XL

The image file size requirements for hoodies are also slightly modified.
Front 4500 X *4050* pixels
Back 4500 x 5400 pixels
Hoodie colors are currently: Heather Gray, Dark Heather, Back, Navy, Royal Blue
Minimum Pricing is currently $32.50 (previously $34.12)

How many designs are listed on Merch By Amazon?
Well, this is always changing, due to the fluid dynamic nature of the platform, but here's a screenshot showing part of their listings: (*711,581* live Merch By Amazon ASINs in March 2017) A year later (March 2018), I would estimate that there are now over 3,000,000 Merch By Amazon designs, however an exact count is no longer possible, as they've changed how the count appears.

MARCH 2017:

Can you make private listing?
Yes. When loading a new design, you have the option on Merch By Amazon to list in draft (for later use), Private link (for hidden from the public), Sell (once approved by Merch By Amazon, it is live for sale on amazon.com)

What if I don't use all my daily Tier max uploads, Do they carry forward?
Nope, the daily tier is set daily at 3AM EST (midnight Pacific Time Zone).

Can I upload more than my daily tier limit?
YES! There's no limit on the number of designs you can load into draft. So if you have some time and designs, but no tier room, upload them anyways. It's also a great way to have designs ready for when you do tier up later.

Can I run PPC on Merch BY Amazon ASIN's?
Not via Seller Central. However, if you're currently in Vendor Central, or Vendor Express (ending March 21, 2018), you can create Sponsored product listings, and drive Amazon traffic to your Merch By Amazon ASIN's (entry to AMS is currently not available). ams.amazon.com

Can I See how much traffic my designs are getting on Merch By Amazon?
Not currently. They do have an analytics section, where you can see 90 days of sales history, as well as download .csv of up to 90 days of sales. This will show you additional information, such as Mens/Womens/Youth, size bought, type of item, currency, color and more.

How much does it cost to joint Merch By Amazon?
It's Free to join, free to list/upload designs.

How long does it take for my designs to get approved for live sale?
This time varies, and could take from a minute, to a few days. Typically lower tiers take longer. Some suggest that some uploads are approved via software, while others are manually reviewed.

If my designs comes down after 90 days of no sales, can I re-upload it again?
Yes you can, however keep in mind, you may want to consider changing the words used in the listing, as it had no sales in the last 90 days.

Can I upload anything?
No, you cannot upload anything that is trademarked in the clothing category with a live Trademark registration number from the USPTO (United State Patent and Trademark Office). You can also not upload swearing, any IP (Intellectual Property Rights) that you don't own (copyright, fonts without licensed permission, celebrities names, etc). For the full details check the Merch By Amazon Terms of Service, and FAQ: https://merch.amazon.com/resource/201859930 **AND** https://merch.amazon.com/resource/201846470

I have more questions!
They're likely answered in the Q& A chapter, or in one of the resources in the community section of this book. Plus, there's new questions all the time. Be sure to read the FAQ (link above), as it answers many of the most common questions.

HQ:
Amazon
410 Terry Ave. North,
Seattle, WA, USA
98109-5210
(It's HQ is actually made up of several buildings, but this will get mail to them if you like)

amazon.com's
Alexa's rankings:
Q1 2018
Global: 10
USA: 5
Q4 2017
Global: 11
USA: 4

etsy.com
Etsy, offers a huge 30+ Million buyers marketplace to sell homemade items. Essentially sellers on Etsy can create one or more storefront(s) to market homemade goods to buyers. What if you want to use a POD platform to fulfill your Etsy listings? YOU CAN! To get started you will need to do some setting up to use for Print On Demand, details below.

Each listings on Etsy costs $0.20 each every 4 months, if you join Etsy using this link, you'll get 40 FREE LISTINGS: http://etsy.me/2nV2rqf Etsy charges a fee for each item sold. Currently it's 3.5%, in case it changes the fee details are located here:
https://www.etsy.com/ca/help/article/136?ref=help_search_result

Here are some of the other fees for selling on etsy to be aware of: link above for details on each.

Fees for Selling on Etsy and Pattern

Here's a breakdown of the **fees for selling** on Etsy:

- Listing an item
- Creating custom items
- Selling an item
- Renewing an item
- Advertising your items
- Shipping Labels and Postage
- Fees for selling on a Pattern site
- Fees not broken out on your Etsy bill

New in 2017, Etsy changed it's rules around integrated apps, opening the door to 3rd party app integration with Etsy. This allows for direct integration with POD services like Printful (here is the direct link to the Printful Etsy App from the Etsy App store: https://www.etsy.com/ca/apps/16100456054/printful-drop-shipping-for-custom-print). This allows you to connect the 2 platforms, and offer automatic fulfillment via Printful on your Easy storefronts. Given Etsy's enormous site traffic (30,000,000+ buyers) , this combination makes Etsy my **# 2 pick** for places to list your designs on.

Before listing on Etsy, be sure you are aware and understand their Seller Policy, which is listed here: https://www.etsy.com/legal/sellers/#allowed (for example they have policies about what can and can't be listed, shop rules, information about cancellations, etc.).

To integrate **Etsy** with ***Printful***:

1. Create a free Etsy Account (use this link for 40 free listings: http://etsy.me/2nV2rqf) Once you've created your free Etsy Account, set up a shop, in order to access your shop manager. (to set up a shop, click shop. You will need to create a first listing. Under Production Partner, choose Printful - see step 4-10, and or the video here: https://youtu.be/f9EghP7-ei4).
2. Create a free account with Printful (done here: https://goo.gl/znYo6o)
3. Authorize Printful's API's on your Etsy Account. (Done in Printful here: https://www.printful.com/dashboard/etsy/register by clicking on the connect button) NOTE: in order to do step 3, steps 1 and 2 must be completed, and I recommend you're signed into both accounts)
4. On Etsy, under settings, select Production Partners.
5. Select Add New Partner.
6. In the Production Partner Field, type in Printful.
7. Deselect Printful's name as showing as your print partner, and type in whatever you would like to have showing on your store, to represent Printful (your Print On Demand Partner).
8. Add One of Printful's 3 printing locations (Chatsworth, California, United States Of America)
9. Type in a description to describe that location (Fulfillment, Warehousing and Shipping service for small online retailers)
10. Select the role of Printful from the 3 dropdown menus, and hit the save button.(I don't have the technical ability or equipment to make..., I design everything myself, They do everything for me).
11. Upload your products onto Printful via your Etsy Store on Printful, then push them to Etsy (note: they load as draft on the Etsy side, you can connect to Etsy from Printful.
12. Complete your Etsy Listings in Etsy, and publish (You connect to Etsy using the orange link on Printful. This moves your design from draft to live, when you publish on the Etsy side.)
13. That's it! Now, when people buy your designs you've listed on Etsy, the orders that are connected to Printful will be created and fulfilled by Printful!

BONUS: You can confirm that the design you loaded to Etsy from Printful is complete, when you see it in your printful account, under your etsy store (if it's synced, go back to stores on Printful, locate your etsy store, and click the sync button).

Once you have completed your first Printful to Etsy Listing, I suggest you have a small party. It's exhilarating! (Don't worry, Redbubble is way simpler ;-))

If you're a bit lost, have a look at the explainer video from Printful here:
Link Here: https://www.printful.com/landing/etsy-print-products-fulfillment

Printful has a more detailed step by step video about these steps above here:
https://youtu.be/f9EghP7-ei4

Your shipping partner info could like like this:

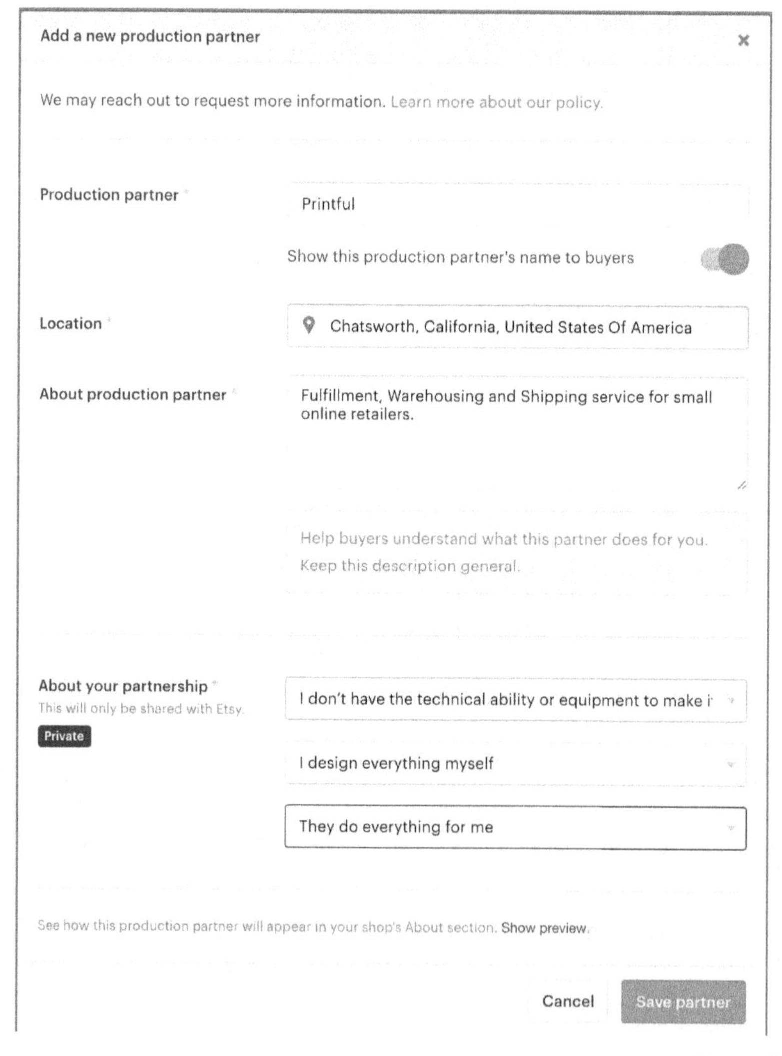

Remember, above is the basics of how to connect Etsy to Printful for POD fulfillment. There can be a lot more details with selling on Etsy, like how to price, discounts, setting up your shipping options, how many Etsy stores to setup, and more. Once you have your accounts set up, here are 2 resources that you may want to consider to learn more about how to get the most out of your Etsy Printful integration:

Additional Etsy Resources:

1: **Course: Etsy Printful Masterclass** by Luke Kelly -> SAVE $100 !!
www.etsyprintfulmasterclass.com (normally $197, but because you have this book, and use this link -> **https://lukekelly.clickfunnels.com/epmcourse?affiliate_id=1010565** , it's ***only $97***) **SAVE $100 using that link** (this book literally is making you money already!)

2: **Book: Etsy Printful Success - Launch Your T-Shirt Business Today** By Monte Werle, Jacob Bates and Jason Huesgen
https://lic.com/a/982168691 ($19.99)
The book includes video lessons, and access to their secret Etsy POD Mastermind Facebook group.

ETSY NOT VIA PRINTFUL:
If you choose to, you can also list on Etsy without Printful. You can integrate directly other POD services such as ***Print Aura*** another platform similar to Printful, which will manufacture and deliver your orders from buyers on Etsy.

To integrate **Etsy** with ***Print Aura***:

1. Create an Etsy Account
Use this link for 40 free listings: http://etsy.me/2nV2rqf (if this is your first listing on Etsy, you'll also need to list your first item, which creates your shop, and gives you access to the shop manager)
2. Register an account with Print Aura
3. Install the Etsy App (on Print Aura)
Instructions here: https://printaura.com/etsy/
4. Select Print Aura as your outside manufacturer on Etsy
(Shop Manager -> Settings -> Production Partners -> Add New Production Partner)
5. Load your designs into Print Aura
6. Sync your Print Aura Designs to Etsy

Here are more details on all the steps, as well as HOW to complete the Etsy Integration on the 'Create a New App' page in Print Aura: https://printaura.com/etsy-install-guide

Want to drive more traffic to your Etsy listings?
Internally:
Promoted listings:
You can use Etsy's Promoted listings, simply set a daily budget, and let the platform drive traffic to your listings. Choose daily limits anywhere from minimum of $1.00/day to Maximum $50.00/day (note, if once your sales start to increase, the maximum can go up, Etsy does this automatically).

Setup Promoted listings here:
https://www.etsy.com/your/shops/me/advertising/promoted-listings

More information about managing your campaigns here:
https://www.etsy.com/help/article/5591

Sales and Coupons:
Etsy allows you to hold sales, and create coupons.
Create a new sale or coupon here: https://www.etsy.com/your/shops/me/sales-coupons?ref=seller-platform-mcnav

ETSY123
Run a sale
Shoppers can discover your sale in search, on your listings, and from shop home. Tips for running sales
Create a coupon
Share it with anyone you like — shoppers can't discover it on their own. Coupons are always applied to the original price, and can be used multiple times. Tips for using coupons

Sale Tips from Etsy:

Sales can help you attract new customers on Etsy and get them to spend more than they would otherwise. A few ideas:

- Attract new customers with a shop-wide sale around a peak shopping time or celebration.
- Clear out excess inventory by offering discounts on select items.
- Get shoppers to spend more with a discount activated by a minimum order.

Coupon Tips from Etsy:

Coupons let you create discounts for specific audiences to encourage purchases, get buyers to spend more, and build loyalty. A few ideas:

- Offer your social media followers a discount on select items.
- Get your newsletter subscribers to spend more by offering a coupon discount activated by a minimum order amount.
- Bring first-time buyers back for more by sending them a “thank you” coupon.

Externally:
Facebook is popular, Pinterest has had good results. You could drive it from anywhere, see Chapter 5 it's all about MARKETING :-)

MAKE YOUR ETSY SHOP PRETTY:
At this point, you have your Shop on Etsy, and it's connected to a POD to load with new products. Take things a bit further, and consider setting up the look and feel of your shop, so that it's inviting and comfortable to buyers, and convoys the message of your brand. Not sure where to start? Check out Etsy's own blog about how to do things right: https://www.etsy.com/seller-handbook/article/the-ultimate-guide-to-telling-your-etsy/22722480541

Does Etsy have mobile apps? Heck yea it does!
Apple iOS Seller App: https://itunes.apple.com/app/sell-on-etsy/id860815329
Android Etsy Seller App: https://play.google.com/store/apps/details?id=com.etsy.android.soe

Apple iOS Buyer App: https://itunes.apple.com/app/etsy/id477128284?_branch_match_id=348568999075461160
Android Etsy Buyer App: https://play.google.com/store/apps/details?id=com.etsy.android&hl

etsy.com's
Alexa rankings:
Q4 2017
Global: 179
USA: 40

HQ:
Etsy
117 Adams St,
Brooklyn, NY
11201, USA

redbubble.com
https://goo.gl/ghe93C (Join Here For Free)
Redbubble offers more than just T-shirts (see list below, in the LETS GET TECHNICAL section), and they ship worldwide, great for sales to Canada, Australia, and Europe!!

FREE GOOGLE SHOPPING ADS:
Superpower: some listings are listed on Google Shopping, at no cost to you! This means that you will see your designs featured in google shopping ads, at no cost to you, paid for by Redbubble! In fact, in 2018 Google authorized Redbubble to list up to 50,000,000 Google Shopping Listings (up from 25 Million). Each listing gives your designs on redouble additional exposure, and effectively free advertising on Google. This leads to MORE organic traffic to Redbubble, and more sales of your designs.

SET YOUR OWN PRICES:
You can set your own prices with Redbubble, by adjusting your percentage of markup, which is accessible under 'artist tools' as 'product pricing' here: https://www.redbubble.com/account/pricing (must have an account with Redbubble to see this page) at this time there appears to be no maximum (up to 1000% was tested, with no errors or warnings), and minimum is 0% markup.

CONNECT TO GOOGLE ANALYTICS:
Also, like many PODs Redbubble wants you to sell as much as possible, and one feature that they give you as a seller, is the ability to connect Google Analytics. By connecting Google Analytics, you can see the broad demographics of all of the traffic that views your designs, as well as which portion of them make purchases. Once you have your free Redbubble account started, follow these simple steps to connect Google Analytics: https://help.redbubble.com/hc/en-us/articles/201774915#settingup

USE THE REDBUBBLE BLOG:
Did you know that Redbubble had a Blog? YES! Check it out in the chapter on Community resources. OR, here's the link to Redbubble's blog: http://blog.redbubble.com/home/

ORGANIZE YOUR REDBUBBLE DESIGNS INTO COLLECTIONS:
Did you know that you can group your Redbubble designs into collections? YUP! To create a new collection, select one or more works on the Manage Works Page and use the 'Collections' dropdown. Here's the direct link to the Manage Works Page: https://www.redbubble.com/portfolio/manage_works

Once you select any image from the Manage Works page, a new menu of choices will appear, it looks like this:

Select Collections, and you'll see this:

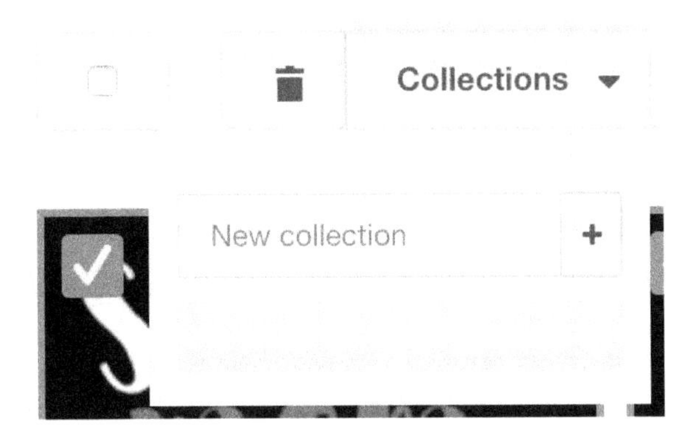

Type in the name of your first collection, and hit the + button to get it started :-)
It will then appear in a list of collections. Select it, and click the Add button to add your selected designs to this collection. There you have it! You've just made a collection!

You can have multiple collections. You can add or delete designs from collections. You can even add a description to your collection! Wait, where's that? … here's how:

Once you have one or more collection setup, you can view it/them by selecting the Collections toggle on the Manage Works Page, it looks like this:

Works | Collections

Manage Portfolio

Need help managing your works?

You can now see a box for each collection, filled with designs! .... Now, select one of them, and click Edit. Here, you can add a description to your collection (in addition to it's name), as well as change the style of the thumbnail, and the order of the collection!

Once you have a collection made in Redbubble, how/where will it appear? You'll find it on your store page (redbubble.com/people/yourstorename). Here's an example of how 4 collections appear together:

In addition to the collections that you create, Redbubble also creates it's own curated collections here: https://www.redbubble.com/discover/collections
Notice that they have top level categories:
Pop Culture
Home Decor
Animals
Patterns
Food
Art Styles
Into The Wild
Funny
Destinations
Hobbies
Seasons
Big Days
For Kids
Halloween
Sticker Packs
Back To School

and several of these top categories have sub categories!
For Example - Big Days is divided into:
Halloween
Christmas
Easter
New Year
Valentine's Day

While Colors is divided into:
Red
Blue
Yellow
Green
Black&White
Pink
Orange
Purple
Greenery
Blush Pink
Ultra Violet

So, have a look through their collections, and consider how you might tag your designs differently, so that they're picked up by one or more collection…
Example:
Red, Valentines Day, Spring, Kids…. etc.

REDBUBBLE Key Keywords:
Redbubble mobile usage grew 58% according to the January 2018 quarterly report (http://shareholders.redbubble.com/site/PDF/1476_1/investorupdateconferencecalltranscript) . One way to Explore the Redbubble mobile app, is by identifying categories you're into. So, when tagging your Redbubble design uploads, I recommend using at least one of the following tags, corresponding to the 'explore' categories Redbubble has available: The TOP 146 Themes of Redbubble are:

Wanderlust	Sloth	Hockey	Forest
Hip Hop	Nature	80's	Water-color
Sitcom	Corgi	Fox	Mountains
Hipster	Science	Nurse	Cartoon
Street Wear	New York	Psychedelic	Happy
Rap	Elephant	90'sCartoon	Kawii
Aesthetic	Travel	Pun	Floral
Funny	Pug	Dragon	Christmas
Dope	Unicorn	Yoga	Nerd
Animated	Scull	Chemistry	Hiking
Cute	Pineapple	Bear	Mexican
Cat	Whale	Panda	Pastel
Anime	Turtle	Animal	Skeleton
Dog	Car	Gaming	Phycology
Cool	Basketball	Trendy	Peace
Singer	Food	Camera	Band

Meme	Love	Pizza	Florida
K-Pop	Beer	Wine	Gay Pride
Flower	Shark	Running	Fashion
Cactus	Ocean	Dinosaur	Graffiti
Horror	Mountain	Sushi	San Fransisco
Space	Moon	Donuts	Astronaut
Japanese	Galaxy	Monster	Softball
Vaporwave	Book	Goat	Song Writer
Trippy	Heart	Geometric	Guitar
Vintage	Retro	Summer	Golf
Feminist	Black and White	Sci-Fi	Ice Cream
Colorado	Wolf	Urban	Owl
Music	Dance	Fantacy	Fishing
TV Series	Avocado	Camping	Girly
california	Good Vibes	Octopus	Pop-Culture
Alien	Football	Tropical	Earth
Coffee	Adventure	Zombie	Plant
Soccer	College	robot	
Computer	EDM	Surf	
90's	Geek	Horse	
Beach	Sport	Programming	

PRO TIP: KIDS SECTION ON REDBUBBLE

Did you know that Redbubble has a Kids section? Are your Redbubble designs there? Did you check off the super secret Kids Clothing checkbox, hidden deep within the design settings? If not, here's how:

1. Under Manage Portfolio, hover over the design you want to add to kids clothing (top left corner), and select Edit:

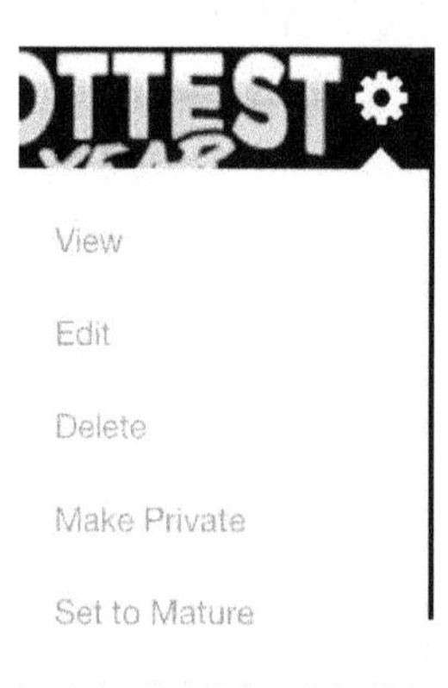

2. Under the Clothing Apparel option, click on the Edit button:

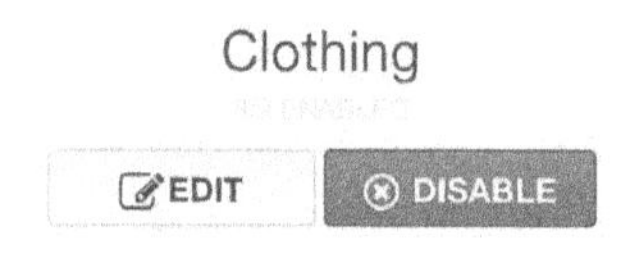

3. Just to the left of the Replace Image button, there are 2 faded out tabs. The top one is called "Image", and the one under it is called "Availability and Markup". Select the bottom one (Availability and Markup).

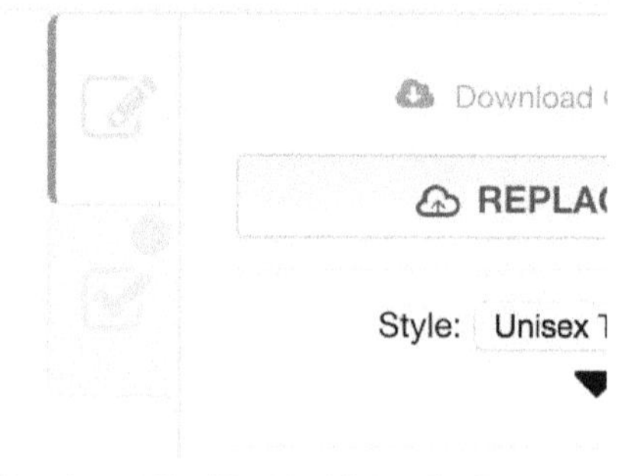

4. Notice that 8/9 items are checked off, but the Kids Clothes is NOT checked off… So

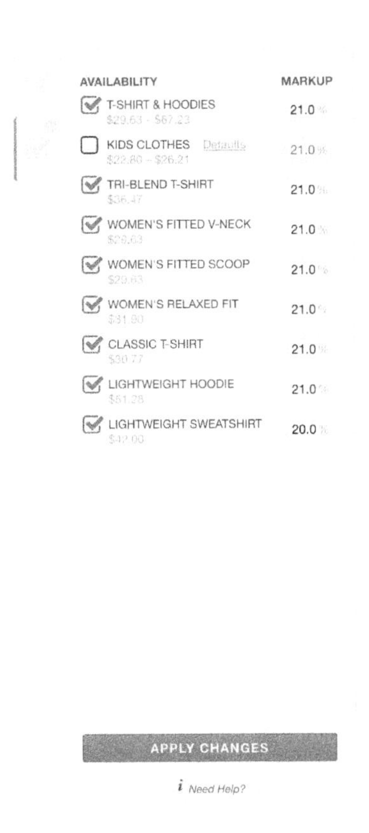

5. This is how it looks when the Kids checkbox is checked:

6. Click the Apply Changes Button:

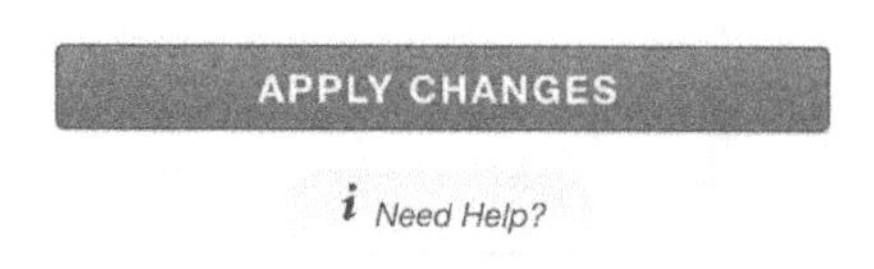

7. Be sure to scroll down the page, and click Save Work:

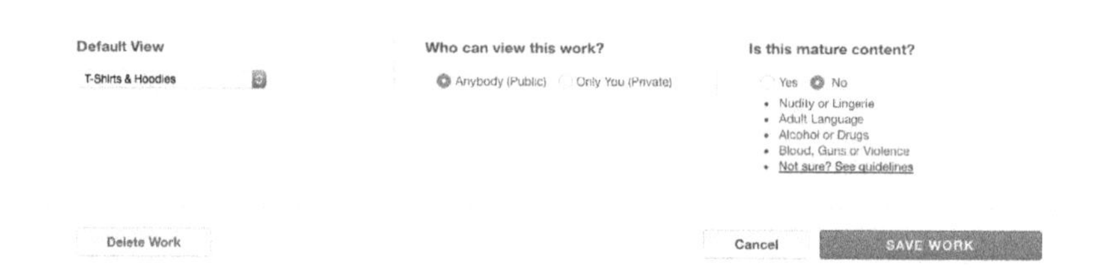

8. Done! Now repeat for all your designs (as long as they are kid friendly designs ;-)). Your design is now available on the Variety of Kids Clothing on Redbubble including:

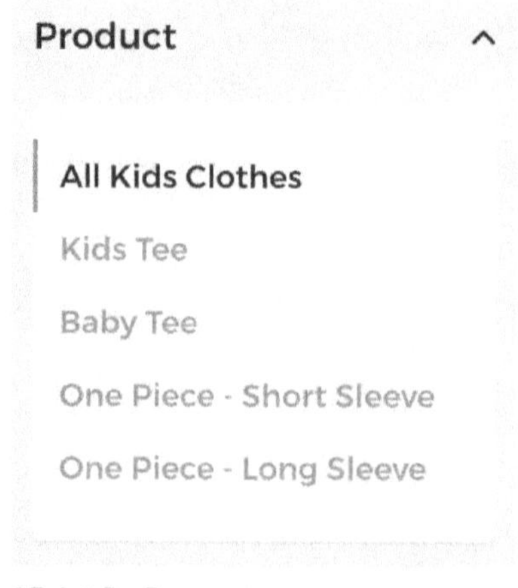

NOTE: You can't sell mature content on the kids shirts. So, if your design contains any of the following things, don't select kids clothing...
Mature content on Redbubble includes:
- Nudity or Lingerie
- Adult Language
- Alcohol or Drugs
- Blood, Guns or Violence

For more info on their guidelines regarding mature content go here: https://help.redbubble.com/hc/en-us/articles/201761545

So... how good of a deal is it to have your designs available in the kids section on Redbubble, isn't everyone selling in the kids section?? NOPE! Running a blank search for kids designs yields: 15,321 results (up from 3,592 results before this book came outMarch 6 2017). A Blank search now yields 107,676 results (Q1 2017 this was 9,874,440), So they must have changed the way the blank search works... At 9,874,440 (as of Q1 2017) under the "recent designs" designation! For the Math geniuses out there... 15,321/9874440 is 0.00155158165... aka, less than 0.2%... so by converting your designs to kids clothing, you remove over 99.7% of your competition, competing on kids designs, on Redbubble!!! Next, some more info on Redbubble numbers...

Redbubble search indicates that their "top selling" shows the top 107,676 designs, which is approximately their top 1% of designs. They have over 600,000 independent artists contributing to their site, lots of variety. Over 200,000 sellers had sales in the last quarter, meaning that plenty of people are not selling, and plenty of people are. In 2017, they had revenue of over $140,000,000USD, meaning of the 200,000 or so sellers who had a sale, on average they had $700. Given that many sellers only have a few designs listed, this is great news if you are considering going Redbubble, and loading some designs.

They have been around for over 15 year, and have paid out over $100,000,000 in profits to sellers.

Here's a fun video by Redbubble, about Redbubble:
vimeo.com/195555159

FUN FACT: Did you know that Redbubble gets almost 7% of it's *referred* traffic from tumblr? Who knew!

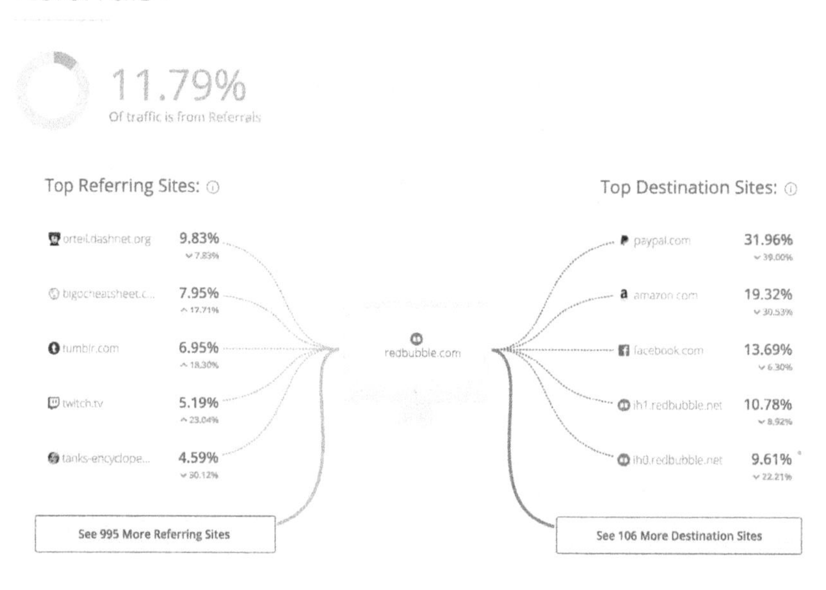

LETS GET TECHNICAL:

When uploading your images to Redbubble, they accept .jpeg and .png file types. You can use your existing 4500x5400 .png Merch By Amazon images, it's no problem!

Their MAXIMUM FILE SIZE is 300MB OR 13500x13500 pixels. They generally do encourage large, detailed images, as they have a **wide variety** of products to place your designs on!

Below is a list of products directly from Redbubble's site, highlighting their preferred minimum image sizes for each product:

NOTE: this list does not include all variations of each product type, I've included that further down)

Greeting Cards:

1300x900 pixels (1 megapixel) more info on cropping, character limits, borders and aspect ratios for cards here: https://help.redbubble.com/hc/en-us/articles/202270749

Framed Prints and Stretched Canvas:
2400×1600 pixels (4 megapixels) for the small print
3240×2160 pixels (7 megapixels) for the medium print
3840×2560 pixels (10 megapixels) for the large print

Metal Prints:
Extra Small - 2400x2400 pixels
Small - 3200x3200 pixels
Medium - 3600x3600 pixels
Large - 3840x3840 pixels
Extra Large - 4800x4800 pixels

Posters:
2500×3500 pixels for the smallest print
3500×5000 pixels for the medium print
5000×7100 pixels for the large print

Calendar images:
2182x1906 pixels for the months
2371x2875 pixels for the cover

Art Prints:
3840x3840 pixels will cover all sizes up to extra large. Art Prints dimensions can change, floating your different shaped images whilst the paper sizes remain the same. More details on Art Print paper sizes will be available in the 'Product Info' section of your product page.

Apparel:
2400×3200 pixels will cover the printable area, although you can resize larger images to fit when uploading. The file must be a PNG for transparencies to be saved.

Mens Graphic tee:
3873x4814 pixels will cover the printable area. There is further information on graphic tees including an artist's template available over here: https://help.redbubble.com/hc/en-us/articles/202270659#Graphic

Women's Chiffon Top:
3711x3814 pixels. There is further information on Women's Chiffon tops, including an artists template over here: https://help.redbubble.com/hc/en-us/articles/202270659#chiffon

Women's Contrast Tank:
3870×4280 pixels There is further information on Women's Contrast Tank, including an artists template over here: https://help.redbubble.com/hc/en-us/articles/202270659#chiffon

Women's Graphic Dress:
4020×6090 pixels. There is further information on Women's Graphic Dress, including an artists template over here: https://help.redbubble.com/hc/en-us/articles/202270659#chiffon
Women's A-Line Dress:
6310x6230 pixels

Stickers:
600x800 pixels for small
1100x1100 pixels for medium
1700x1700 pixels for large
2800x2800 pixels for x-large
The file must be a PNG for transparencies to be saved. We recommend uploading a file with the maximum pixel requirements (2800x2800 pixels) to ensure your design is available on all 4 sticker sizes

Phone Cases & Skins:
1187x1852 pixels will cover the printable area, however you can resize larger images to fit

iPhone Wallet
2087×1956 pixels

Laptop Skins & Studio Pouches:
4600x3000 pixels will cover the printable area, however you can resize larger images to fit
Please note slight cropping of the image on the smaller pouches will occur.

Laptop Sleeves:
4125x2956 pixels

iPad Cases & Skins:
2696x3305 pixels will cover the printable area

Throw Pillows:
2188x2188 pixels for the small pillow
2438x2438 pixels for the medium pillow
2788x2788 pixels for the large pillow

Tote Bags:
2175x2175 pixels for the small tote bag
2625x2625 pixels for the medium tote bag
2950x2950 pixels for the large tote bag

Drawstring Bags:
2475x2775 pixels for drawstring bags
Duvet Covers (125 max DPI):
8570x11250 pixels for the twin duvet (including bleeding)
11000x11000 pixels for the queen duvet (including bleeding)
13500×11462 pixels for the king duvet (including bleeding)

Mugs:
2700x1624 pixels for standard & tall mug
2376x2024 pixels for travel mug

Leggings:
4350x4032 pixels for leggings

Scarves:
5748x5748 pixels for scarves

Pencil Skirt:
2152x2502 pixels for pencil skirts

Spiral Notebooks:
1756x2481 pixels for spiral notebooks

Hardcover Journals:
3502x2385 pixels for hardcover journals

Wall Tapestries:
13500 x 11462 pixels

Clock:
2940 x 2940 pixels

Acrylic Block:
4 x 4 & 6 x 6: 1860 × 1860 pixels

NOTE: The above list of Redbubble products and dimensions is from their webpage here: https://help.redbubble.com/hc/en-us/articles/202270679-Dimensions-Format-and-Color AND they have even more tips for their site, as well as design tips there, worth taking a read if you want additional information about their suggested design tips, and perspective.

REDBUBBLE MEGA DETAILS:
Below you will find different variations in item type, as well as colors which match each type (included because they may have the same number of colors... but THE COLORS ARE DIFFERENT... sneaky Redbubble!)

Clothing options:

✓ Unisex T-Shirt
Unisex Tank Top
Women's T-Shirt
V-Neck
Racerback Tank
Baseball ¾ Sleeve
Long Sleeve
Sweatshirt
Hoodie (Pullover)
Hoodie (Zipper)

Unisex T-Shirt (18 colors)

Unisex Tank Top (7 colors)

Women's T-Shirt (18 colors)

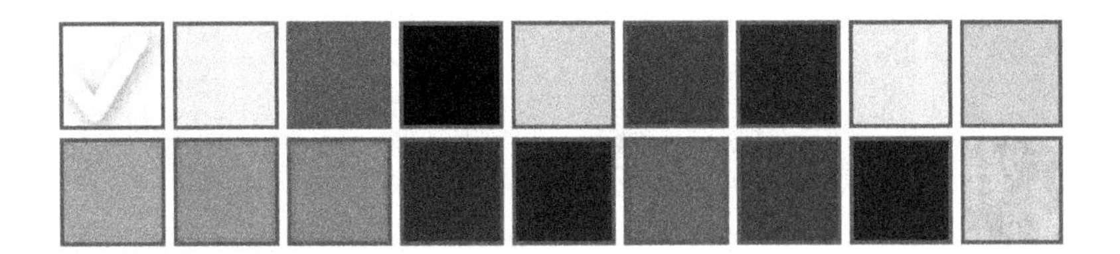

V-Neck (8 colors)

Racerback Tank (3 colors)

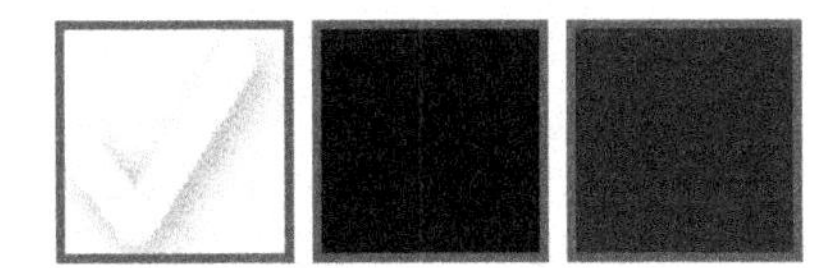

Baseball 3/4 sleeve (7 colors)

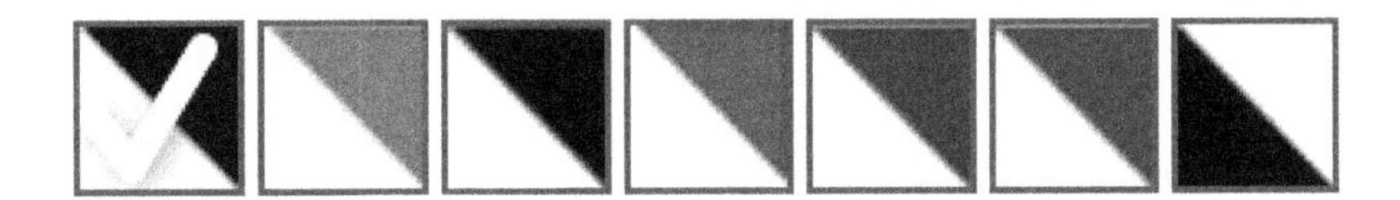

Long Sleeve (6 colors)

Sweatshirt (6 colors)

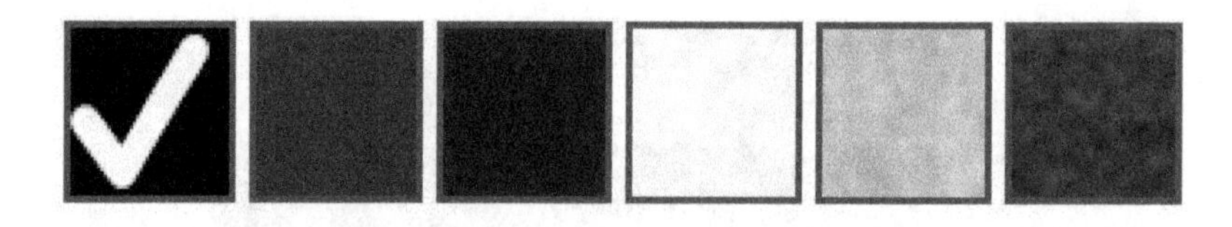

Hoodie (Pullover) (6 colors)

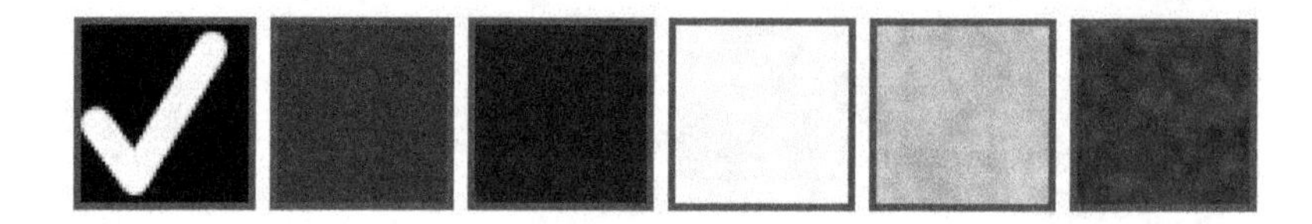

Hoodie (Zipper) (6 colors)

(for the next 5 choices, you choose your own color by dragging selection or RGB/HEX#)

HELPFUL LINK: Want to pre-select your RGB[Hex#] colors? Here's a link for that: http://www.w3schools.com/colors/colors_picker.asp

Contrast Tanks
Women's Chiffon Tops
Graphic T-Shirt Dress
Graphic T-Shirts
A-Line Dress

Stickers

On Redbubble, stickers ship with a white background, and are cut to match the shape of the design.

Phone Cases & Skins

(Available for the following 45 variations - Samsung and Apple iPhones only) Including the newly added iPhone 8, iPhone 8 Plus, and iPhone X, Galaxy S8, Galaxy S8 Plus

✓ Samsung Galaxy S7 Edge - Snap
Samsung Galaxy S7 Edge - Tough
Samsung Galaxy S7 - Snap
Samsung Galaxy S7 - Tough
Samsung Galaxy S6 Edge Plus - Snap
Samsung Galaxy S6 Edge Plus - Tough
Samsung Galaxy S6 Edge - Snap
Samsung Galaxy S6 Edge - Tough
Samsung Galaxy S6 - Snap
Samsung Galaxy S6 - Tough
Samsung Galaxy S5 - Snap
Samsung Galaxy S5 - Tough
Samsung Galaxy S5 - Skin
Samsung Galaxy S4 - Snap
Samsung Galaxy S4 - Tough
Samsung Galaxy S4 - Skin
Samsung Galaxy S3 - Snap
Samsung Galaxy S3 - Tough
iPhone 7 - Snap
iPhone 7 - Tough
iPhone 7 Plus - Snap
iPhone 7 Plus - Tough
iPhone 6s - Snap
iPhone 6s - Tough
iPhone 6s Plus - Snap
iPhone 6s Plus - Tough
iPhone 6 - Snap
iPhone 6 - Tough
iPhone 6 - Skin
iPhone 6 Plus - Snap
iPhone 6 Plus - Tough
iPhone 6 Plus - Skin
iPhone SE/5s/5 - Snap
iPhone SE/5s/5 - Tough
iPhone SE/5s/5 - Skin
iPhone 5c - Snap
iPhone 5c - Tough
iPhone 5c - Skin
iPhone 4s/4 - Snap
iPhone 4s/4 - Tough
iPhone 4s/4 - Skin

Phone Wallets
(available on the following 4 iPhone variations)

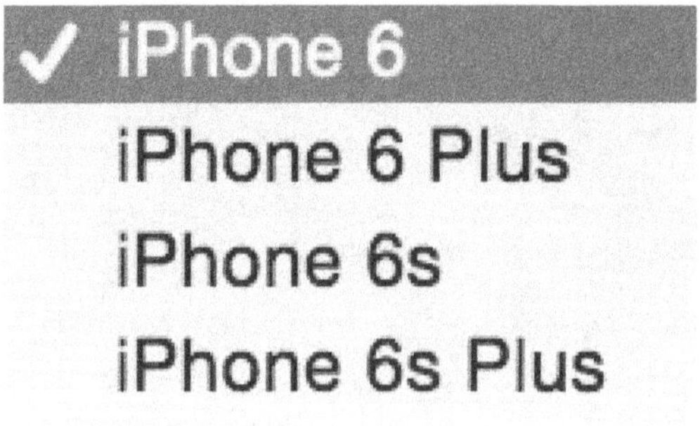

✓ iPhone 6
iPhone 6 Plus
iPhone 6s
iPhone 6s Plus

Prints, Cards & Posters
Pillows & Totes
Pouches, Laptop Skins & Sleeves
Duvets
- King
- Queen
- Twin

Mugs (tall and standard)
Travel Mugs
Leggings
Mini Skirts
Scarves

Tablet Cases & Skins

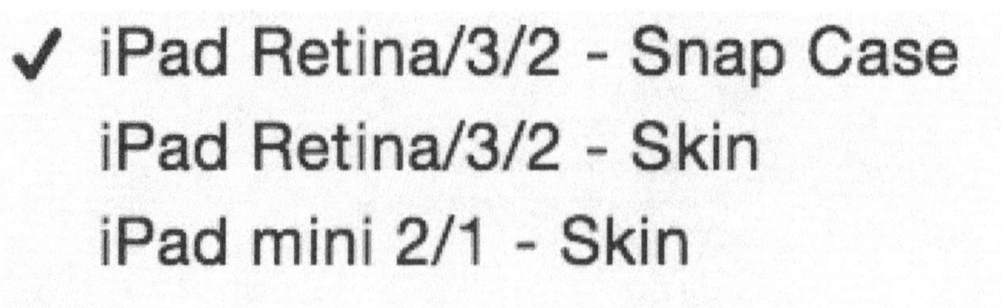

✓ iPad Retina/3/2 - Snap Case
iPad Retina/3/2 - Skin
iPad mini 2/1 - Skin

Drawstring Bags
Spiral Notebooks
Hardcover Journals
Clock
Art Board
Acrylic Block
Wall Tapestry

PRO TIP: Did you know that Redbubble has templates? Yes! They have templates for nearly every one of the items that they sell! In addition to the templates, they also have quick videos showing you how to use the templates. Great for marketing your designs!
https://blog.redbubble.com/templates/

Does Redbubble Have a Mobile App?
Yes! For Apple iOS: https://itunes.apple.com/app/apple-store/id1145737091?mt=8
You can use it to browse products, see collections, save favorites for later, and best of all find inspiration for things you may want to design :-)

redbubble.com's
Alexa's rankings:
Q12017
Global: 2,003
USA: 861
Q4 2017
Global: 1,366
USA: 481

Head Quarters:
Redbubble
111 Sutter St.
San Francisco, California 94104
U.S.A.

Redbubble
Level 3, 271 Collins Street
Melbourne, Victoria 3000
Australia

zazzle.com
Zazzle offers loads of product choices (OVER 1,400 PRODUCTS TO CHOOSE FROM!), and have a different look and feel. Zazzle has been around since 2003 (15 years old).

Choose the percentage of royalties you would like to receive, and you will see an estimated amount, based on the design you are viewing. Some designs will be marked as sold out if the stock is not available at the time of listing. During the upload process you have many bulk options such as: Dark designs only, Light designs only, Mens/Womens/Kids designs only, and more!

ZAZZLE BLACK:
Ordering lots of samples, or want faster shipping, FREE shipping via Zazzle? Check out their paid premium service offerings via Zazzle Black: https://www.zazzle.com/zazzleblack for a small annual fee ($995/year Standard Zazzle Black, or $39.95/year Zazzle Black 2 Day), you get all the normal Zazzle, plus more!

The best way to shop or sell on Zazzle!
Get free shipping, exclusive discounts, and much more.

Zazzle Black
Standard
$9.95/year (Most popular!)

- Unlimited **FREE Standard Shipping** on all orders for qualifying products*

Get a free 30-day trial and save on your order today!

Start a FREE trial

You will have the opportunity to opt out of automatic enrollment before your trial period ends.

Zazzle Black
2-Day
$39.95/year

- Unlimited **FREE 2-Day Shipping** on all orders for qualifying products*
- Unlimited **FREE Standard Shipping** on all orders for qualifying products*

Sign up for 2-Day

By clicking "Sign up", you agree to be charged $39.95 for Zazzle Black 2-Day Shipping program membership.

Like Redbubble, Zazzle lists your designs on Google shopping, which drives more traffic to your listings!

Here is a quick link to Zazzle's own video about how to create on their platform:
https://youtu.be/bdcGV4RNwJ0 It all starts with the Create your Own button! As a seller, be sure to select the 'sell it' option, of course!

PRO TIP: Want to earn commissions off of other people modifying your designs? You can! Try making some "Create your Own" designs, and when people choose your design, and modify it to their own, you get paid! (one of the best kept secrets in POD land)

Some Zazzle categories: (there's even more than these!)

- Expressions
- Holidays
- Occasions
    - Anniversaries
    - Baby & Expecting
    - Birthdays
        - Belated
        - Best Friends
        - By Year
            - 1st to 105th...
        - Children
        - Family
            - Aunt & Uncles
            - Daughters & Sons
            - Fathers
            - Grandparents
            - Mothers
            - Sisters & Brothers
        - For All
        - From the Group
        - Funny
        - Over the Hill
        - Romantic
        - Sports Related
        - Sweet 16
        - Work Related
    - Care & Concern
    - Celebration
    - Divorce
    - Graduations

New Home & Pet
Religious Events

Other

NEW For a FULL list of all the things that Zazzle offers, Check out their sitemap, here: https://www.zazzle.com/sitemap

Here are just **SOME** of the Products offered on Zazzle:

Categories

Invitations, Cards & Postage

Cards
Greeting Cards
Anniversary Cards
Birthday Cards
Thank You Cards
Sympathy Cards
Get Well Cards

Congratulations Cards
Baby & Pregnancy Cards
Graduation Cards

Holiday Cards
New Year's Cards
Chinese New Year Cards
Valentine's Day Cards
Easter Cards
Thanksgiving Cards
Hanukkah Cards
Christmas Cards

Invitations & Announcements
Wedding Invitations
Holiday Invitations
4th of July Invitations
Halloween Invitations
Thanksgiving Invitations
Christmas Invitations

Graduation Announcements
Graduation Invitations
Graduation Party Invitations

Baby & Pregnancy Invitations
Baby Shower Invitations
Baby Boy Shower Invitations
Baby Girl Shower Invitations
Birth Announcements
Gender Reveal Invitations
Pregnancy Announcements

Religious Celebrations
Baptism & Christening Invitations
Bar Mitzvah Invitations
Bat Mitzvah Invitations
Confirmation Invitations
First Communion Invitations

Response Cards
Change of Address Cards
Moving Announcements
Retirement Party Invitations
Grand Opening Invitations

Birthday Invitations
1st Birthday Invitations
40th Birthday Invitations
50th Birthday Invitations
60th Birthday Invitations
Quinceañera Invitations
Sweet 16 Invitations

Envelopes
Invitation Belly Bands
Return Address Stamps
Return Address Labels

Postcards
Postage

Crafts & Party Supplies

Gift Wrapping Supplies
Gift Bags
Gift Boxes
Gift Tags
Stickers & Labels
Tissue Paper
Wrapping Paper

Party Supplies & Décor
Favor Bags
Favor Boxes
Hand Fans
Banners
Bunting Flags
Guest Books
Table Numbers
Diaper Raffle Tickets

Napkin Bands
Paper Cups
Paper Napkins
Paper Placemats
Paper Plates
Table Card Holders

Sports, Toys & Games

Baseballs
Basketballs
Hockey Pucks
Soccer Balls
Softballs
Footballs

Golf
Golf Balls
Golf Head Covers
Golf Gloves
Golf Ball Markers

Beer Pong Tables
Cornhole & Bag Toss
Frisbees

Cribbage
Playing Cards
Poker Chips

Skateboards
Yoga Mats
Coolers
Beach Towels

Dartboards
Mini Basketball Hoops
Ping Pong Balls
Ping Pong Paddles

Musical Instruments
Drumsticks
Guitar Picks
Guitar Cases

Stuffed Animals
Puzzles

Electronics

Cases
iPhone Cases
iPhone X
iPhone 8/7
iPhone 8 Plus/7 Plus
iPhone 6/6s
iPhone 6/6s Plus
iPhone SE/5/5s
iPhone 5C
iPhone 4/4S

Speck Cases
OtterBox Cases
Lifeproof Cases
Case-Mate Cases
Uncommon Cases
Carved Cases
Incipio Cases
Zazzle Cases

Computer & Laptop
Keyboards
Mouse Pads
Wireless Mouse
USB Flash Drives
Speakers
Headphones

Chargers
Power Banks
USB Charging Stations
Apple Watch Bands

Samsung Cases
Galaxy S8
Galaxy S8+
Galaxy S7
Galaxy S7 Edge
Galaxy S6
Galaxy S6 Edge
Galaxy S6 Edge Plus
Galaxy S5
Galaxy S4
Galaxy Note 5
Galaxy Note 4

Google Cases
Nexus
Pixel
Pixel XL
Laptop Cases
Laptop Sleeves
Tablet Cases
iPad Cases
iPad Covers
iPad Sleeves
iPod Cases

Skins
Phone Skins
System Skins
Computer Skins
iPod Skins
Laptop Skins & Decals
Tablet & eReader Skins

Clothing & Shoes

Men's Clothing
Men's T-Shirts
Men's Tank Tops
Men's Activewear
Men's Hoodies
Men's Sweatshirts
Men's Jackets
Men's Jerseys

Women's Clothing
Women's T-Shirts
Women's Tank Tops
Women's Activewear
Women's Hoodies
Women's Sweatshirts
Women's Jackets
Women's Jerseys
Women's Polo Shirts

Kids' & Baby Clothing
Kids' T-Shirts
Kids' Hoodies
Kids' Sweatshirts
Kids' Shoes
Kids' Flip Flops

T-Shirts
Tank Tops
Polo Shirts
Jerseys
Hoodies
Sweatshirts
Jackets & Coats
Dresses

Men's Polo Shirts
Men's Underwear
Men's Boxers
Men's Shoes

Maternity Shirts
Plus Size
Women's Leggings
Women's Underwear
Hot Shorts
Sports Bras
Boyshorts
Thongs
Women's Shoes

Baby Clothes
Baby Tops & T-Shirts
Baby Bodysuits & One-Pieces
Diaper Covers
Baby Girl Dresses

Activewear
Performance T-Shirts
Underwear
Socks
Shoes
Flip Flops

Accessories

Bags, Wallets & Luggage
Backpacks
Drawstring Bags
Gym & Duffel Bags
Fanny Packs
Reusable Grocery Bags
Tote Bags
Cosmetic Bags

Luggage & Travel
Accessory Bags
Luggage
Luggage Handle Wraps
Luggage Tags
Passport Covers & Holders

Jewelry
Bracelets
Charms
Earrings
Necklaces
Rings
Watches

Hats & Caps
Embroidered Hats
Trucker Hats
Headsweats
Visors & Sun Hats
Graduation Cap Toppers
Athletic Headbands
Hair Ties

Clutches & Evening Bags
Wristlets
Crossbody Bags
Laptop & Messenger
Wallets
Checkbook Covers
Money Clips

Buttons
Button Covers
Belt Buckles
Belts

Suit Accessories
Ties
Tie Bars
Cufflinks & Shirt Studs
Lapel Pins

Keychains & Lanyards
Sunglasses & Eyewear
Scarves
Bandanas

Home

Seasonal Holiday Décor
Ornaments
Snow Globes
Stockings
Tree Skirts

Food & Drink
Candy & Jelly Belly Tins
Candy Jars
Chewing Gum Favors
Chocolate Boxes
Drinks & Drink Mixes

Barware & Bar Tools
Bottle Stoppers & Corks
Bottle Openers
Wine Charms
Coasters
Lighters

Bath & Beauty
Bathroom
Bath Towels
Bath Accessory Sets
Bath Mats & Rugs
Bathroom Scales
Shower Curtains

Home Décor
Photo Blocks
Photo Cubes
Photo Plaques
Photo Statuettes
Picture Frames

Chocolates & Treats
Brownies
Cake Pops
Cookies
Frosting Rounds

Flasks
Decanters
Steins
Shot Glasses
Wine Glasses

Beauty
Compact Mirrors
Lip Balm
Nail Art
Temporary Tattoos

Lamp Shades
Lamps
Night Lights
Outlet Covers
Wall Plates

Kitchen & Dining
Food & Drink Labels
Beer Labels
Water Labels
Wine Labels

Refrigerator Magnets
Recipe Binders
Recipe Cards

Bedding
Bed & Body Pillows
Duvet Covers & Bedspreads
Pillowcases & Shams

Decorative Tiles
Knobs & Pulls
Door Hangers
Door Signs
Hangers
Key Racks

Serving Platters
Serving Trays
Trivets
Cake Toppers
Cake Stands
Cutting Boards
Cheese Boards

Bowls
Plates
Can Coolers
Lunch Boxes
Mason Jars
Wine Tote Bags & Carriers

Pet Clothing
Pet Tags
Pet Bowls
Dog Beds
Dog Collars
Dog Leashes

Poufs
Throw Pillows
Outdoor Pillows
Blankets & Throws
Throw Blankets
Fleece Blankets
Sherpa Blankets
Wall Tapestries
Candles
Trinket Trays
Indoor Mats & Rugs
Doormats & Rugs
Yard Signs

Drinkware
Coffee Mugs
Travel Mugs
Tumblers
Pitchers
Water Bottles
Teapots

Aprons
Kitchen Towels
Placemats
Table Runners
Tablecloths
Napkins

Car Accessories
Bumper Stickers & Decals
Car Flags
License Plates
Trailer Hitch Accessories
Air Fresheners
Car Floor Mats

Again, for a FULL list of all the things that Zazzle offers, Check out their sitemap, here: https://www.zazzle.com/sitemap

BRANDS ON ZAZZLE:
In addition to all the above types of items on Zazzle, there are also a LOT of MEGA-Brands including: Disney, Marvel, Looney tunes, Harry Potter, Sesame Street, My Little Pony, Dreamworks Studios, Warner Brothers, Sports Teams from NCAA teams, to Greek's Sorority's, Fraternity's, NBA, and MORE! This is great for bringing traffic to the platform, and making happy buyers. On the Consumer side, all these brands and teams offer customization-able designs. So you could for example make a Micky Mouse loves XYZ on ABC product, etc. CRAZY!

MAKERS ON ZAZZLE:
In addition to all the products they make, and the brands they have licences for to sell, they also have a new and growing stable of 3rd Party Makers. Everything from custom bicycles, hammocks, Bound Journals, Carved Smartphone cases, Custom buttons for button-up shirts, whiskey glasses, wooden cutting boards, even Faux Taxidermy.... the makers get prettttttty creative. At the moment, the Makers are all US based, however Zazzle has announced privately that they intend to open up the maker marketplace to international makers as well... so in the near future, you might see Etsy or Amazon handmade having a run for it's money, with Zazzle...

Does Zazzle have a mobile app? YES they do!
Here is their Apple iOS App:
https://itunes.apple.com/us/app/zazzle/id736836912
Here is their Android App:
https://play.google.com/store/apps/details?id=com.zazzle

zazzle.com's
Alexa's rankings:
Q1 2017
Global: 2,552
USA: 881
Q4 2017
Global: 3,309
USA: 794

Head Quarters:
Zazzle
Located in Redwood City, California

teespring.com

TeeSpring is a "mega POD", meaning it's been around for a while, and it's driven millions of dollars in sales. It also has advanced features and capabilities found on no other POD. Teespring offers campaigns, with countdowns, allowing you to synchronize your shipments out, which is great for events, or time sensitive releases. Tee spring also drives ads via the Criteo ad network, on websites such as inc.com.

BUYER EMAIL:

TeeSpring offers you as a seller/designer access to your buyer's e-mail information. In addition to a direct buyer messaging tool they have (more in the TeeSpring services section below), they also allow you to bulk download your buyer's email addresses for use elsewhere. Here's how: Go to "Messages" in your Teespring dashboard, choose "Create a group" to group the campaigns you'd like to download your buyer emails from. Download buyer emails or Hashed Buyer Emails (HBE's) from past 6 months within your Teespring Dashboard.

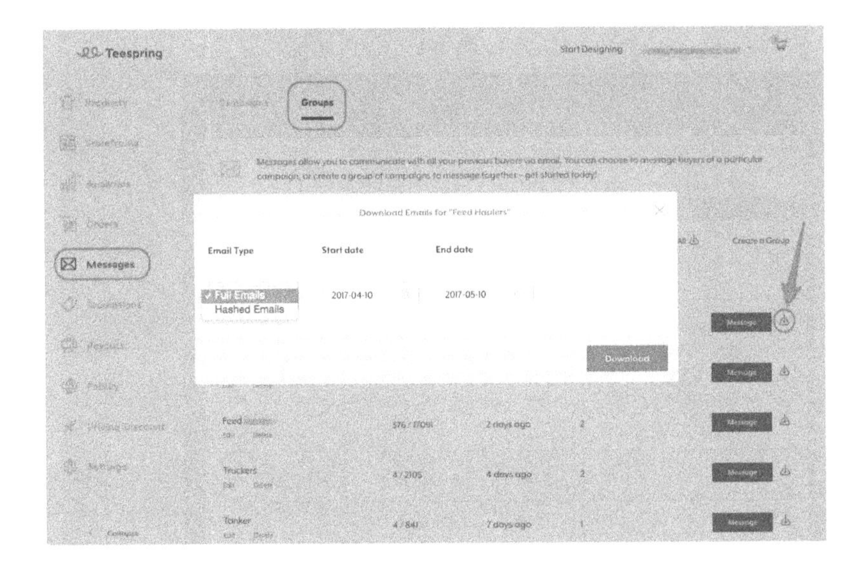

UPSELLING:
This is when you can incent your buyers to buy more items in one order (kind of like an on the spot bundle). Here's where you create these: On your dashboard, navigate to the "promotions" section. Locate the "Up-sells" tab. Use it to create an upsell. More info here:
https://community.teespring.com/answers/up-sells/

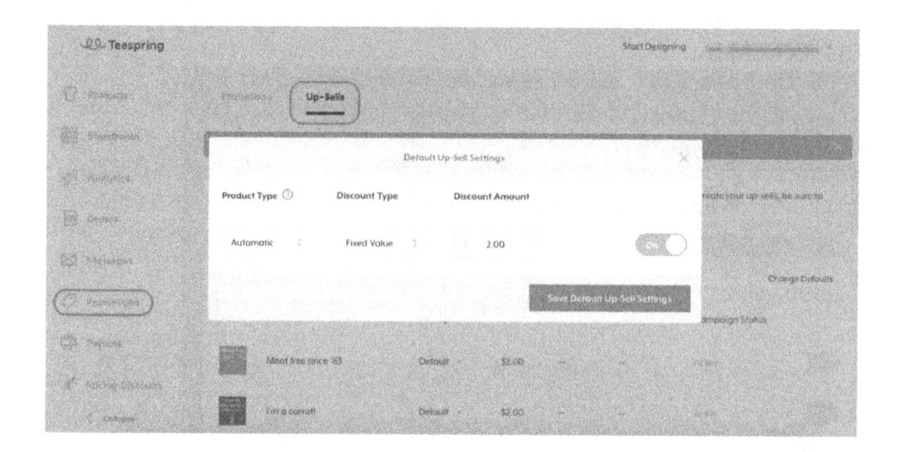

CROSS SELLING:
Cross selling allows you to showcase similar products you offer to your buyers at several key places. They can be shown in 3 places on TeeSpring: campaign pages, checkout pages, and the thank you page after purchase. Cross selling boosts the exposure of your designs to your buyers. In addition to the 3 places you can show cross selling, there are 5 types of things that TeeSpring allows you to cross sell by:

Featured: We will suggest the products you've "starred" (featured within your store) to shoppers.

Bestselling: This is a useful setting if you want to push your most popular products.

Shuffle: Teespring randomly suggests products from your store to shoppers.

Newest: We'll suggest the latest products added to your store.

Oldest: We'll suggest the oldest products added to your store.

Find and setup cross selling in your dashboard under the storefronts section, under the cross sell tab:

More info on Cross selling here: https://community.teespring.com/answers/cross-selling/

FACE BOOK CART ABANDONMENT TOOL:
TeeSpring now offers an innovative way to bring buyers back, who have left things in their cart... by Facebook Messenger Bot!

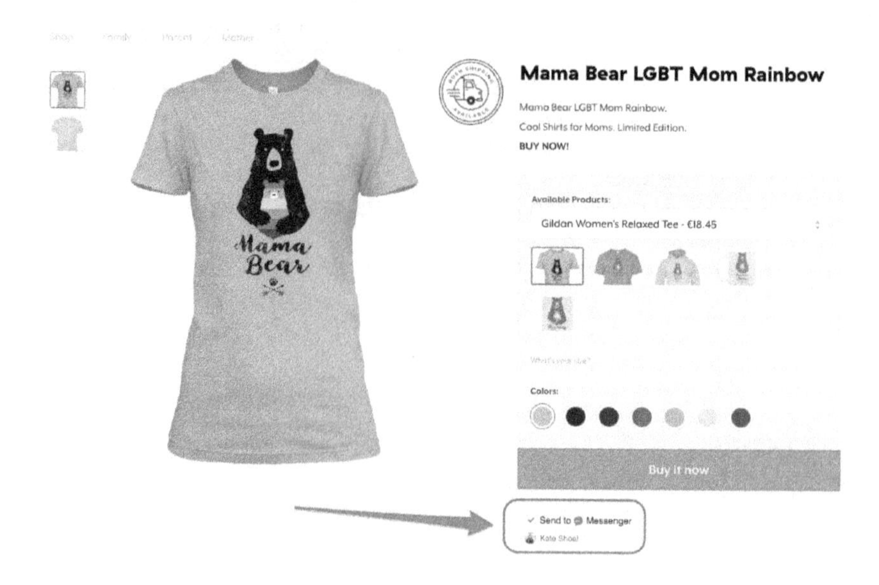

When a shopper visits your campaign page (while logged into Facebook) they'll see a messenger icon and their name below the "Buy Now" button. If the buyer adds one of your products to their cart (with the messenger option ticked) and does not check out, TeeSpring will be able to send them a message reminding them to complete their purchase. This message will include a link they can click to complete checkout on teespring.com. Initial results look promising and TeeSpring plans to continue testing this feature site-wide in the months to come.
Here's what they'll see in Facebook Messenger:

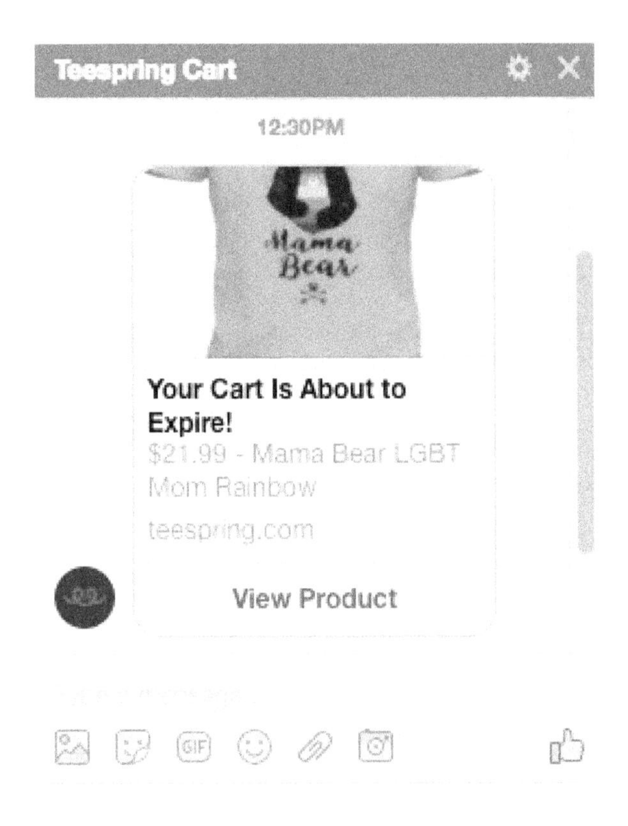

SUPER RUSH SHIPPING: (Faster than Amazon Prime with Merch By Amazon…)

Added in late 2017, TeeSpring has a new shipping option which gets products into buyers' hands within two to three days of ORDERING. Available at checkout on select products, this is one of the FASTEST SHIPPING OPTIONS AVAILABLE ANYWHERE (yea, it's way faster than Amazon Prime's 1 day Shipping… because Merch By Amazon can sometimes take 2-3 days to make the orders, before they even ship them)

PROMOTIONAL CODES:

Want to offer buyers a big sale, or use a promotional code, you can with TeeSpring!

They make it easy, in 3 steps:

1. In your Teespring Dashboard, select the "Promotions" section

2. Create your "Promo ID" and select your discount amount (i.e. free shipping, monetary discount such as $5, or a percentage discount like 15%), you can create a custom discount name (i.e. FREESHIP, 50OFF, etc.) or just use the auto-generate button. Set an expiration date for the discount code, or make it "never ending". Ensure your discount code's status is switched to "on".

3. To add the discount code to the end of your campaign URL. Type this text before pasting it in the code: "/?pr=".

More Info here: https://community.teespring.com/training-center/teesprings-promotions/

FREE PlaceIt Images through TeeSpring - NO LONGER OFFERED :-(
Blast from the past here's how it used to work…

~~HOW TO GET FREE PlaceIt HIGH RES IMAGES VIA TEESPRING: once you have created your TeeSpring listings, click the gear to go into settings. Scroll down to the bottom of the settings, and you will see a section called Social Share Image ->Teespring Creative… here is an example of what it looks like:~~

TeeSpring's T2 LAUNCH:
What about the Spring 2017 TeeSpring T2 launch, which promised to automatically link
all your TeeSpring listings to amazon.com? It was a massive failure. It ran for a very short period of time in 2017, before being modified to only be available for sellers meeting a minimum selling volume. Then it was paused. Then it disappeared... so yes, PODs can and do change, and sometimes more rapidly than you would like. ... So what followed the T2 Launch? Glad you asked! They now have modified their boosted network, and still have access to cross-list to Amazon.

TeeSpring's Boosted Network:

In 2017, TeeSpring launched it's "new" T2 push, which allowed sellers to Amazon via TeeSpring - here is one of their announcements at the time:

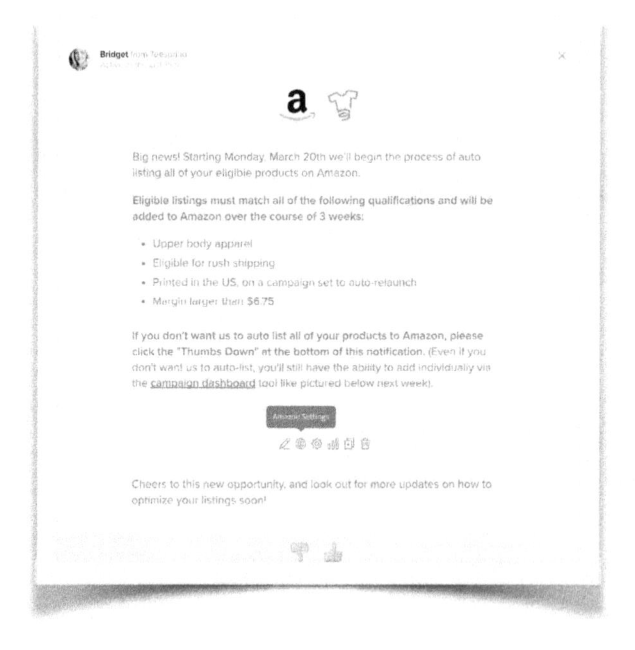
Bridget

Big news! Starting Monday, March 20th we'll begin the process of auto listing all of your eligible products on Amazon.

Eligible listings must match all of the following qualifications and will be added to Amazon over the course of 3 weeks:

- Upper body apparel
- Eligible for rush shipping
- Printed in the US, on a campaign set to auto-relaunch
- Margin larger than $6.75

If you don't want us to auto list all of your products to Amazon, please click the "Thumbs Down" at the bottom of this notification. (Even if you don't want us to auto-list, you'll still have the ability to add individually via the campaign dashboard tool like pictured below next week).

Cheers to this new opportunity, and look out for more updates on how to optimize your listings soon!

T2 was replaced by the much better, much clearer Boosted Network (they had boosted network before, but before T2, it was a number of multiple websites that TeeSpring owned and ran, in addition to their main platform). So, the Boosted Network added Amazon, Walmart, Ebay and Wish. Powerful huge marketplaces, where your designs can be both seen and sold - if you know how to use / enter the Boosted Network ;-)

How to join TeeSpring's Boosted Network:

1: Your design must comply with Boosted Network Design Guidelines located here: https://community.teespring.com/training-center/boosted-network-design-guidelines

2: Your campaign needs to offer one or more rush eligible product(s) detailed here:
https://community.teespring.com/answers/rush-shipping-product-options

3: Your campaign's lifecycle needs to be set to always available or continuous relaunch. Here's how to do that: https://community.teespring.com/answers/campaign-length-and-relaunches

4: The secret 4th step not in their infographic below... Opt into the Boosted network! You'll find this in your TeeSpring Account Settings (image below)
Located here: https://teespring.com/dashboard/settings

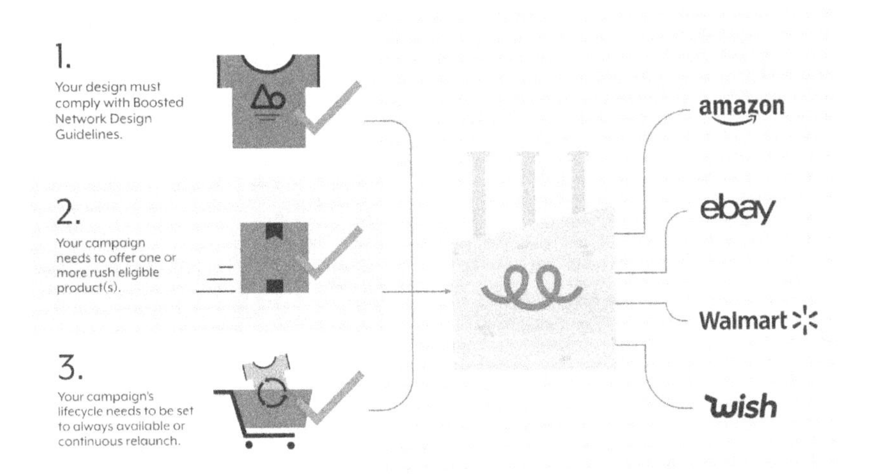

PRO TIP: One really important factor as part of the 1st criteria (meeting the **boosted network's** designs guidelines, is that your designs also happen to comply with Facebook's Ad network policy! Explainer slide show located here: https://community.teespring.com/training-center/why-does-ad-quality-matter/

Facebook's Ad Policy here: facebook.com/policies/ads

Facebook's Ad learning centre here: facebook.com/business/help
(this has LOADS of FREE info on how to make better performing Facebook ads)

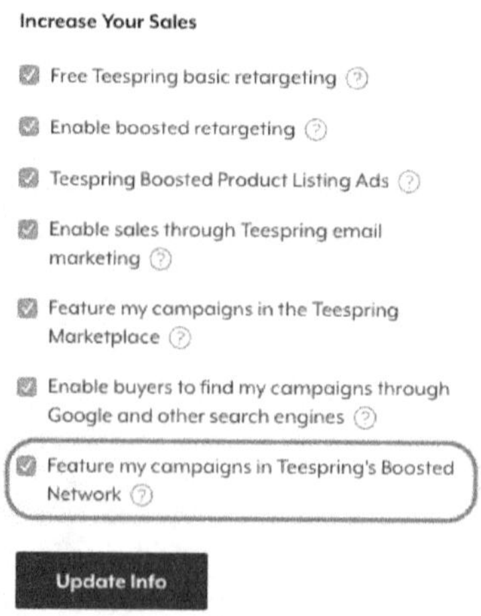

Increase Your Sales

- Free Teespring basic retargeting
- Enable boosted retargeting
- Teespring Boosted Product Listing Ads
- Enable sales through Teespring email marketing
- Feature my campaigns in the Teespring Marketplace
- Enable buyers to find my campaigns through Google and other search engines
- Feature my campaigns in Teespring's Boosted Network

Update Info

TEESPRING SERVICES you may not know of:

1: TRANSLATION SERVICES: TeeSpring offers FREE language translation services for sellers that have sold over 100 designs on the platforms! Yea!!! German, French, Italian, Spanish, Polish… you name it! FREE -> https://community.teespring.com/training-center/teespring-languages-department/ NOTE: TeeSpring Translation services are available from Monday to Friday and queries will receive a response within 24 – 48 hours.

2: EUROPEAN SALES: That's right, TeeSpring offers European fulfillment in addition to it's USA fulfillment. Access the over 614 million internet users and over 300 million Facebook users in Europe! To offer your designs via TeeSpring's European boosted network: ***Duplicate your US based campaign, and then Change the fulfillment region to EU.*** Go a step further by using their translation service (above), or if you're not yet qualified for it (100+ sales to qualify for free translation services from TeeSpring), use google translate, or pay a VA or other service to translate to the languages you wish to target. For even more traffic make sure you've got some rush eligible products selected. More info here: https://community.teespring.com/training-center/welcome-to-teespring-europe/

3: DESIGNER SERVICES: You can have teeSpring help you with making your designs, and more. Just one of the services offered when you plan a campaign of 100+ designs… apply for a quote here: https://try.teespring.com/direct

4: MESSAGE BUYERS IN BULK: That's right, TeeSpring allows you to connect to your buyers in bulk, by campaign via their messages section in your dashboard. Imagine sending out emails to all your previous buyers! YOU CAN! More info here: https://community.teespring.com/training-center/teesprings-buyer-message-tool/

5: DIRECT BUYER PICKUP: Lets say you have an event - a conference, a party, a show, etc. and you want people to order their own things ahead of time, and pick up their order's at your event… you can, with TeeSpring! Just let them know in advance, and they'll have the orders from your campaign delivered to the location you choose. Added benefit: they back out the delivery cost from your profits, so you earn more $$, and it's a great way for you to meet your buyers with their custom orders, at your own event!

More info here: https://community.teespring.com/answers/allowing-for-pick-up/

BOOSTED NETWORK UPDATE: ASIA!
March 6 2018: TeeSpring announces that the Boosted network will be expanding to Asia (with no details on where, or exactly when), their post does include icons from some BIG BIG Asian marketplaces: jd.com (ranked in top 20 websites worldwide, and #7 in China), tmall.com (ranked top 15 worldwide, and #4 in China), and rakuten.co.jp (ranked top 125 worldwide, and top 10 in Japan). Together, these are powerful sales distribution channels that you will be able to access in the near future via TeeSpring!

Information overload? I know, TeeSpring is a monster... but there's MORE!

VOLUME DISCOUNTS:
TeeSpring offers seller discounted pricing based on # of sales made in a month on campaigns.
(AKA YOU EARN MORE PER ITEM WHEN YOU SELL MORE).

Here are the tiers: Save from $0.40 to $4.80 PER DESIGN, when selling in volume).

Increase your monthly sales to get a bigger discount!

Units	Discount (US)	Discount (EU)
100 - 499	$0.40	$0.40
500 - 999	$1.00	$0.70
1,000 - 2,499	$1.90	$1.00
2,500 - 4,999	$2.80	$1.50
5,000 - 9,999	$3.40	$2.30
10,000 - 19,999	$3.80	$2.80
20,000 - and up	$4.80	$3.50

PRO TIP: Authenticate your Facebook Ads account to get an extra $0.50 discount PER SALES from the start! **<——— FREE MONEY PEOPLE!**

TEESPRING FULFILLMENT SHOPIFY APP:
Jan 2017: CANCELED!! wa wa wa… :-(
http://shopifystorepro.com/teespring-pulls-plug-on-shopify-integration/

So you know that TeeSpring has a sales marketplace, of course that's what this whole section has been talking about. … However, did you know that TeeSpring also had a "back end" fulfillment option? Ya! You could have your Shopify store listings fulfilled by TeeSpring! Here's a link to the TeeSprings Fulfillment: https://teespring-fulfillment.readme.io/docs/getting-started
Step By Step walk-though of their Shopify Fulfillment App:
https://docs.google.com/presentation/d/1Ud_nfww6alNcHb0lMUpxypewfHCwMW5tqynzknquxk8/edit#slide=id.g12e3752548_0_88

Already have your Shopify Store up and ready to add TeeSpring fulfillment? Here's the Shopify TeeSpring app: It was here: http://apps.shopify.com/teespring-fulfillment
NO LONGER EXISTS :-(

Here was their full product pricing: https://teespring-fulfillment.readme.io/docs/pricing-and-payments Still exists, so you can see their products and pricing ;-)

CHANGE:
With such a large and changing POD platform, you can almost always find more happening on TeeSpring through their Blog here: https://community.teespring.com/blog/

TeeSpring Mobile Apps? Yup, they have 3 of them!
1: Apple iOS Seller App:
https://itunes.apple.com/us/app/teespring-seller/id1129017989?mt=8

2: Apple iOS Buyer App:
https://itunes.apple.com/us/app/teespring-shopping/id1144693237?mt=8

3: Android Seller App:
https://play.google.com/store/apps/details?id=com.androidteespring&hl=en
Sorry Android users, there's no buying app, only selling… if you want to get the buying app, use Apple, LOL!

teespring.com's
Alexa's rankings:
Q1 2017
Global: 3,888
USA: 1,715
Q4 2017
Global: 3,757
USA: 1,363

Head Quarters:
TeeSpring
77 Geary St 5th floor,
San Francisco, CA 94108, USA

society6.com
Also features designs via Google shopping!
Society6 in general is very much focused on artists, and art based designs (similar to Designed By Humans). It offers both google shopping paid ads for your designs, as well as really engaging drip email marketing (most all PODs use drip email marketing to reach out to buyers, and sellers, however I have found society6's to be fairly engaging compared to others). Yes, organic sales can be found via Society6, although I would stand by Redbubble as the king of pure organic sales (after Merch By Amazon, of course).

Like most other PODs, Society6 offers worldwide shipping, however, one thing that sets it apart is **FREE** returns.

Use this link for $15 off your first Society6 order: https://share.society6.com/x/dSMWup

Like many PODs which offer affiliate programs, Society6 offers a curator program, which pays you up to 10% on most items. This is one way to boost your earnings, as it's on top of other commissions you would normally receive from sales on your own designs. More details here: https://society6.com/curator Unlike some other PODs… it also provides a 30 day cookie for buyers, which gives you the curator commissions on anything they buy for the next 30 days! :-)

Society6 also has a student discount program, which gives registered students a 15% discount from the site. This helps drive more traffic to the site, and is another reason to get people to use them versus other PODs. More info here: http://society6.studentbeans.com/

Want to send a friend, family member or anyone a Society6 gif card? You can here:
https://society6.com/product/gift-card makes a nice gift around the holiday season.

Society6's
Alexa's rankings:
Q1 2017
Global: 5,441
USA: 2,213
Q4 2017
Global: 4,696
USA: 1,574

Head Quarters:
Society6
1655 26 Street
Santa Monica, CA
90404

fineartamerica.com
Fine Art America (FAA) at first seems like a site very focused only on Fine Art Canvas sales, however once you look at the product offerings that it offers, you soon realize that it really focuses on people looking for unique artwork, aka designs. So you, being a seller on Print On Demand platforms, hopefully either have, or are about to have a boatload of designs. Designs that work just as well on a canvas, as they would on a T-shirt. Plus, they also carry T-Shirts, as well as all kinds of other Print On Demand items you've come to love, like phone cases, sweatshirts, onesies, beach towels, canvas prints, coffee mugs, and more!

PRO TIP: *Your artwork is not shown on FAA's website, until you upload a headshot (or a design in place of a headshot). So, be sure to load an image or design to your profile page, otherwise you're not going to be shown on the site...*

In fact, you may be surprised to hear that they claim to be:
the world's largest art marketplace and print-on-demand technology company
In addition to driving millions of buyers to it's own sites monthly, you can also connect your designs to a Shopify store, here is the link to it's Shopify app:
https://apps.shopify.com/pixels?ref=developer-48887da66368ae70

Now, lets get into some of the additional reasons you may want to list with FAA:

- They have a licensing program with ABC to potentially show your artwork on ABC's popular TV shows.
- You can use their API and/or SDK to build your own integration.
- You can drop your store onto an existing website.
- Premium members can have their own pre-build white label website made for them.
- You can sell directly through Facebook.
- You can sell though 150+ retail outlets via their partner network.

Of course, your designs are also featured on their own website, as well as their mobile apps for both Apple iOS and Android. They have a 30 day money back satisfaction guarantee. You set your own prices, so you can have as much or as little margin as you like on top of the base manufacturing costs for each item.

The POD is free to join and use, but for $30 a year (that's $2.50USD/month), you can access additional premium features. You can also add Google Analytics, although they also offer built in analytics to see traffic and other demographic info on the traffic to your pages. The site has built in mass emailing systems, which send and receive using your email address. They allow you to issue press releases on their own site. You can upload images one at a time, or use their bulk uploader to load up to 5 at once.

Manufacturing is done from one of 16 partner factories, located in Canada, USA, Europe, UK and Australia. Each location prints certain items, the full list is here:
https://fineartamerica.com/global-print-on-demand-manufacturing-network.html

Globally based printing locations:

Detroit, MI United States | Chicago, IL United States | Atlanta, GA United States | Atlanta, GA United States | Los Angeles, CA United States | Charlotte, NC United States | Hendersonville, NC United States | Austin, TX United States

Toronto, Ontario Canada | London, England United Kingdom | Glasgow, Scotland United Kingdom | Boxtel, Netherlands Europe | Sydney, NSW Australia | Brisbane, QLD Australia | Hawthorne, CA United States | Denver, CO United States

Below is a list of items offered on the platform:

Wall Art
Art Prints
Posters
Canvas Art
Framed Art Prints
Metal Prints
Acrylic Prints
Wood Prints
Mail & Frame
Painted Portraits

Art Media
Paintings
Photos
Drawings
Digital Art
Mixed Media

Home Decor
Throw Pillows
Fleece Blankets
Duvet Covers
Shower Curtains
Bath Towels
Hand Towels
Coffee Mugs

Phone Cases & Tech
iPhone Cases
Galaxy Cases
Mobile Battery Chargers

Lifestyle
Yoga Mats
Tote Bags
Weekender Tote Bags
Carry-All Pouches

Apparel
Men's T-Shirts
Women's T-Shirts
Long Sleeve T-Shirts
Tank Tops
Sweatshirts
Baby Onesies

Stationery
Greeting Cards
Spiral Notebooks

Beach
Beach Towels
Round Beach Towels
Weekender Tote Bags
Carry-All Pouches
Mobile Battery Chargers

Miscellaneous
Gift Certificates
Sample Kits
Limited Time Promotions
Create Your Own Products

Fine Art America items available for Print On Demand:

Wall Art:
Art Prints
Posters
Canvas Art
Framed Art Prints
Metal Prints
Acrylic Prints
Wood Prints
Mail & Frame
Painted Portraits

Art Media:
Paintings
Photos
Drawings
Digital Art
Mixed Media

Home Decor:
Throw Pillows
Fleece Blankets
Duvet Covers
Shower Curtains
Bath Towels
Hand Towels
Coffee Mugs

Phone Cases & Tech:
iPhone Cases
Galaxy Cases
Mobile Battery Chargers

Lifestyle:
Yoga MatsNEW
Tote Bags
Weekender Tote Bags
Carry-All Pouches

Apparel:
Men's T-Shirts
Women's T-Shirts
Long Sleeve T-Shirts
Tank Tops
Sweatshirts
Baby Onesies

Stationery:
Greeting Cards
Spiral Notebooks

Beach:
Beach Towels
Round Beach Towels
Weekender Tote Bags
Carry-All Pouches
Mobile Battery Chargers

Miscellaneous:
Gift Certificates
Sample Kits
Limited Time Promotions
Create Your Own Products

fineartamerica.com's
Alexa's rankings:
Q1 2018
Global: 6,433
USA: 3,168

HQ:
Fine Art America
2415 N. Geneva Terrace
Chicago, IL 60614 USA

customink.com
Marketed as a POD service for public use (people go here to make their own custom shirts, not to buy other designers designs). There is no design marketplace. Offers unique programs for Team sponsorships, fundraising, hundreds of products. Great option for anyone looking to deliver products for on site sales (fundraisers, local businesses, etc.), or for sports teams looking to offset apparel costs by showing corporate sponsors. Covers USA and Canada (ca.customink.com). CANNOT currently edit or remove designs automatically (it is available by e-mailing them at: artist@dizinga.com). Custom ink is working on automatic artist edits and removals (as of Q1 2017).

customink.com's
Alexa's rankings:
Q1 2017
Global: 8,509
USA: 1,772
Q4 2017
Global: 7,146
USA: 1,789

Head Quarters:
Custom Ink
2910 District Ave
Fairfax, VA
22031

spreadshirt.com

SpreadShirt like many large PODs offers international production (not just international shipping, these goods are MADE IN EUROPE, USA, and multiple locations in each), so when you think SpreadShirt, think Europe! Spreadshirt's CEO has publicly stated that they would like to be a $1+ Billion dollar company, with new efforts to push harder into the US market (where they have been since 2004), you can rest assured that SpreadShirt will be actively expanding their marketshare… which means YOUR market reach. They ship to over 150 countries worldwide. They also offer a GREAT resource/tool for marketing their shirts - a HUGE selection of model stock photography (great for creating mockups) for you to use! Just be sure to mention the source when using these images FOR YOUR SPREADSHIRT DESIGNS! Here's the link: https://www.flickr.com/photos/spreadshirt/albums/72157615586234425/page1

SpreadShirt features designs via Google shopping, which means that you can get some organic sales via SpreadShirt, as Google Shopping will put your designs in front of more eyes, and market you designs better via organic SEO search!

In 2017, the company's global revenue was over $117 million and over 48 million items had been printed. Spreadshirt also had over 70,000 selling partners.

Above you see some of the countries and currencies that SpreadShirt operates in, with each of the above having its own URL domain, they have presence in many countries. They have printing production facilities in 5 locations: Germany, Poland, Czech Republic, and 2 in the USA.

SpreadShirt gives you several selling options, including selling on your own storefront or theirs. Selling on YOUR storefront gives you higher commissions, full control over your storefront's look and feel, and control which items and designs are for sale at the times you control. Selling on THEIR storefront gives you access to their global traffic (80,000+ daily visitors), as well as access to both Amazon and E-bay. See their over 10,000+ designs on Amazon here:
https://www.amazon.com/s/ref=lp_8542977011_st?srs=8542977011&rh=i%3Aspecialty-aps&qid=1521058374&sort=review-rank

SpreadShirt also allows you to earn commissions from selling other sellers' items. This gives you an opportunity to make big sales from marketing popular designs of existing sellers. As a seller, it encourages you to create compelling great selling designs, as once your design starts to gain traction on sales, other sellers will start driving traffic to your design, and you will also earn some commissions from their sales. To locate your own Affiliate ID, login to Spreadshirt, find a design that's not your, click the share button, choose email. At the end of the URL, you'll find the code ?affiliateId=XXXX (where XXXX is YOUR affiliate ID #). Add that bit of code to any designs on Spreadshirt that you wish to market to, and you will start earning the affiliate commissions. More info on their affiliate commissions, payouts, and tiers here:
https://help.spreadshirt.com/hc/en-us/articles/207233389-Affiliate-Commission Oh, and if you want to deselect your affiliate # when sharing you can do that as well, same link above. Affiliate commissions are paid monthly at the end of the month.

To help you sell even more, SpreadShirt also has created what they call a Success Guide for shop owners. it is a 48 page downloadable .pdf file that covers strategies, pricing, products, and promotion. Personally, I found their promotion section the most useful section, as a seller. Why not download it directly yourself, and see if there is some additional info to boost your sales via SpreadShirt.
Link Here:
https://image.spreadshirtmedia.com/content/v1/CMS/SSP/PDF/success_guide.pdf
NOTE: Although their guide is written with SpreadShirt in mind, many of the points within it can also be applied to other PODs, so it's worth a read through as well.

ADVANCED: Spreadshirt offers an API (https://developer.spreadshirt.net/display/API/Home), which allows you to drop a spreadshirt store on your website, and more! Here's one of the neatest applications of this I have seen: http://funtranslations.com/morse on this site you can translate English into multiple other forms of communications (morse code, braille, pig latin, etc.). But what really stands out, is that when they offer the translation, they have a button to put it on a shirt! See image below:

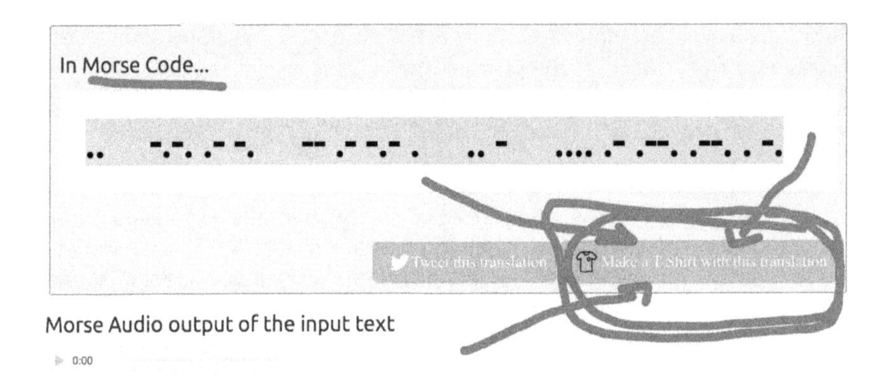

SPREADSHIRTS SPREAD SHOP:
Spreadshirt is so committed to helping your do well on their platform, that they even have a design service within their Spread Shop portal, where you can buy professional designs! Pricing ranges from $19 to $99, for many types of design work. More info here:
https://www.spreadshop.com/premiumdesign/?affiliateId=8054

Choose the package that best suits your need.
The Vendor
SpreadShop Styling
SpreadShop colors and banner styling
Access to our design team
read more
$25.00
Order Now
The Designer
Custom Shirt Design
One-of-a-kind custom shirt design
Access to our design team
read more
$49.00
Order Now
Designer PLUS
Custom Design PLUS
One-of-a-kind custom shirt design
Custom social media shareable
Access to our design team
read more
$59.00
Order Now
EntrePROneur
Deluxe Package
Shop styling
Social promos
Team access
2 custom shirt designs
read more
$99.00
Order Now
The Quick Fix
Basic Design
Design adjustments and optimization
read more
$19.99
Order Now

Mobile apps?

iOS Sales Tracking App: https://itunes.apple.com/us/app/spreadshirt-sales-stats/id1040510583?mt=8

Android Spreadshirt sales tracking App: https://play.google.com/store/apps/details?id=de.itcampus.mobile.trackspread

spreadshirt.com's

Alexa's rankings:
Q1 2017
Global: 8,426
USA: 3,511
Q4 2017
Global: 7,430
USA: 2,848

There are 5 Spreadshirt production sites:

HQ:
Spreadshirt Headquarters
Gießerstraße 27
04229 Leipzig
Germany

ui Slubickaz
59 - 220 Legnica
Poland

Pod Dolni drahou 105
417 42 Krupka
Czech Republic

1572 Roseytown Road
Greensburg, PA 15601
USA

1100 Mary Crest Road, NV
89074
USA

More ways to contact Spreadshirt (phone, production locations, offices, and more - could be useful for VAT tax production sites, and other uses): https://www.spreadshirt.com/branch-offices-C3138

cafepress.com

Founded in 1999 Cafe Press is one of the oldest POD platforms -19 years! Similar to Zazzle, they offer many many product choices, hundreds of products (345+)! Cafe Press, is publicly traded on the NASDAQ (NASDAQ:PRSS), and it's worth over $23 Million dollars by market cap! Although this is a huge number, it should be noted that it's around half of where it was a year ago, and has been trending downward, as fierce competition from Zazzle, Redbubble, Society6, and even Merch By Amazon have eaten away at it's once market dominance. That being said, they're still selling $80+ million in revenues per year, so you can be sure that they are getting plenty of traffic. They also claim to have over 2 million independent designers, so you can be sure that there are lots of people making designs for Cafe Press. Combining existing designs with all their products, you could create over 1 Billion items.

Cafe Press also will list designs on Google shopping, and some designs it also lists on Amazon (over 300,000 Cafe Press products live on Amazon right now: https://www.amazon.com/s/ref=sr_st_review-rank?srs=2586636011&rh=i%3Aspecialty-aps&qid=1521048339&sort=review-rank)!

Cafe Press has multiple paths to listing your designs. You can sell on it's market place, or you can open one or more Shops (places where you control what products are shown, and you can take a slightly higher profit per sale). Another advantage to the Shops is that Cafe Press handles returns and customer service. You can also market to other people's designs via their affiliates program (up to 15%), allowing you to earn income without any designs of your own.

More on Cafe Press Shops:

CAFE PRESS SHOPS:

What do I get in a CafePress shop?

Your own online shop to customize any way you want
Your choice of 250+ products to sell (with your own designs)
Design & shop management tools
Reliable shopping experience for your customers
Royalty earnings on every sale

You manage & market your shop.
CafePress takes care of the rest:

Handles all payment transactions
Produces each item using our high-quality print technologies
Ships products worldwide (no cost to you)
Provides expert customer support 24/7
Manages returns & exchanges
Sends you royalty payments for your sales earnings

T-SHIRTS & CLOTHING:
Men's
Women's
Plus Sizes
MaternityT-Shirts
Long Sleeve T-Shirts
Sweatshirts
Hoodies
Pyjamas
Tank Tops

KIDS:
Kids T-Shirts
Baseball Jerseys
Sweatshirts & Hoodies
Kids Accessories

BABY:
Baby Clothing
Bibs
Blankets
Diaper Bags

ACCESSORIES:
Baseball Hats
Jewelry
Scarves
Neck Ties
Watches
Men's Accessories

DRINKWARE:
Mugs
Water Bottles
Flasks
Drinking Glasses
Shot Glasses
Acrylic Tumblers

HOME:
Shower Curtains
Kitchen Accessories
Home Décor
Pillows
Bedding
Office Accessories
Area Rugs
Duvet Covers
Ornaments

HOBBIES:
Buttons
Stickers
Magnets
License Plate Frames
Car Magnets

WALL ART:
Posters
Framed Prints
Wall Decals
Photo On Canvas
Canvas Art
Clocks
STATIONERY:
Greeting Cards
Note Cards
Invitations
Calendars
Journals

BAGS:
Canvas Tote Bags
Lunch Bags
Messenger Bags
Totes & Shoulder Bags

CASES & COVERS:
Phone Cases
iPad Cases & Covers
Laptop Covers

As fair commentary, Cafe Press's site layout, and seller side design could benefit from some modern updates to design and usability. That being said, of the 21 POD platforms I sell one, its one of the top for making actual sales, so I must recommend it as one you should definitely add to your stable of platforms.

Cafe Press has 4 main domains (Australia, Canada, UK, USA), and like most PODs, ships worldwide.

Cafe Press offers an API, which allows you to add a Cafe Press shop to your existing site, and can be used to program bulk uploading, to a certain level. I'm confident that it would be part of any current or future Multi-Uploading solutions that people have. To access the API, or develop software to work with Cafe Press, here's the link to their developer site: http://www.cafepress.com/cp/developers/

cafepress.com's
Alexa's rankings:
2017 Q1
Global: 5,306
USA: 1,569
Q4 2017
Global: 7,931
USA: 1,572

Head Quarters:
Cafe Press
11909 Shelbyville Road
Louisville, KY 40243

teepublic.com
http://tee.pub/lic/uhsusqxoUmw (affiliate link, no cost to you)

Teepublic has fixed pricing, typically $14 for the first 3 days, then $20 afterwards. They also have occasional sales, which attracts new buyers organically. Payments to you as a seller, can be made to either Paypal, or Payoneer accounts, and happen on the 15th of the month after the sale occurs. For example: money made during sales in February will be paid out on March 15th.

When listing on TeePublic, they have a great auto-suggest function built right into their keywords, so when you put in a keyword, it suggests many more which might fit your design. This is also a great way to see generally what other designs in the similar niche might be, and can even be a great ideas generator to give you inspiration for your next batch of designs! TeePublic also has Albums, which are groups of your designs that you curate. They will appear in the left side of your store. To edit albums, under My Account you'll see a link to My Albums. There you can make new ones, delete them, even arrange them as you like.

TeePublic uses Kornit DTG printers for their shirts, and sublimation for their home goods products. In terms of colors, they offer over **60 choices**, which can be found in the uploader for the product you're wondering about. Printing is on the front of all their shirts, except for zip up hoodies, where back printing is offered.

TeePublic also has a handy "prep guide" for how to best prepare your designs for optimal printing via DTG, located here:
https://assets.teepublic.com/assets/pdfs/designing-for-dtg-8c868f5d17631694f6ca25bbf96bdb80a34ec1cb54eb708674490512151738c5.pdf
These rules would also work for other PODs who also use DTG printing, such as Merch By Amazon for example, which also happens to use Kornit DTG printers…

TeePublic does run some ads for its sellers for free, which over time will lead to organic traffic.
NOTE: Sellers have had mixed results with Teepublic. Some get a lot of sales. Some get very few. So it can be a polarizing POD platform. Personally I very much enjoy it's design loading process, and they do offer a large and growing assortment of items to print your design onto.

TeePublic Products:
T-Shirts
Tank Tops
Long Sleeve T-Shirts
Baseball T-Shirts
Kids T-Shirts
Crewneck Sweatshirts
Hoodies
Wall Art
Phone Cases
Laptop Cases
Notebooks
Mugs (coffee Mug and Travel Mug)
Stickers
Pillows
Totes
Tapestries
Kids Hoodie
Kids Long Sleeve T-Shirt
Onesie

A whopping 60+ color choices! Here are 41 of them:

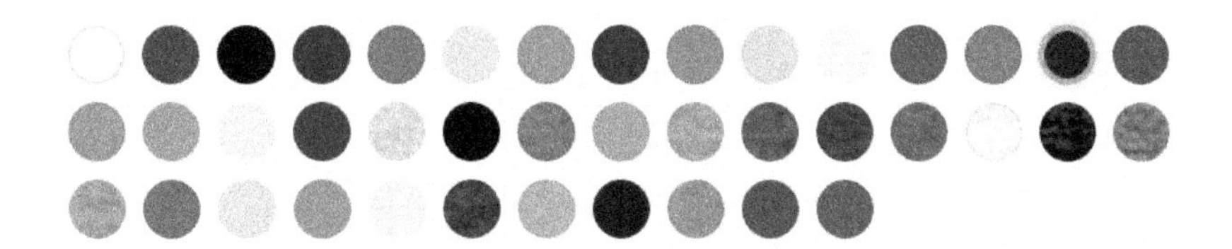

In addition to great pricing, and organic traffic, TeePublic also tries to assist sellers by listing out trending topics on each of it's items sold. The full list is updated regularly, and can be found here: https://www.teepublic.com/trending-tags
(HINT: great place for inspiration on what niche to tackle next, although it also contains many of the brands it carries (Disney, Marvel, DC comics, etc.), so not all of them can be used across other PODs).

DESIGNERS:
Another interesting not so talked about part of TeePublic is their Commission a designer space, where you can find other designers who are willing to make designs for other sellers like yourself. Pick a designer that you would like to work with, and contact them using the form posted below. Check it out here: https://www.teepublic.com/commission-a-designer

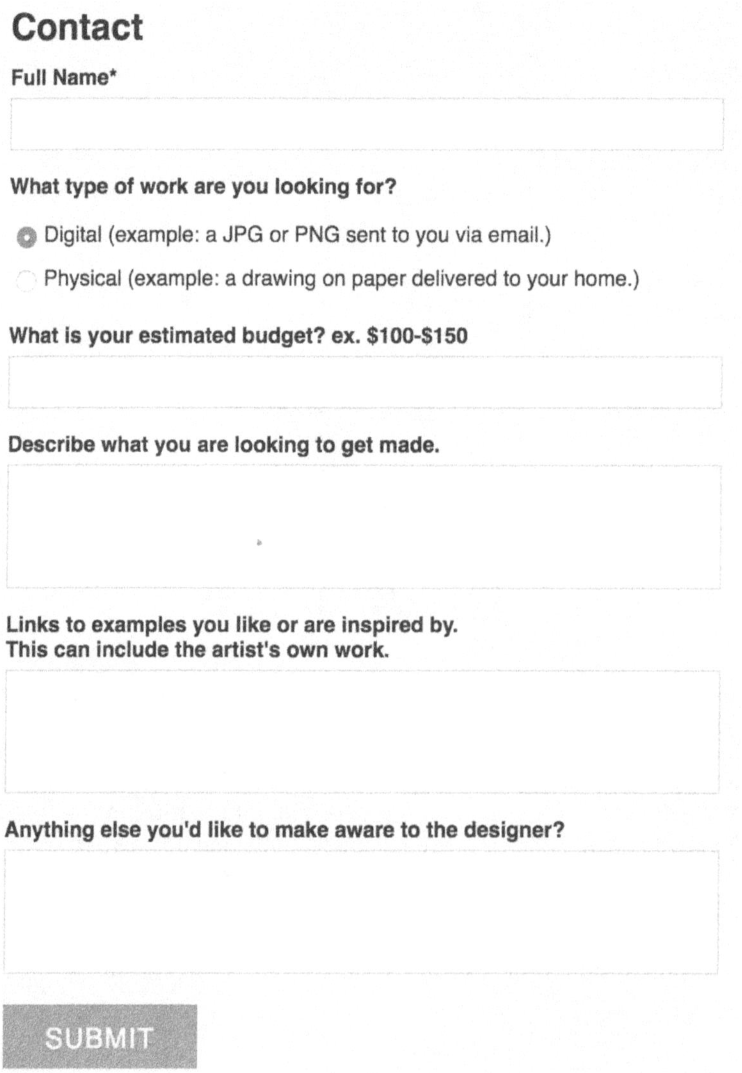

Contact

Full Name*

What type of work are you looking for?

- Digital (example: a JPG or PNG sent to you via email.)
- Physical (example: a drawing on paper delivered to your home.)

What is your estimated budget? ex. $100-$150

Describe what you are looking to get made.

Links to examples you like or are inspired by.
This can include the artist's own work.

Anything else you'd like to make aware to the designer?

SUBMIT

TeePublic does offer a unique affiliate and referral program for sellers. Once you create your account and have made sales, you will see a small link called Make $100, or Make $1000. Here's how it works: If you refer a friend who becomes a TeePublic Designer, you'll get $1 for every product they sell up to $1000. Your friend still gets their full commission. Share your custom link with friends to get paid. So, if you are thinking of creating your own FREE TeePublic account, please use this affiliate link (at no cost to you): http://tee.pub/lic/uhsusqxoUmw For more info about their affiliate program, under MY ACCOUNT, there is a link called make $1000.

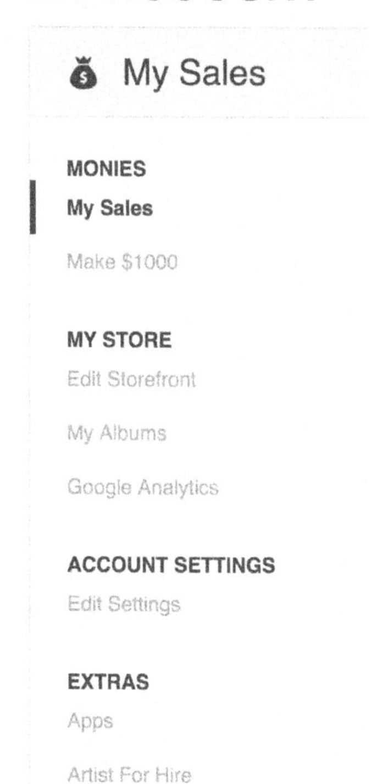

In addition to the above referral program, they also offer affiliate commissions for referred buyers to the site. You can earn up to 31% commissions on your own designs, and up to 11% on other people's designs (curated designs). For more info on TeePublic's partner program go here: https://www.teepublic.com/stores/learn-more

How Do You Make Money?

Create
Create a custom storefront with your merch and/or designs you curate from TeePublic.

Share
Share your merch with your fans using TeePublic tracking links.

Promotions
Engage with your fans through promotionals, giveaways, and more.

Commision A Designer
Earn a commission on every product you sell, including merch that isn't your own.

For more information about how affiliate links work in general, there is a section about affiliates near the end of the book.

AFFILIATE PARTNERS

About the Affiliate Program:

Receive 11% commission on all products.

30 day cookie duration

Access to all Entire Design Catalogue

11% Commission applies to both your own designs and existing TeePublic designs

Paid Search Terms & Conditions:

Search marketing on TeePublic brand terms is prohibited. Keywords include, but are not limited to: teepublic, tee public, teepublic.com, teepublic store, teepublic coupon code, tee public store, tee public coupon, brand + coupon related terms, and any brand misspellings.

This policy is strictly enforced. Failure to comply with our search policies may lead to the removal of the program and the reversal of commissions.

All TeePublic brand terms must be negative matched.

Paid Search Terms & Conditions:

Publishers are not permitted to use "TeePublic" in their domain unless it is an extension. For example, www.yourwebsite.com/bustedtees or www.yourwebsite.com/teepublic.

Publishers are not permitted to use TeePublic in any press releases without prior approval. Please send an email to affiliate@teepublic.com for approval.

All TeePublic brand terms must be negative matched.

teepublic.com's
Alexa's rankings:
Q1 2017
Global: 16,481
USA: 6,017
Q4 2017
Global: 10,044
USA: 2,504

Head Quarters:
Teepublic
36 E 20th St,
New York, NY
10003, USA

Phone: 1-844-233-5033 weekdays 10am-6pm EST.

printful.com
Printful can connect to your E-Commerce platform (Shopify, WooCommerce, Gumroad, Shipstation, etc.)
Printful has multiple ways to integrate their POD platform into amazon.com One way is via Shopify, which in turn connects to amazon.com. The other is directly from Printful to Amazon. This may sound like a simple choice, just connect directly from Amazon to Printful, and cut out the percentage and per unit costs that Shopify would charge to fulfill your orders, right? Well, this is one of those cases of "it depends". Shopify is more than just a domain and host for your website, it is a full scale e-commerce platform, this means that it offers you full scale commerce platform features such as record keeping apps, marketing apps, and the ability to capture customer order information when they order from Amazon… Wait what? That's right! Because an Amazon order coming from amazon.com via Shopify to Printful is a Merchant Fulfilled order… that means that your Shopify enabled site can capture that data on it's way through, and you can use this information to market to your customers later (allowing the site to cross market to them, or learn their buying preferences, etc).

Shopify integration essentially connects you to a whole world of additional e-commerce applications that a direct to Printful connection does not offer. Another thing to consider, is how to manage you're order flows, if you have multiple POD's connected to Shopify and then to Amazon, would you prefer to have Printful off in it's own spot, or would you prefer to have the Printful connection happily playing through your Shopify backend, along side other POD services such as CustomCat, Print-Aura, TeeLaunch, and others?

New in 2017, Etsy allows manufacturing and fulfillment via Printful. This means that you can now also connect your Etsy store to Printful, and have Printful manufacture and fulfill your Etsy orders directly.

Here's how: (also referenced in the Etsy section ;-)

To integrate **Etsy** with ***Printful***:
1. Create a free Etsy Account (use this link for 40 free listings: http://etsy.me/2nV2rqf) Once you've created your free Etsy Account, set up a shop, in order to access your shop manager. (to set up a shop, click shop. You will need to create a first listing. Under Production Partner, choose Printful - see step 4-10, and or the video here: https://youtu.be/f9EghP7-ei4).

2. Create a free account with Printful (done here: https://goo.gl/znYo6o)

3. Authorize Printful's API's on your Etsy Account. (Done in Printful here: https://www.printful.com/dashboard/etsy/register by clicking on the connect button) NOTE: in order to do step 3, steps 1 and 2 must be completed, and I recommend you're signed into both accounts)

4. On Etsy, under settings, select Production Partners.

5. Select Add New Partner.

6. In the Production Partner Field, type in Printful.

7. Deselect Printful's name as showing as your print partner, and type in whatever you would like to have showing on your store, to represent Printful (your Print On Demand Partner).

8. Add One of Printful's 3 printing locations (Chatsworth, California, United States Of America)

9. Type in a description to describe that location (Fulfillment, Warehousing and Shipping service for small online retailers)

10. Select the role of Printful from the 3 dropdown menus, and hit the save button.(I don't have the technical ability or equipment to make…, I design everything myself, They do everything for me).

11. Upload your products onto Printful via your Etsy Store on Printful, then push them to Etsy (note: they load as draft on the Etsy side, you can connect to Etsy from Printful.

12. Complete your Etsy Listings in Etsy, and publish (You connect to Etsy using the orange link on Printful. This moves your design from draft to live, when you publish on the Etsy side.)

13. That's it! Now, when people buy your designs you've listed on Etsy, the orders that are connected to Printful will be created and fulfilled by Printful!

BONUS: You can confirm that the design you loaded to Etsy from Printful is complete, when you see it in your printful account, under your etsy store (if it's synced, go back to stores on Printful, locate your etsy store, and click the sync button).

Once you have completed your first Printful to Etsy Listing, I suggest you have a small party. It's exhilarating! (Don't worry, Redbubble is way simpler ;-))

If you're a bit lost, have a look at the explainer video from Printful here:
Link Here: https://www.printful.com/landing/etsy-print-products-fulfillment

Printful can also fulfill orders coming from a wide variety of platforms including:
Amazon
Storenvy
BigCommerce
Gumroad
TicTail
Big Cartel
Ecwid
Weebly
Squarespace
Inktail
ShipStation
Etsy
Not sure which one is for you, They have a great video giving you some pros and cons to each of these integrated partners here: https://youtu.be/X9vtoRD7u-E

As well as a detailed chart comparing each of them here:
https://www.printful.com/landing/overview-print-products-fulfillment

Ecommerce platform comparison chart

	Live shipping rates	Price	Personal server required	Products pushed to store	Order import	Shipping status update	Displays "out of stock" notice	Marketplace	Ease of installation
Shopify	Yes	% of revenue + subscription, starts at $29/month.	No	Yes	Immediately	Automatically	Yes	No	Fast
Etsy	No	3.5% transaction fee + $0.20 fee to publish products	No	Yes	Every 15min	Automatically	No	Yes	Fast
WooCommerce	Yes	Free	Yes	Yes	Immediately*	Automatically	Yes	No	Normal
Storenvy	No	Free, but you'll be charged commission fees on marketplace sales.	No	Yes	Immediately	Automatically	Yes	Yes	Fast
BigCommerce	No	Subscription, starts at $29.95	No	Yes	Immediately	Automatically	Yes	No	Fast
Gumroad	No	8.5% + $0.30 per transaction or $10/month subscription	No	No	Immediately	Manual	No	No	Fast
Tictail	No	Free, but you'll be charged commission fees on marketplace sales	No	Yes	Every 30min	Manual	No	Yes	Fast
Big Cartel	No	Free - $29.99 monthly	No	No	Immediately	Automatically	No	No	Fast
Ecwid	Yes	Subscription, starts at $15.99/month	No	Yes	Every 15 min	Automatically	Yes**	No	Fast
Amazon	No	Subscription + referral fees - starts at $39.99	No	Yes	Hourly	Automatically ***	No	Yes	Complex
Weebly	No	Subscription + transaction fees, starting at $8/month	No	Yes	Immediately	Automatically	Yes	No	Fast

* Using the latest version of WooCommerce

** Available for Ecwid Business and Unlimited plan users

*** Amazon will transfer your profit to your bank account once a day after your orders have shipped out

NOTE: a few marketplaces do not integrate directly to Printful, but you CAN still connect them to Printful... and I think you may want to, when you see who they are, and how to do it ;-)

ShipStation (which DOES have an integration with Printful) can connect you to the following Marketplaces:

Walmart.com (https://www.shipstation.com/partners/walmart/)

Jet.com (https://www.shipstation.com/partners/jet-com/)

Yahoo (https://www.shipstation.com/partners/yahoo/)

Ebay (https://www.shipstation.com/partners/ebay/)

Bonanza (https://www.shipstation.com/partners/bonanza/)
9 million visitors/6months

Sears (https://www.shipstation.com/partners/sears/)
25 million visitors/6 months

PrestaShop (https://www.shipstation.com/partners/prestashop/)
4 MIL visitors/6 months

Plus several more! Find them all here:
https://www.shipstation.com/partners/

So for example:

Walmart

1: Setup Printful for FREE here: https://goo.gl/znYo6o
2: Setup and integrate Shipstation to your Printful store, and select whichever plan you choose (starts at $9/month, join here: http://mbsy.co/shipstation/29968195)
3: Apply for and get accepted to become a Walmart Partner here (https://info.shipstation.com/walmart) - as part of this application, you will have Shipstation selected as your fulfillment Partner, and in ship station, you will choose Printful as your fulfillment channel to fulfill your Walmart orders.

Keep in mind that Shipstation does have monthly fees, however depending on your sales volume, connecting to marketplaces like Walmart, Ebay, Yahoo, Sears, PrestaShop and others may be well worth it!

Join Shipstation here: http://mbsy.co/shipstation/29968195

Plans that meet your needs

STARTER $9 PER MONTH	BRONZE $29 PER MONTH	SILVER $49 PER MONTH	MOST POPULAR GOLD $69 PER MONTH	PLATINUM $99 PER MONTH	ENTERPRISE $159 PER MONTH
50 Shipments per month	500 Shipments per month	1,500 Shipments per month	3,000 Shipments per month	6,000 Shipments per month	Unlimited Shipments per month
All Selling Channels (unlimited stores)	All Selling Channels (unlimited stores)	All Selling Channels (unlimited stores)	All Selling Channels (unlimited stores)	All Selling Channels (unlimited stores)	All Selling Channels (unlimited stores)
1 User	1 User	2 Users	3 Users	5 Users	10 Users
Branded Labels & Packing Slips	Branded Labels & Packing Slips	Customized Packing Slips & Branded Labels	Customized Packing Slips & Branded Labels	Customized Packing Slips & Branded Labels	Customized Packing Slips & Branded Labels
E-mail & Community Forum Support	E-mail & Community Forum Support	Live Chat, E-mail & Community Forum Support	Live Chat, E-mail & Community Forum Support	Live Chat, E-mail & Community Forum Support	Live Chat, Phone Support, Email & Community Forum Support

All prices in USD. Plans subject to applicable taxes, if any.

No matter what ShipStation plan you choose, you'll get the ability to link up your own Canada Post, Purolator, UPS, FedEx, and other carrier accounts, fantastical user support, access to import your chosen selling channel's orders, automation rules, and a crazy amount of time savings from all our features.

Access all ShipStation features for free today and then simply choose a plan at the end of your 30-day trial.

Start Your Free Trial Now!

NOTE: Printful has opened it's European manufacture site (Latvia), in addition to it's 2 USA based manufacturing sites (California, North Carolina), you may want to brush up on your VAT taxes knowledge, printful has a helpful video here: https://youtu.be/uFEHGAgeqRE

printful.com's
Alexa's rankings:
Q1 2017
Global: 140,135
USA: 13,371
Q4 2017
Global: 12,027
USA: 3,464

Head Quarters:
Printful
19749 Dearborn Street
Chatsworth, CA
91311

designbyhumans.com
Designed By Humans (DBH), much like Society6 contains sellers who really seem to specialize on the design side of their artwork, much more than text based designs, or trending designs found on Merch By Amazon, or other large PODs. Unique about the process, is that you will need to submit a portfolio of your design work, and be vetted by their curation team in order to open an account here. Mature content is allowed on this POD, and can be turned on or off by buyers.

Alternatively, if you have a large following on Youtube, or other social media platforms, this is an alternate path to joining this platform. DBH offers curated designs, by way of it's voting structure. Designs are voted on by users of the site. They also hold regular contests, and special events to help grow the community of artists.

DBH also has a portion of their site called the TeeGrinder, where sets of randomly generated t-shirts are offered in sets of 3 shirts, at a discount (3 for $60). Link here: https://www.designbyhumans.com/TeeGrinder/

Student discounts offered by Student Beans of 20% off for cardholders. Link here: https://www.designbyhumans.com/student-discount/

You could even win prizes for submitting photos of yourself wearing or using products bought on DBH, see gallery of customers here: https://www.designbyhumans.com/fan-photos/

Charities looking to use a POD to fundraise can also use DBH, and many do. 25% of proceed go to charities using this program. More info here: https://www.designbyhumans.com/charity

DBH has an ambassador program, where you can earn commissions for promoting any item on the site, including their vast selection of branded designs (think Avengers, Jurassic Park, NASA, Star Wars, Disney, FIFA, Cartoon Network, Coca Cola!!! ... and more), more info here: https://www.designbyhumans.com/ambassador-program/

designbyhumans.com's
Alexa's rankings:
Q1 2017
Global: 25,464
USA:14,142
Q4 2017
Global: 13,529
USA: 4,710

Head Quarters:
Designed By Humans
7 Holland
Irvine, CA
92618

threadless.com

Treadless is artistically driven. Here you will find many design-only non-text based designs, similar to Society6, and Designed By Humans. One factor that sets Threadless apart from virtually all other major Print On Demand platforms is their voting system.

Once you are on the platform, and have loaded your design, it is then available to be voted on for printing, using 1-2-3-4-5 rating system. If you design is voted up for printing, then they will print off your design, and pay you a relatively large commission of typically over $1,000. Enough to motivate you and others to compete for the best designs to be showcased on the platform. Also, remember not only is your design available for voting, but you also can vote for other seller's designs.

threadless.com's

Alexa's rankings:
Q4 2017
Global: 13,607
USA: 3,984

Head Quarters:
Threadless
406 N. Sangamon St.
Chicago, IL 60642

teechip.com
TeeChip, operates on campaigns with countdowns. Choose from between 1day and 25 day campaigns. Once the campaign has ended the shirts are made and shipped to buyers. I prefer to keep my countdown days as low as possible to be able to ship to my buyers as quickly as possible, however there are benefits of longer campaigns, such as time to build hype and momentum around a listing. Longer campaigns are also useful if you expect your buyers to tell all their friends, or to broadcast that they are buying your design. Longer campaigns also can serve as a way to build anticipation, and increase buyers returning to your listing to check how much longer until their shirt is made.

Campaigns can be set to auto restart or to expire. Expiring is an opportunity to promote a sale with a limited time offer. You always have the option to bring the design back at a later date, and create another limited time offer. I prefer to have as many of my designs available across as many platforms, so I typically set this to auto restart.

TeeChip has really low base prices. With TeeChip the shirt retail cost is $13 (minimum), the base shirt cost is only: $7.74. The remaining difference of $4.89 is profit back to you. So you can either pass the savings on to your clients, or make more $ per sale, your choice! Even shipping is low cost with TeeChip for example: Most items are $3.99 for one item + $1.99 per additional item. More detils here: https://pro.teechip.com/faq
TeeChip listings allow you to have your own custom URL suffix. When uploading designs, TeeChip gives you a maximum of 3000 characters for your description.

New in 2017, TeeChip launched TeeChip Pro. TeeShip Pro later ended... It provided you slightly modified seller experience, details found here: https://pro.teechip.com (now forwards back to TeeChip). It was great while it lasted TeeShipPro!

teechip.com's
Alexa's rankings:
Q1 2017
Global: 6,616
USA: 2,816
Q4 2017
Global: 16,070
USA: 8,585

sunfrog.com
Sun Frog has one of the largest number of designs available in a single site for Print On Demand (over 11,000,000 designs). It also has an amazing affiliate marketing program (starts at 40% affiliate payout). Add this to the 5.5% artist payout, and you could be making 45.5% of every sale, for traffic you direct (that sells) to your designs! If that isn't incentive enough, after certain volume levels the percentage goes even higher!

SunFrog Academy:
SunFrog even has their own sellers academy setup to help sellers at all levels to sell better. It's free, no monthly fee, no one time cost, FREE! The content is great.
Video Link Here: https://www.facebook.com/SunFrogSellers/videos/257849214666995/
Link to the FREE seller academy here: http://academy.sunfrog.com/

Upload your designs, or create them using Sun Frog's on site design creator (select, fonts, colors, outlines, centre on vertical or horizontal, left centre or right justify, size text as you like, etc.). Or upload your own designs; Sun Frog accepts the following file types: .svg, .png and .jpg then pick your shirt types, listed as the following:

Here are all the available items on **Sunfrog** as of Q1 2018:

Select Design Type

- ✓ Guys Tee
- Ladies Tee
- Youth Tee
- Hoodie
- Sweat Shirt
- Guys V-Neck
- Ladies V-Neck
- Unisex Tank Top
- Unisex Long Sleeve
- Leggings
- Coffee Mug (colored)
- Coffee Mug (white)
- Coffee Mug (color change)
- Posters 16x24
- Posters 24x16
- Posters 11x17
- Posters 17x11
- Canvas 16x20
- Hat
- Trucker Cap

NOTE: Color changing mugs, posters, canvases, hats and trucker caps are ALL NEW in the last year - Another sign, that POD's are always changing, and adding more/faster/cheaper/better/etc,

Guys Tee (17 colors)

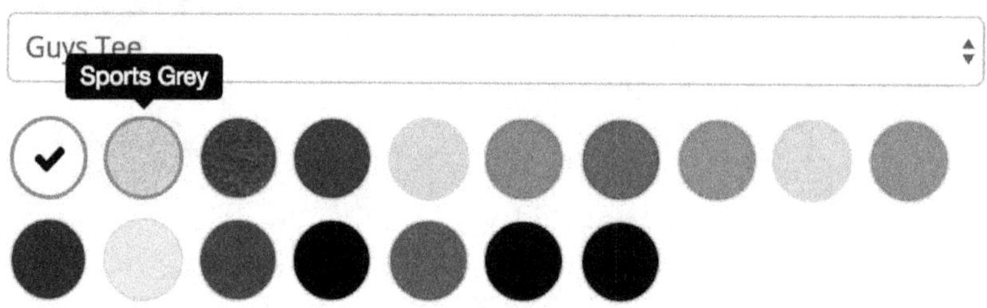

Ladies Tee (17 colors)

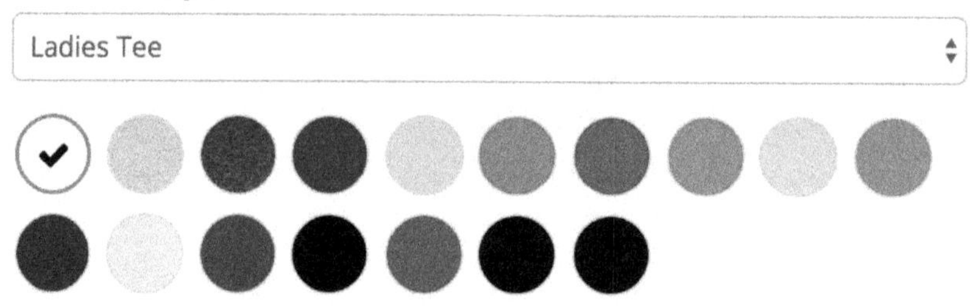

Youth Tee (7 colors)

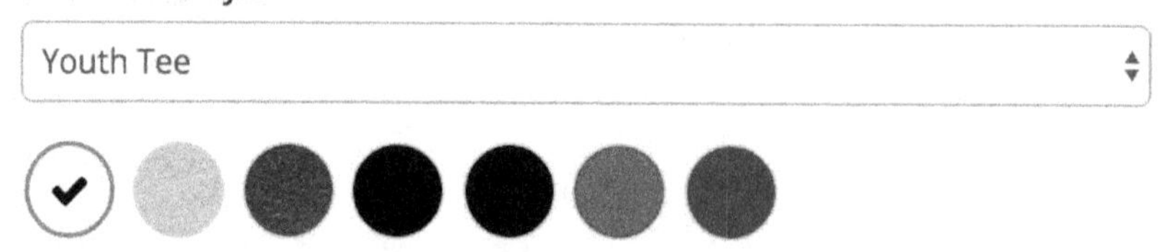

Hoodie (10 colors)

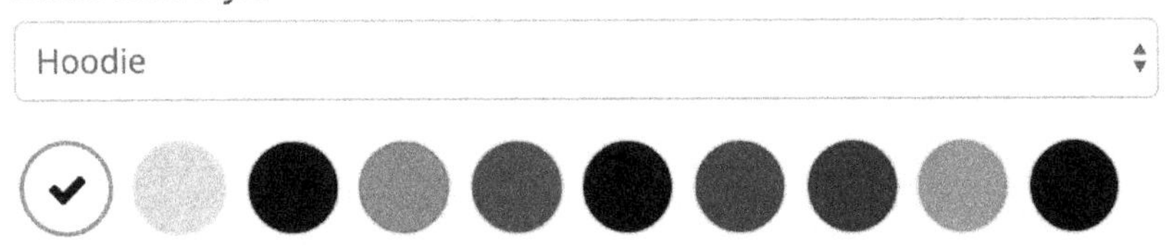

Sweat Shirt (7 colors)

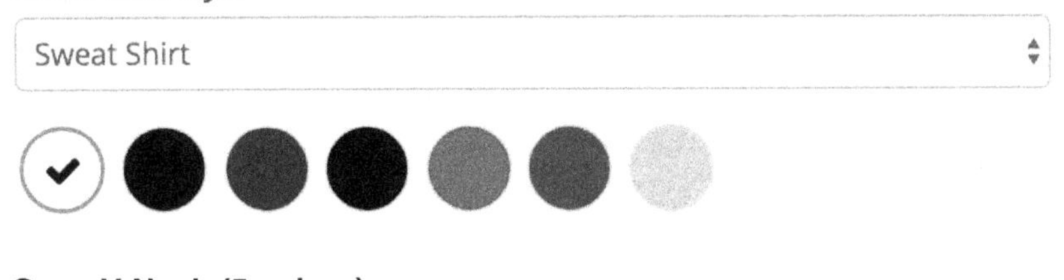

Guys V-Neck (5 colors)

Ladies V-Neck (7 colors)

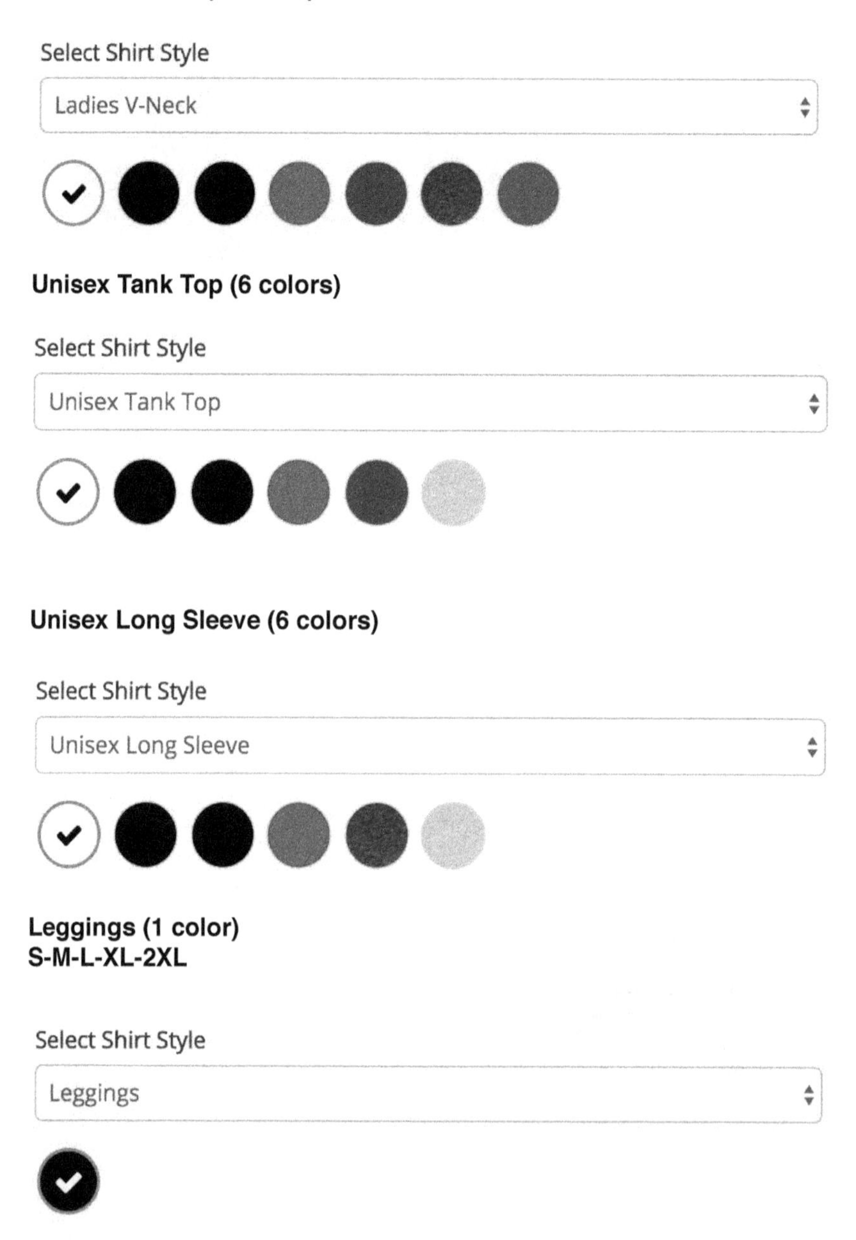

Select Shirt Style
Ladies V-Neck
Unisex Tank Top (6 colors)
Select Shirt Style
Unisex Tank Top
Unisex Long Sleeve (6 colors)
Select Shirt Style
Unisex Long Sleeve
Leggings (1 color)
S-M-L-XL-2XL
Select Shirt Style
Leggings

Plus all the new items just added this year, you see all the details when you create a new design. It's a boatload of new options and choices.

Where available, choose 1 up to 5 colors for each style above. Then it's off to the rest of the listing info:

Title
Category from 23 choices: (Automotive, Birth Years, Drinking, Events, Faith, Fitness, Funny, Gamer, Geek-Tech, Hobby, Jobs, Lifestyle, Movies, Music, Names, Outdoor, Pets, Political, Sports, States, TV Shows, Zombies)

✓ --Select--
Automotive
Birth Years
Drinking
Events
Faith
Fitness
Funny
Gamer
Geek-Tech
Hobby
Holidays
Jobs
LifeStyle
Movies
Music
Names
Outdoor
Pets
Political
Sports
States
TV Shows
Zombies

Description (up to 30 words)
Tags (up to 3)
Agree to terms and conditions

Once the design is loaded, it's live and ready for sale. However, you have a few more options to choose from if you would like to edit the listing further! You can adjust the price of each item selected (for each shirt/hoodie/etc.). You are also supplied with the listing URL.

NOTE: Always include the 4 digits after the .html?XXXX, as this is YOUR affiliate code, meaning any Sun Frog items sold with YOUR 4 digit code after the full Sun Frog code, gets you more $$! You can even use your affiliate code to promote other people's Sun Frog designs, and you will get 40% commission (or more) with every sale that uses your affiliate code. AKA earn $$ with ZERO of your own designs, totally legally :-)

Some additional options that you can add/change to the listing:

More about Facebook Pixel ID, and Google Analytics Pixel ID later in the book.

Think of all the possibilities with a time defined private listing… sell for an event, make a special shirt for a promotion, offer to a select group of people (like maybe people who buy your product, or like your Facebook page or something… get creative, try different strategies).

PRO TIP: You could run the same design at different prices, and offer it to different groups!

NOTE: SunFrog offers short videos throughout their site to help assist sellers with feature options. From their YouTube page, you can also subscribe to their channel, and see new tricks and tips from the platform, as they become available. Great learning resource. Link Here: https://www.youtube.com/user/sunfrogshirts/videos

Along those lines, don't forget about these small icons throughout Sun Frog's site:

1: The first orange one, shows you traffic statistics at the single design level, and you can even track traffic over specific dates.
2: The second blue icon shows you additional information about the page you're on.
3: The third red icon, when clicked, will launch a small pop-up, and play a video clip about the page you're on.

Look for other small icons throughout Sun Frog's site for additional information, and helpful spots!

Things to keep in mind with Sun Frog: Descriptions are *limited to 30 words.* Organic public facing searches do not work well with multi-word searches. Only 3 keyword tags are allowed.

NEW THINGS ADDED:
Sun Frog added leggings, and as of Feb 26th, 2017, they now also have both dark and light colored mugs!! (This is a big big game changer given Sun Frog's massive affiliate marketing community, and site traffic). Mugs start at an unadjusted buyer price of $8.99, and at that price you won't make too much $, but it's great exposure for your designs. I recommend upping the price to a point where you can attract some of Sun Frog's legendary affiliate sellers... with their 40% starting level Affiliate commission payout, they were once one of the fastest growing POD's in the world, they are also already pretty huge in terms of traffic. Once ranking in the top 250 highest traffic'd websites in the USA.

PRO TIP:
To get out of the single word for each keyword tag, you can copy and past your multi-word keywords into Sun Frog, then press the space bar, and BOOM! you just got a multi-word single keyword in Sun Frog... BAM!

SunFrog.com's
Alexa's rankings:
Q1 2017
Global: 1,018
USA: 193
Q4 2017
Global: 26,692
USA: 11,217 <—— I'm not sure what happened here Sunfrog???

Head Quarter Location:
1782 O'Rourke Blvd
Gaylord, MI 49735

represent.com
https://represent.com/?ref=x3eAIk5uLhzLQO2BcLAI <—Join Free Here
You can connect represent directly through your Shopify storefront (https://apps.shopify.com/represent). Adding additional benefits and reasons to using Shopify as one of your fully integrated product pipelines. In addition to Shopify integration, here are some other unique aspects of represent:

GREAT MARGINS
From Represent via Shopify:

Let the numbers speak for themselves: if you sell a Gildan Short Sleeve Tee for $29.99 + $3.99 domestic shipping, we'll charge you just $8.50 + shipping, with the remaining $21.49 going as profit to you. **That's an insanely awesome 71.6% profit margin.**

- **Gildan Short Sleeve Tee** (S - 5XL) for $8.50
- **Next Level Unisex Fitted Tee** (XS - 3XL) for $9.75
- **Bella Canvas Short Sleeve Tee** (Female S - XL) for $10.00
- **Next Level The Boyfriend Tee** (Female XS - 3XL) for $10.50
- **Bella Canvas Flowy Racerback Tank** (Female S - 2XL) for $12.50
- **Gildan Pullover Sweatshirt** (S - 5XL) for $15.50
- **Gildan Pullover Hoodie** (S - 5XL) for $18.50
- **Phone cases** starting at $17.99:
    1. **iPhone** 6/6+/6S/SE/7/7+
    2. **Samsung** Galaxy S6/S7/Edge/Edge Plus)

Shipping: $3.99 Domestic, $8.99 International

CAMPAIGN STORY
Rather than a limited description spot, you are encouraged to tell a story for your products (unlimited space), and can include embedded items like *tweets*, *additional images*, and *YouTube videos*. One of the few platform PODs which allow these extra features to sell your designs, and tell your story. You can also capture fan's email addresses by including an email capture field in your 'about' section.
PROMOTIONS
Boost sales to products or campaigns by adding specials or time limited promotions, example: $15 off.

EMBEDDING
If you have an existing website, or space on the web, and are looking to add POD fulfilled manufacturing and shipping from represent, you can! Just grab the short embed code generated from a new represent campaign, and drop a buy now button onto your existing website. A fast an easy way to add merch to your brand or existing website.

PAYOUT DETAILS
Payouts are via Paypal. Profit from your campaigns will be available for payout 24 hours after your campaign ends (higher-margin campaigns) or 12 hours after an order is placed (faster-shipping campaigns). Once you have made a sale and request a transfer of your earnings, the payout will be processed immediately.

Products available include:
T-Shirts
Hoodies
Raglans
Tank Tops
Long Sleeve Shirts
Youth T-Shirts

Printing with represent is done via both screen printing, and DTG, based on the size and type of items ordered during the campaigns.

Represent campaigns can be run with goals as well. This can encourage support from your fan base, and act as an additional measure for sales to convert. Some sellers also choose to show how many items were sold during a campaign. This is great for buyers to see that others are buying an item, and as a seller, it can give you some insights into the popularity of a design. Running a campaign also gives some urgency to a design, and can be useful for creating more sales via scarcity.

They also have an affiliate program that's open to anyone using the platform, located under the referrals tab on the main dashboard. represent will pay you $0.75 from each item sold by anyone that you bring into the platform for their first year. If you would like to join Represent for free, please do use this affiliate link: **https://goo.gl/eNHyfW**
It costs you nothing extra (free) and the affiliate amount does not affect your payouts or margins in any way.

Someone once asked me if anyone uses Represent. Yes. It's a great platform, especially if you have an audience. One great example is Pewdiepie. Pewdiepie, if you're not familiar is a youtuber, with the highest number of subscribers for any person on the platform, **OVER 60,000,000+** people are subscribed to his youtube channel. Some of his campaigns have over 4,000+ units of each product selling. It's certainly a platform working well for PewDiePie. Have a look at his store, get some ideas on how your store might look or feel: https://represent.com/store/pewdiepie

Alexa's rankings:
Q1 2017
Global: 44,043
USA: 18,070
Q4 2017
Global: 31,420
USA: 9,429

Head Quarters:
Represent,
#400, 1680 Vine St
Los Angeles, CA 90028, United States
leo@represent.com

gearbubble.com

Gearbubble is one POD service to watch. With explosive growth, and some ground setting integration options, Gearbubble is one of the 21 PODs platforms I am currently listing with. In the top 10,000 ranking of all website in the USA, it's also an American focused service, that knows it's market, and is willing to innovate to grow its share of the POD pie. (which is a huge pie). Open to the public since 2015, this newbie on the block already has over 60,000 sellers, and over 500,000 customers in 2016 alone!

Gearbubble Is Growing...

From Unisex T-Shirts to Necklaces

Select a Product You Would Like to Create and Start Selling

GearBubble makes it easy to sell on almost anything. Simply select one of the products that we have and you can have something up and selling within minutes. That simple, that easy.

It doesn't end there, in addition to being a regular POD, and being able to sell via their marketplace, GearBubble also allows integrations with several other sales platforms, including Amazon, Ebay, Shopify and soon Etsy. Here is the link to the Amazon integration, for example:
https://www.gearbubble.com/amazon
To add a new marketplace (dropship store) within your gear bubble account, you can do so here:
https://www.gearbubble.com/dropship_stores/new

For step by step video training on exactly how to each each of the marketplace platform integrations, check out Gearbubble's training area here: https://www.gearbubble.com/trainings

This means that you can load your designs to GearBubble, then connect your GearBubble account to other sales platforms, and have the designs cross listed there. When people order your products on say Amazon, eBay, Etsy or Shopify, the order is passed through to GearBubble, who then makes and ships the product to your buyer. Here is more info on their drop shipping program via Shopify: https://www.gearbubble.com/dropship_users/new

PRO TIP: Gear bubble's top seller's page, shows you how many of each item has sold, giving you a great insight into just how popular some products, and some designs can become. $285,000+ in revenue from a single Mug from a single platform? YES! (link here: https://www.gearbubble.com/wifelv) Get your design on the top seller list by selling a lot, and you will benefit from the added exposure of this feature. As a new seller, it's also interesting to note just how many non-shirt items sell well! From thermal mugs to necklaces, Gear bubble definitely has some unique offerings not found commonly elsewhere. See their top sellers, Link Here: https://www.gearbubble.com/category/top-sellers ... One current top selling item has over $600,000 in sales ... on ONE product (its a necklace, check it out: https://www.gearbubble.com/from-dad-to-son)!

If you are interested in using GearBubble as your POD for your Etsy store, you now can (NEW as of March 2018): Plans and details are here: https://www.gearbubble.com/etsy

Join Etsy for FREE, Plus get 40 FREE listings here: http://etsy.me/2nV2rqf

Gearbubble Pro ($297/month), launched in mid 2017 takes all of the experience for GearBubble, and creates a unique selling portal for sellers.

Here are some of the features that **Gearbubble Pro** offers:

- Full Store Builder
(private products, on-demand products, banners, sliders, search, sort, categories, menu's, etc)
- Direct To Checkout Sales Pages
(optimize for CONVERSIONS)
- Cart Based Order Pages
(optimize for Average Order Value)
- Create, Sell, Manage Monthly Box Offers
(rebills and stable revenue)
- 45+ On-Demand Products

- 1 Page Checkout Forms
(higher conversions)
- 1 Click "Smart Upsells"
(smarter checkouts, higher order value)
- Global Upsells & Related Products
(automated upsells)
- Full Featured Page Builder
- Fully Automated Cart Abandonment
- Email Broadcaster
- Automated Review Collection And Filtering
- Automated Receipts With Related Products
- Optimization Enhancers
(stock count, amount sold, timer, etc)
- Customer Photo Upload Technology
- Customer Input Fields For Customized Products
- Custom Domain Capabilities
- SSL Encryption
- Fraud Prevention
- Unlimited Products
- Unlimited Sub-Users
- Analytics - Facebook Pixel, Google Analytics, 3rd Party
- Advanced Reporting
- International Language & Currency Supported
- Order Management System
(manage 10,000+ orders/day)
- Email Integrations: Aweber, Mailchimp, GetResponse, ConstantContact
- Payment Integrations: Paypal & Stripe
- Other Integrations: Stamps.com
Videos, and more info here: https://www.gbrecommends.com/pages/pro

Gearbubble Pro, simply offers more great ways to drive more sales.

gearbubble.com's
Alexa's rankings:
Q1 2017
Global: 21,888
USA: 8,678
Q4 2017
Global: 28,982
USA: 9,327

Head Quarters:
6440 SkyPointe Dr. 140-361
Las Vegas, NV 89131 USA

teezily.com (USA and European focus)
It's big in Germany! TeeZily has both a marketplace, and does back end POD fulfillment (connect it to Shopify for example with their Shopify app, here: https://apps.shopify.com/teezily-plus) One thing that makes this appealing is their low base pricing, both in Europe, and the USA:

Estimated Profits (EU)	Estimated Profits (US)
Product: Selling Price - Cost (using Teezily Plus) = €€€ (profit margin)	Product: Selling Price - Cost (using Teezily Plus) = $$$ (profit margin)
T-shirt R-Neck Unisex: 24,99€ - 6€ = 18,99€ (76%)	T-shirt R-Neck Unisex: 24,99$ - 6$ = 18,99$ (76%)
T-shirt V-Neck Unisex: 25,99€ - 8€ = 17,99€ (69%)	T-shirt V-Neck Unisex: 27,99$ - 10$ = 17,99$ (64%)
T-shirt Long Sleeves: 25,99€ - 8€ = 17,99 (69%)	T-shirt Long Sleeves: 28,99$ - 11$ = 17,99$ (62%)
Tank Top Unisex: 24,99€ - 8€ = 16,99 (68%)	Tank Top Unisex: 26,99$ - 10$ = 16,99$ (63%)
Hoodies: 34,99€ - 14€ = 20,99€ (60%)	Hoodies: 39,99$ - 17$ = 22,99$ (57%)
Sweater: 34,99€ - 13€ = 21,99 (63%)	Sweater: 39,99$ - 17$ = 22,99$ (57%)
T-shirt R-Neck Woman: 24,99€ - 8€ = 16,99€ (68%)	T-shirt R-Neck Woman: 26,99$ - 10$ = 16,99$ (63%)
T-shirt Kid: 24,99€ - 8€ = 16,99 (68%)	T-shirt Kid: 25,99$ - 9$ = 16,99$ (65%)
Hoodie Kid: 34,99€ - 15€ = 19,99€ (57%)	Hoodie Kid: 39,99$ - 17$ = 22,99$ (57%)
Onesies: 24,99€ - 8€ = 16,99 (68%)	Onesies: 25,99$ - 9$ = 16,99$ (65%)
Tank Top Woman: 24,99€ - 8€ = 16,99 (68%)	Tank Top Woman: 26,99$ - 11.25$ = 15,74$ (61%)
T-shirt V-Neck Woman: 25,99€ - 8€ = 17,99 (69%)	T-shirt V-Neck Woman: 27,99$ - 11$ = 17,99$ (67%)

TeeZily also allows you to earn commissions from any existing designs on it's platform earning up to 80% of THE PROFIT on each sale. Their affiliate program is also cookie based, so you not only earn commissions from the traffic you send to the platform, but you also each the affiliate commissions on any additional purchases made by those buyers for up to 30 days after the initial click to their site. This can be great as a designer as well, as others might be willing to promote your designs so they can earn their affiliate commissions. For more details on their affiliate program go here: https://www.teezily.com/affiliate

To see TeeZily's Shopify backbones POD TeeZily Plus in action, here's a short video showing you exactly how to add it to your Shopify store, and add products: https://youtu.be/mTMvWaMG7Fs

teezily.com
Alexa's rankings:
Q1 2017
Global: 12,773
Germany: 3,006
Q4 2017
Global: 33,071
Germany: 5,286

Head Quarters:
103 Rue La Buétie
75008 Paris

6dollarshirts.com

The name kind of gives it away. These guys have really cheap $6 shirts. Order in bulk, and you can get 10 for $5 each... They also offer premium Tees for $12 each. Their big draw is price, but they do sell huge volumes, so if you can get your designs on this POD, you can stand to make some real $. Their shirts are silk screened, rather than DTG. This allows them to keep costs very low, with large production runs on a limited number of high selling popular designs. For base shirts, they tend to use Delta, Gildan, and Tultex shirts. The also offer some additional items for sale, beyond their very cheap t-shirts:

6dollarshirts is more like competition, and an interesting place to see popular selling designs, than it is a POD that you can load designs onto.

SHOP BY STYLE

- GUYS TEES
- GIRLS TEES
- KIDS TEES
- GUYS TANKS
- GIRLS TANKS
- SWEATSHIRTS
- HOODIES
- PRINTS

SHOP BY CATEGORY

- NEW DESIGNS
- TV & MOVIES
- PETS & ANIMALS
- SCIENCE & MATH
- GEEK & GAMING
- GRAPHIC & VINTAGE
- FUNNY
- FOOD & COFFEE
- MUSIC
- PARTYING
- POP CULTURE
- POLITICS
- SPORTS & WELLNESS
- HOLIDAYS & COSTUMES
- SHOP ALL TEES

SHOP BY PRICE

- TEES FOR $6
- TEES FOR $9
- TEES FOR $12
- 10 FOR $50 TEES
- GIFT CERTIFICATES
- CLEARANCE

6dollarshirts.com's
Alexa's rankings:
Q1 2017
Global: 77,189
USA: 18,267
Q4 2017
Global: 51,104
USA: 9,881

Head Quarters:
Thread Pit Inc / 6dollarshirts
2708 NE Waldo Rd,
Gainesville, FL
32609, USA

viralstyle.com
ViralStyle offers both a back end POD service (integrates with e-commerce solutions such as Shopify ViralStyle Shopify app link here: https://apps.shopify.com/viralstyle-fulfillment) and an online marketplace of it's own where people can buy you items. Full product pricing available here: https://viralstyle.zendesk.com/hc/en-us/articles/115000686090-Product-Pricing-Shipping-Costs

They also have a great Seller Academy to help you learn ways to sell more. It contains multiple full video courses, case studies, and weekly webinars on how to drive more sales. All FREE! Located here: http://sellers.viralstyle.com

ViralStyle ships over 1,000,000 printed items per year, and is well known as a trusted POD partner. They have a wide variety of items that can be POD fulfilled including Kozies, Dog Tags, flip flops, and of course all the T-shirts you would expect - from brands such as Anvil, Bella + Canvas, Gildan, Hanes, LAT and Next Level and more!

They print DTG, and All-over dye sublimation, so you can get your repeating patters, and full image shirts made easily, with this fully automated fulfilment option.

viralstyle.com
Alexa's rankings:
Q1 2017
Global: 31,572
USA: 14,295
Q4 2017
Global: 51,663
USA: 24,375

Head Quarters:
4618 Eagle Falls Pl.
Tampa, FL
33619

rageon.com
RageOn! is the full sublimation (full coverage) POD. Thousands of licensed brands. RageOn! has one of the best mobile apps for any POD I've ever seen.
iOS app available here: https://itunes.apple.com/us/app/rageon/id1031607191?mt=8

It allows you to take a picture of anything using your phone, and turn it immediately into a design listed across multiple types of items, from T-Shirts, to underwear, bikini's, socks, towels, and more!

RageOn again, is really the go to source for All-Over-Prints, they have done such a great job in this area, that if your designs lend well to full garment prints, this is one POD you should really consider asap. Again, its free, and only takes a few moments to join.

PRO TIP: Want to make a LOT MORE SALES with your existing RageOn account? convert your free account into one of the super secret paid Rageon Plans, and watch your sales follow. There are 4 levels: FREE, $4.99/month, $49.99/month, Enterprise.
More info here: https://www.rageon.com/pages/plans

RageOn! paid plans give you access to the following additional features:

Training Course
Featured Brand
White Labeling
Dedicated Support
Newsletter and Promotion
Custom Product Images
IP Protection
Discount Codes
Set Your Own Pricing
Store Customization
Advanced Web Marketing
Advanced IP Protection

SUPERLIKES
With RageOn, when you spearlike an item, you earn a small commission each time anyone on the site buys that item. It's a creative way for them to drive traffic to popular designs, and allows everyone to use the platform to earn extra cash for helping to identify great designs.

Mobile App?
Apple iOS Seller and Buyer App: https://itunes.apple.com/us/app/rageon/id1031607191?mt=8

rageon.com's
Alexa's rankings:
Q1 2017
Global: 58,276
USA: 18,360
Q4 2017
Global: 55,096
USA: 12,777

Head Quarters:
RageOn!
1163 E 40 Street
Suite 211
Cleveland, OH
44114

bonfire.com
Bonfire allows you to create custom pages. It is geared towards fundraising for charities and non-profit organizations. It ran the main T-shirt campaign/delivery for the Women's March on Washington, in January 2017; one of their designs sold over **$500,000** worth of shirts in under 2 weeks! This is a great platform to use, if you have a passionate audience who is willing to support your cause. For a full list of their catalogue go here: https://www.bonfire.com/catalog/

bonfire.com's
Alexa's rankings:
Q1 2017
Global: 118,835
USA:14,315
Q4 2017
Global: 86,096
USA: 18,469

HQ:
Bonfire
10128 W Broad St Suite A,
Glen Allen, VA
23060, USA

printaura.com
Print Aura is a back end POD, meaning it connects to Shopify, Etsy, WooCommerce, and more. Print Aura will receive your orders via your e-commerce site, and take care of the manufacturing, packing and shipping. So, your customers buy a shirt for example on your Shopify store, and Print Aura takes this order, and makes it for you and ships it to your buyers. Because your buyers are paying you through your e-commerce platform, and the orders are happening on the back end, you will need to ensure that you have funds or a payment method to pay for the items being made by Print Aura. You can then cover these costs with the money your customers paid you, and you keep the difference.

One of the advantages to using a large back end POD like Print Aura, is a wide assortment of products to offer your buyers. Print Aura has over 100+ products to offer, listed here: https://printaura.com/products

Multiple types of:
T-Shirts
Bags and Totes
Mugs
Phone Cases… lots of Phone cases!
Snap Cases, Clear Cases, Tough Cases, BAKPAK style cases, Folio style cases… for many phone types: iPhone 6, 6+, 6S, 6S+, 7, 7+, 8, 8+
Galaxy S6, S6 Edge, S6 Edge+, S7, S7 Edge, S8, S8+
Galaxy Note 5
LG G5, G6
Google Pixel, Pixel XL
Posters
Hoodies… Lots of Hoodies!
Multiple hoodie styles from each of these brands: Gildan, Bella+Canvas, Alternative, Next level, Royal Apparel, Hanes, Independent trading
Aprons
Pocket T-Shirt Prints
Embroidered Hats
Pillows

One of the stand out brands in the list above is Royal Apparel, as it offers organic T-Shirts. One of only a few places that do, and Print Aura is one of the few places that offers Royal Apparel.

Again, as mentioned in the section on Etsy:
To integrate Etsy with ***Print Aura***:

1. Create an Etsy Account (use this link for 40 free listings: http://etsy.me/2nV2rqf) (if this is your first listing on Etsy, you'll also need to list your first item, which creates your shop, and gives you access to the shop manager)
2. Register an account with Print Aura
3. Install the Etsy App (on Print Aura) (Instructions here: https://printaura.com/etsy/)
4. Select Print Aura as your outside manufacturer on Etsy (Shop Manager -> settings -> Production Partners -> Add new production partner)
5. Load your designs into Print Aura
6. Sync your Print Aura Designs to Etsy

Here are more details on all the steps, as well as HOW to complete the Etsy Integration on the 'Create a New App' page in Print Aura: https://printaura.com/etsy-install-guide

printaura.com's
Alexa's rankings:
Q1 2017
Global: 100,925
USA: 31,460
Q4 2017
Global: 100,466
USA: 31,738

Head Quarters:
PrintAura
2 Wurz Avenue
Yorkville, NY
13495 USA

customizedgirl.com
Customized Girl is primarily a Marketplace, with no back end POD fulfillment option. It has printed over 200,000 items last year, and expects to continue to grow. It offers FREE 3 day shipping on orders over $60, and specializes in group orders making it a great option of groups and teams. Speaking of which, it offers discounts on group orders of 5 units or more, and it allows individual customization such as nicknames or team numbers. It has developed a great audience of mostly women buyers, so you may want to cater to this audience with more feminine designs, although you can see any sort of design here, as you would on other PODs.

customizedgirl.com's
Alexa's rankings:
Q1 2017
Global: 89,117
USA: 24,769
Q4 2017
Global: 106,232
USA: 19,892

Head Quarters:
eRetailing Associates, LLC
2282 Westbrooke Dr.
Columbus, OH
43228
Phone: 1.800.345.0345 Ext 108
Email: pthibault@eretailing.com

customcat.com
Can connect to your Shopify store. 24-48 hour shipping. Over 200 products, it is based in Detroit, Michigan.

CustomCat is a 'back end' POD, meaning it integrates with an online e-commerce platform, such as Shopify (https://apps.shopify.com/customcat-fulfillment). It offers very fast fulfillment, low per product costs, and white label packaging (meaning you can put your branding on the package). All great features that set CustomCat apart from other PODs. One thing that also sets it apart from other POD services, is that it charges a monthly fee of $30USD per month, billed monthly. They also have a 14 Day free trial period, so you can see it in use for FREE before committing to the $30/month fee.

If you are just starting out with a back end POD making and shipping your items, sold on another platform like Amazon, etsy, or Shopify, you may want to start with something with no monthly fee, like Printful. However, once your volume increases, and you are getting consistent orders from month to month, CustomCat makes a great alternative to Printful, with better base product pricing, shipping times, and shipping costs.

Print On Demand offers industry leading Aeoon Printers producing up to 1200DPI printing resolution on its apparel. Low cost domestic shipping: CustomCat charges $3.99 for the first item+ $1.50 per each additional product added to that order shipped domestic and $7.50 for the first item + $5.95 per each additional product to the rest of the world. However, note that CustomCat does not accept returns due to user error such as incorrect selection of sizes, designs, colors, etc. Although they do offer 100% guarantee on it's workmanship, and offers no charge replacement on any defects.

Some unique products not commonly found on other PODs include: button up short sleeve work shirts, flannel pants, fleece pants, 22oz beer stein, 20 oz stainless steel water bottles, doggie bandanas, scarfs, backpacks, microfiber golf towels, dog tags, flip flops, and many more! Here is portal to access all products and base pricing from CustomCat: http://www.customcat.com/?t=h.catalog

CustomCat also offers several in depth tutorials about a variety of subject from getting started, to creating grouped listings, manual orders via Shopify, and more here: http://www.customcat.com/?t=h.faq_tutorial

customcat.com's
Alexa's rankings:
Q1 2017
Global: 184,598
USA: 51,496
Q4 2017
Global: 109,771
USA: 27,033

Head Quarters:
CustomCat
1300 Rosa Parks Blvd
Detroit, MI
48324

moteefe.com (European focus)
Moteefe appears to have a European focus compared to other PODs, it also caters to sellers by offering daily payouts, and fast product uploads (under 60 seconds).
Moteefe is Available in 7 languages - English, German, French, Italian, Dutch, Spanish, and Portuguese.

Like TeeSpring, Moteefe is a campaign based POD, so orders will be taken for a period of time, then shipped to all buyers at the conclusion of the campaign. Offer your campaigns in 3, 7 or 10 day default campaigns, or create a custom time frame that matches your marketing. Campaigns can be set to automatically renew at their end.

PRO TIP: Use shorter campaigns for happier customers and faster delivery. Use longer campaigns for greater profit (volume reduces base costs, giving you more profits per campaign), or to match large launches (new design, new product, conferences, etc.).

HUGE MARGINS

Sample Pricing: $15.99USD gives $9.49USD Profit (Base costs of $6.50 for single t-shirt order), price gets better with higher volume, yielding $10.79USD profit for total order volume of 50 shirts. Pricing is much lower compared to Merch By Amazon, giving you the option of taking more profit at the same prices, OR offering lower customer prices, while maintaining the same profit margins you would see elsewhere.

Items Available on Moteefe:

Like many of the other PODS, they offer more than just t-shirts, and have a variety of multiple t-shirt suppliers as well.

Here's some of their offerings:

Classic Men's T-Shirt
Premium Men's T-Shirt
Men's V-Neck T-Shirt
Men's Tank Top
Classic Women's T-Shirt
Premium Women's T-Shirt
Women's V-Neck T-Shirt
Women's Tank Top
Men's Long Sleeved T-Shirt
Women's Long Sleeved T-Shirt
Baby T-Shirt
Kids T-Shirt
Babygrow (onesie)
Unisex Sweatshirt
Women's Hoodie
Unisex Hoodie
Kids Sweatshirt
Kids Hoodie
Samsung Galaxy Case (S3-S7EDGE)
iPhone Case 4/4S
iPhone Case 5/5s/5c
iPhone Case 6-7+
White Mug
Magic Mug
Black Mug
Women's Flowy Tank Top
Towel
Cushion (Rectangular)
Cushion (Square)
Tote Bag

Small - Medium - Large Portrait Canvas
Small - Medium - Large Landscape Canvas
Small - Medium Square Canvas
Portrait Puzzle <—this is pretty unique among PODs…
Landscape Puzzle

Descriptions and or sizing for each product is available to buyers when an item is selected. Multiple items can be viewed by the buyer on the design page for each design. for example:

Sizing Guide

Classic Men's T-Shirt

Allow for a tolerance level of 2cm/0.8in. It is always better to choose the larger size in the case of doubts. Feel free to contact us at support@moteefe.com if you have any questions.

? Fullchest	CM	INCHES
S	91.4	36
M	101.6	40
L	111.8	44
XL	121.9	48
XXL	132.1	52
3XL	143.4	56
4XL	153.6	60
5XL	163.8	64

? Body Length	CM	INCHES
S	69.9	27.5
M	73	28.8
L	75.6	29.8
XL	78.1	30.8
XXL	81.3	32
3XL	169	66
4XL	174.1	68
5XL	179.2	70

moteefe.com's
Alexa's rankings:
Q1 2017
Global: 176,635
Germany: 27,877
Q4 2017
Global: 109,565
Germany: 33,532

gearlaunch.com
Relatively new, and with big ambitions, this back end POD service was one of the featured speakers at the 10X Merch Conference fall of 2017 in New Jersey. The GearLaunch founder and CEO is Thatcher Spring. It can be connected to Shopify. You select items to sell, they do the rest. GearLaunch helps clients create online storefronts, and handles back-office and logistic tasks. They offer an assortment of items which you can fulfill via your Shopify store (done by application here: http://info.gearlaunch.com/gearlaunch-shopify-app), or your own storefront on your own domain.

Some things that set GearLaunch apart from other POD services (such as Printful, PrintAura, TeeLaunch, etc.), are that they offer PERSONALIZED CUSTOMER SERVICE. That's right, when buyers call for customer service, they are greeted by YOUR BRAND, not GearLaunches. From a buyer's perspective the banding is 100% yours. GearLaunch provides full access to purchaser emails, allowing you to build out personalized email campaigns, and know who is buying. They also have one page product creation, which speeds up loading your listings, and they offer Flags! ***Not too many other PODs have flags ;-)***

GearLaunch offers tiered pricing for volume sellers. Tier pricing starts with the first unit sold, and the top volume tier is 20,000+ units.
For example here is their lowest cost T-Shirt:
Hanes Tagless Tee model # 5250
Blue $8.95
Bronze $8.25
Silver $7.65
Gold $7.25
Platinum $6.85
Diamond $6.15

Here's their full catalog with pricing: https://www.gearlaunch.com/product-catalog

Here's What some of the products Look like:

Apparel:

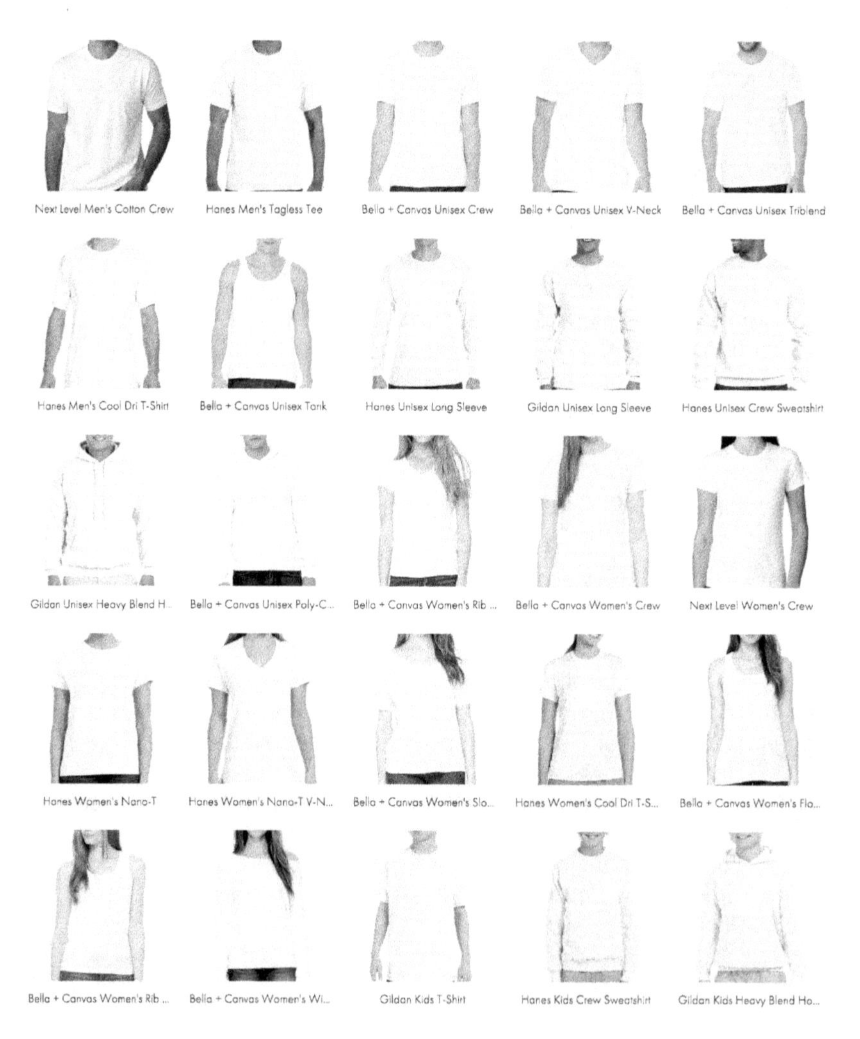
APPAREL
Next Level Men's Cotton Crew
Hanes Men's Tagless Tee
Bella + Canvas Unisex Crew
Bella + Canvas Unisex V-Neck
Bella + Canvas Unisex Triblend
Hanes Men's Cool Dri T-Shirt
Bella + Canvas Unisex Tank
Hanes Unisex Long Sleeve
Gildan Unisex Long Sleeve
Hanes Unisex Crew Sweatshirt
Gildan Unisex Heavy Blend H...
Bella + Canvas Unisex Poly-C...
Bella + Canvas Women's Rib ...
Bella + Canvas Women's Crew
Next Level Women's Crew
Hanes Women's Nano-T
Hanes Women's Nano-T V-N...
Bella + Canvas Women's Slo...
Hanes Women's Cool Dri T-S...
Bella + Canvas Women's Flo...
Bella + Canvas Women's Rib ...
Bella + Canvas Women's Wi...
Gildan Kids T-Shirt
Hanes Kids Crew Sweatshirt
Gildan Kids Heavy Blend Ho...

GearLaunch Drinkware:

DRINKWARE

11 Oz. Ceramic Mug

15 Oz. Ceramic Mug

22 Oz. Beer Stein

14 Oz. Travel Mug

14 Oz. Travel Mug

30 Oz. Tumbler

20 Oz. Water Bottle

GearLaunch Accessories:

ACCESSORIES

Five Panel Trucker Cap

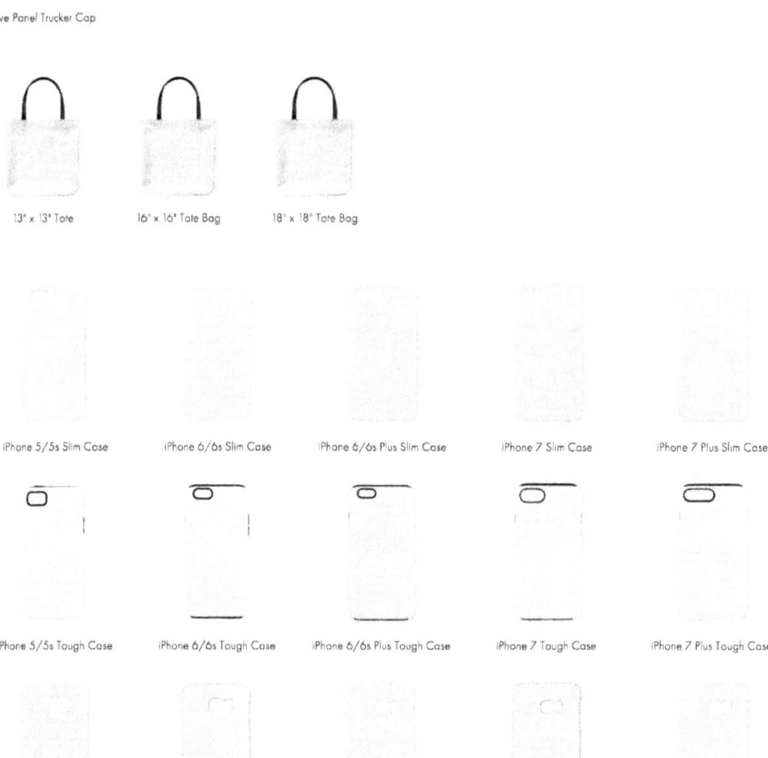

Home Decor:

HOME DECOR

16" x 16" Outdoor Throw Pillow

18" x 18" Outdoor Throw Pillow

16" x 16" Indoor Pillow

18" x 18" Indoor Pillow

Standard Pillowcase

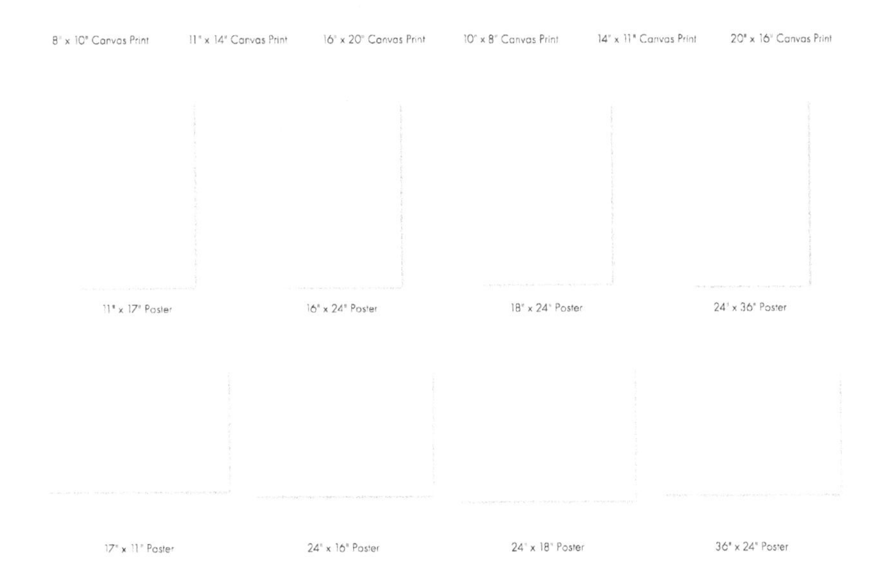

To see all of their current product offerings visually, click here: https://www.gearlaunch.com/products

GearLaunch also has one of the best resources pages, including seasonal and monthly reports to help you sell more: https://www.gearlaunch.com/resources/

Alexa's rankings:
Q1 2018
Global: 149,464
USA: 73,883

Head Quarters:
GearLaunch
234 Front Street,
3rd Floor,
San Francisco,
CA 94111, USA

teelaunch.com
Connect to Shopify (https://apps.shopify.com/teelaunch-1). Select items to sell. They do the POD. Here's a video on how to add items to your Shopify store:
https://www.youtube.com/watch?time_continue=95&v=qF9EMFzsXOI
More about this coming up later in the book ;-)

teelaunch

PRICE SHEET

PRODUCT	PRICE	SHIPPING (U.S)
3"x4" Sticker	$2.00	$1.50
11oz Mugs (White)	$3.50	$4.50
16" Pillow Cover	$4.50	$2.50
15oz Mug (White)	$5.00	$4.50
11oz Mugs (Black)	$5.00	$4.50
Mousepad	$5.00	$3.00
Dog Bowl	$10.00	$8.00
Tote Bag	$10.00	$4.50
Cell Phone Cases	$11.00	$2.00
Beer Stein	$12.00	$4.50
Cutting Board	$15.00	$3.00
Small Blanket	$15.00	$5.00
Medium Blanket	$25.00	$10.00
Yoga Mat	$30.00	$10.00
Shower Curtain	$30.00	$8.00
Large Blanket	$35.00	$10.00

Up to date pricing here: https://files.teelaunch.com/products/price_sheet.pdf

TeeLaunch also includes White label shipping, so your name is on the shipping label.
Here is a FULL list of teeLaunch's Products: https://teelaunch.com/collections/products

In addition to Shopify, TeeLaunch also offers Etsy integration. More info here: https://teelaunch.com/pages/etsy

Here is the direct link to the Etsy Store TeeLaunch app: https://www.etsy.com/apps/182574138636/teelaunch-helping-over-32k-store-owners Here are the exact steps/instructions on how to connect TeeLaunch to your Etsy store: https://teelaunchhelp.zendesk.com/hc/en-us/articles/115014905408-installing-Etsy-integration

Alexa's rankings:
Q1 2017
Global: 164,315
USA: 41,025
Q4 2017
Global: 152,672
USA: 50,592

Head Quarters:
1100 E 15th Street
Sioux Falls, SD
57104-5271

skreened.com
Skreened donates returned apparel to Planet Aid, prints with water based inks, and uses minimal packaging for a reduced environmental impact. Skreened also maintains a blog, so you can keep up to date on it's latest trends, and offerings, Link Here: https://skreened.com/blog/

skreened.com's
Alexa's rankings:
Q1 2017
Global: 134,036
USA: 44,534
Q4 2017
Global: 156,819
USA: 42,963

Head Quarters:
Skreened
3327 N High Street
Columbus, OH
43202-1115

artsadd.com

"Arts Add is the Chinese K-Pop of POD yo ;-) "

Arts Add is a unique POD as far as some of the items that it allows you to offer. Items like umbrellas, kids lunch boxes, boots, backpacks, lunch bags, and more! It offers integrations with Shopify (See how its done here, with the soulful tunes of the arts Add crew: https://youtu.be/hzaB5Bi3rCo) and WooCommerce, as well as custom API, so you can add artadd's items to virtually any website you have.

With Arts Add you set your own commission % (similar to Redbubble), and you can choose from 1% to 100% markup. They also offer referral fee on driving sales of other listed items on it's platform of 5%. Meaning, if you drive traffic to another design on the platform (with your referral code on the URL), and it sells, you will receive 5% of the price the customer pays. This can be a great option if you're looking to add additional designs to a website or marketplace you're driving traffic to.

This POD operates in multiple ways unlike other PODs, so be sure to read through their FAQ (http://www.artsadd.com/help), so that you fully understand both what they offer, and on what terms. For example, earning can only be withdrawn via Paypal, and only if the balance owed to you exceeds $100USD. However, if your balance owing is less than $100USD, you can use this owed amount as credit towards purchased items on the platform.

For a small added fee, they also offer branding both on package (a sticker on your shipping package for $1 per order), or in-item label (a small label sewn into your items with your brand on it, for $2 per order).

Here are some of the items offered by ArtsAdd:

129 Accessories including:

Umbrella
Watches
Mousepads
Air Smart Phone Holder
Aprons
Carry-All Pouch
Clocks
Fidget Spinner
Headband
Lunch Box
Mugs
Neckties
Neoprene Water Bottle Pouch
New Pet Car Seat
NoteBook
Pet Bed
Scarves
Sleeping Mask
Electronics

65 Home Decorations:

Beach Supplies
Tablecloths
Wall Tapestries
Posters
Canvas Print
Doormat
Coasters
Art Print
Canvas Print Sets
Garden Flag
License Plate

79 Home Set items:

Pillow Cases
New Window Curtain
Window Curtain
Area Rug
Bath Rug
Bedding Set
Blanket
Duvet Covers

Placemat
Shower Curtain
Table Runner
Towel
Hooded Bath Towels

152 Footwear / shoe items:
Custom Boots
Light Up Shoes
Running Shoes
High Top Shoes
Low Top Shoes
High Top Leather Shoes
Low Top Leather Shoes
Casual Shoes
Women's High Heels
Flip Flops
Socks

107 Bag Items:
Backpacks
Laptop Sleeves
Tote Bags
Laptop Handbags
Saddle Bag
Sling Bags
Handbags
Messenger Bags
Wallets
Travel Bags
Drawstring Bag
Lunch Bag
Cosmetic Bag

111 All Over / Sublimation Clothing items including:
Hoodies
Leggings
Sweatshirts
Hooded Blankets
Dresses
Jackets
Pants
T-Shirts
Underwear

Swimwear
Skirts
Shorts
Tops

42 Direct Print Clothing Items:
Hoodies
Sweatshirt
Dresses
T-Shirts
Jackets
Polo Shirts
Shirts
Tops
Baby Onesies
Jeans
Hats

One thing to keep in mind when using ArtsAdd (like with any POD platform), is production time. Here are the production times for some of the items offered by this unique and interesting POD platform:
*Shoes Production Time: 5-7 days

*Bags Production Time: 4-6 days

*All-Over-Print Apparels Production Time: 4-7 days

*All-Over-Print Legging Production Time: 4-6 days

*All-Over-Print Hoodies Production Time: 4-7 days

*Umbrella Production Time: 3-6 days

*Accessories Production Time: 3-6 days

*Home Products Production Time: 3-6 days

*Generally speaking, we will strive to print & produce all orders within a week.
*Mix & Match order requires even longer production time due to across-department manufacturing processing.

Because of the wide variety of the products that they offer, they use multiple DTG printers, from multiple brands, including: Konit Storm, Epson, MUTOH VJ-1924, ROLAND FH740.

For more answers to questions about this interesting POD platform, here is a direct link to their extensive FAQ: http://www.artsadd.com/help

Artsadd's
Alexa's Rankings:
Q1 2018
Global: 190,929
Spain: 9,883

Artsadd's HQ: UNLISTED....
Secret location somewhere near
Licheng District, Kuokou Community
Putian, Fujian 351100 China

teescape.com
Useful to integrate into your Shopify store(https://apps.shopify.com/teescape-fulfillment) Which you can then connect to Amazon, for automated POD delivery of Amazon orders. Teescape offers exceptionally competitive POD pricing, and runs things a bit old school. Here is a quick 3 minute video on how to add TeeScape products to your Shopify Store: https://youtu.be/QcljHVcJ0mw

teescape.com's
Alexa's rankings:
Q1 2017
Global: 689,992
USA: 196,046
Q4 2017
Global: 616,192
USA: 141,802

Head Quarters
636 River Drive
PO Box 37
Princeton, IA
52768

inktale.com

One of the newest Print On Demand platforms, it's slogan is "Simplest online print product marketplace in existence"... What makes it great? Access to your customer list, great quality prints and items for sale at low base prices (for example a T-Shirt has a base price of $13, so if you're selling it for $20, you make $7 profit), discount codes (friends and family, or custom % off codes, your choice - both can be turned on or off). Get your payouts by request anytime within 3 days, once your balance (Inktale wallet) reaches at least $25. Payouts are pushed to your Paypal account.

Currently Inktale offers the following product categories:
t-shirts, tank tops, all-over t-shirts, all-over tank tops, sweatshirts, hoodies, phone cases, coffee mugs, throw pillows, wall art, tote bags, drawstring bags, leggings and towels.

Like most PODs, Inktale also has a Blog - Link Here: https://inktale.com/blog/category/artist-guide Where Inktale offers helpful advice and tips on how to sell more and build your business. One that I especially enjoyed was how to use Facebook ads to drive more traffic to your site, including how to setup Facebook Pixel: https://inktale.com/blog/inktale-101-step-by-step-facebook-ads-for-beginners#more-837 This is especially useful on Inktale, as it allows you to connect your account to Facebook Pixel, allowing you to gather additional information about your audience, and build lookalike audiences to market to in the future.

Although Inktale is one of the newest PODs, they are looking to build in additional features to help drive more sales, such as plans to integrate with Amazon Payments, allowing users one click payments via their Amazon account. They are also looking to create integration with Instagram, so that you can connect your Instagram photos directly onto products with Intake in the future.

Interesting Fact: Inktale orders are currently fulfilled via Printful at one of Printful's 3 locations: Los Angeles, CA, Charlotte, NC and Riga, Latvia.

inktale.com's

Alexa's rankings:
Q1 2018
Global: 333,019
USA: 166,908

Head Quarters:
Inktale, Inc.
611 Anton Blvd., Ste. 1400, Costa Mesa,
CA 92626
hello@inktale.com
Twitter: @inktale

dizinga.com
UK and USA sales. Worldwide shipping, est. 5-7 day shipping times. Centralized delivery points in Canada, USA, and Europe. Select prices on page by US dollars, UK pounds, or Euro. 12.5% artist royalties, and 18% affiliate commissions, combined, can give you 30% earnings off each sale you bring in! Pays via Paypal, no minimum payout amount. Prices are SET BY THEM, meaning you cannot set your own prices. They feature your designs via Google shopping!

dizinga.com's
Alexa's rankings:
Q1 2017
Global: 251,824
UK: 18,175
Q4 2017
Global: 686,366
USA: 231,101

Head Quarters:
Dizinga
99-93 Mabgate Business Center
Leeds, LS9 7DR
United Kingdom

jackofalltradesclothing.com

Est. 2010. Specialists in high quality shirts. Jack of all Trades Clothing has an affiliate program, so you can make money promoting other designer's clothing. Categories they specialize in include: Comic Book, Pop-Culture, Rock N' Roll, Art & Lifestyle, Fashion Basics. They have Trademark licenses with: DC Comics ; Warner Bros. Entertainment Inc. ; A Beatles™ Product Apple Corps Ltd. ; BS Productions Limited. ; The Doors Apparel Company, LLC The Doors is a registered trademark of The Doors Property, LLC ; Black Frog Entities, Inc. ; Authentic Hendrix LLC. ; Queen Productions Limited; and Musidor B.V. and more!

Alexa's rankings:
Q4 2017
Global: 2,094,313
India: 367,279

booster.com

Encourages fundraisers for non-profits

Alexa's rankings:
Q1 2017
Global: 109,315
USA: 22,519
Q4 2017
Global: 4,321,933

Head Quarters:
Booster
Riverside Centre
275 Grove Street, Suite 1 305
Newton, MA
02466

END OF CHAPTER 4

CHAPTER 5: Marketing

Connecting your shoppers to your products...

Marketing Intro:
Before we start to get into the weeds on marketing, a subject that itself alone has thousands of books, thousands of videos, and thousands of courses all of the world, and for hundreds of years of history, theory and millions of ways to market, lets look at the purpose of marketing, and what you are looking to achieve when marketing your Merch By Amazon, or other POD designs, and anything related to on demand...

Marketing 101 - The Basics:

Marketing in the context of this book, is creating a path of least resistance between buyers and sales. Think of yourself. I imagine that if you're reading this now, that you have bought more than one thing in your life. So look around you and see things that you have bought. Shoes, socks, shirts, pants, shorts, underwear, your tablet, your smartphone, your computer, the building you might be in right now... all these things were likely bought, or are being bought. The ground beneath your feet, or maybe the airplane seat in front of you, or the trees in the park you're sitting in right now... Maybe you bought them, or maybe someone you know bought them, or maybe your local state or federal government bought the things around you. Now think about shopping, when you search for the things you have bought, or plan to buy.

Think about the process you took to get the things you shopped for. Maybe you connected to the internet and bought something online (like this book), or maybe you went to one of the largest online retailers in the world - Amazon to buy something? Or maybe you drove to a convenience store, and found something on the shelf, like chips, or baby wipes, or gas for your car... As you think about buying and shopping and having things, I want you to know that they all have something in common. They are all things that you found. Or things that found you. ***At the point of purchase, there is always a connection between things that people want, and things that people buy.*** It is this connection between buyers and sellers, the thing that connects the two that is called marketing. What are some examples? Lets take ads as an example. TV Ads, billboards, social media ads, email marketing, YouTube pre-roll videos, signage posted on the street or even airplane banner ads... these are ways to connect buyers to products.

The goal as a seller should really be: how can I identify a need that my buyer has, or a need that they want fulfilled, or something that will satisfy their desires to a point at which they will part with something they cherish - their money - and exchange it for something you can offer to them, your stuff (T-shirt, leggings, custom wall clock), whatever you're wanting to sell. Since many of us are selling our 'stuff' via online - via on demand channels - it's logical to use these same channels to connect with our buyers. It's not the only way, but online is a great way to reach many buyers. It targets ways, with scale and at scale, in a way that offers buyers value. Greater value than the money they use to exchange for your goods. I know, this is pretty wordy, but I promise I get into the details shortly. I wanted to be sure that we're all on the same page though. Know that marketing is really about connecting your buyers, in the ways that are important to THEM, to the things that you would like THEM to buy. This can't be understated...

Marketing 201 - How to know what people want:

Now that the basics are covered, how do you know what buyers want, so that you can give them what they want? This is on the one hand very hard, and on the other hand very easy.

On the one hand, there's no magical tool that can pry into someone's mind, and see what they want... but there are LOTS of tools that can show us what people have bought before, and ways to see what people tend to buy, and methods to view that give us some indications of how much people buy things. Those are all covered in the tools and resources section.

Before you skip off and go straight to the tools, I believe it's important to know why your buyers want anything to begin with. What are their needs? Needs typically precede wants... so what do people need, or think they need?

PLEASE NOTE: Not all buyers will buy a T-shirt for the same reasons. Different buyers will buy the same niche for multiple "meta-reasons", or values.

10 THINGS BUYERS VALUE:

Different buyers value the things you sell in different ways. I touched on this on one of the live videos recorded and on replay before this book launched (Google: Merch Jacob Topping, or Jacob Topping Merch), and you should get multiple recorded videos, blogs, podcasts, webinars and more, where I discuss these things. But I'll save you some time, and list some important buyer values right now:

Buyers everywhere tend to value one or more of these things when considering buying a T-shirt, or other item online. Different PODs are better or worse at some or multiple of these buyer values. I will cover each value in more detail under the list.

1. **Time**
2. **Price**
3. **Convenience**
4. **Quality**
5. **Exclusivity**
6. **Variety**
7. **Customization**
8. **Mitigating Remorse**
9. **Surprise**
10. **Reputation**

Time:

For some buyers, the time between when they place their order, and when they get their item is the most important factor. Here's an example: you need a T-Shirt to be ready for Dad's 75th birthday, and it happens on Sunday. It's Thursday night.... but you promised your Mom you would have that shirt for Sunday... and Merch By Amazon doesn't deliver to Canada, and you're in Canada too ... at that moment, time may be this hypothetical buyer's biggest concern. How will our buyer actually get that shirt done, and delivered in time? Does this buyer care about cost at this moment? Not really.

But, but... what about Convenience? Everyone likes more convenience, but at that moment, time is the valuable factor. So, the buyer goes to the local print shop 5 minutes from his house, drops it off at 11am, heads out for lunch, and picks up a custom heat pressed vinyl T-Shirt later that day around 2:30pm. In this case, very very few online POD platforms could have fulfilled this order in under 6 hours. Is it possible? Yes! 'What' you say? Impossible... no, it's possible. Be creative. Seek out the answers. Here's another solution that may have worked: Make your own. Walmart sells blank T-shirts, and iron on designs you can print at home. Not at all convenient, and not even cheap, sometimes a buyer doesn't care. They want it now. ... or in a few hours, or minutes.... yes, I said it, in minutes (faster than Amazon Now)... crazy fast....

GAME CHANGER ALERT

Uber Rush:

Link here: https://rush.uber.com/how-it-works/
Available in limited cities: New York, Chicago, and San Fransisco (at the time of publication)
Uber Rush allows your company to collapse time and distance, and offer your buyers an On Demand, hyper fast delivery service that can deliver just about anything that fits in the Uber driver's car, to buyers in your (or that) local area. Hyper fast delivery, meaning minutes, not days or hours. For example, get a custom shirt delivered to your customer within 30 minutes or less. GAME CHANGER!

... Taking this a step further... why not locate the POD platforms located in the areas with overlapping Uber Rush coverage, and offer On Demand Hyper Fast, Hyper local customer fulfillment. How? Use Shopify. They offer an app which allows you to connect your business to Uber Rush, and provide hyper fast delivery to your buyers in certain locations. Want to set this up locally, and you live outside of New York City, Chicago, or San Fransisco? Why not contact a local Uber Driver, and make some custom deals... Not as seamless, but it's close. Hate Uber? Try it with Lyft, or a local pizza delivery service.
Have customers that really value time over money, also see Roadie: https://www.roadie.com/

The observant seller, will notice that I have conveniently included the addresses of almost every POD in chapter 4... connect the dots... take action... shoppers want their custom new shirts in less than an hour from click to doorstep (MAKE IT HAPPEN).

Price:

Some buyers value price among all other factors. They are looking for a low price, even if they need to wait for it, and even at the cost of other factors like convenience, or quality for example. Amazon get this, and this is one reason they let you offer Merch By Amazon shirts for as little as $12.88 (previously as low as $10.96). At this price, you're not likely to make much commission, and buyers who use Amazon to buy t-shirts on more than likely value and convenience over price, but it's an option. If you want to offer the lowest price, you can do this by carrying an inventory (international blank T-shirt rates are very low, and you can get blank T-shirts at some quality levels for well under $2 each. But this isn't really a book about making your own t-shirts, right? This is about Merch and the World of POD. So what is a POD service that offers very low pricing? TeeChip is very good for this at low volumes. With TeeChip shirt retail costs of $13 (minimum), the base shirt cost is:$7.74. The remaining difference of $4.89 is profit back to you. Scaleable Press is very good for bulk orders, with pricing on some shirts as low as $2.55 each (for a finished shirt with design on it, not just blanks! - on orders of 1,000+, and some other conditions), there are POD services at prices that even price sensitive buyers can appreciate. Teezily Plus for example has shirts starting at just $9 (price is lower down to $6 with volume)- and this POD you can connect to Shopify (https://apps.shopify.com/teezily-plus) , and then connect Shopify to Amazon. Using this method, you could literally have t-shirts listed on Amazon .com for under $12, and make a profit after fees! That's PRICE + Convenience!

Convenience:

So we've covered Price and Time, now it's time to discuss Convenience. Convenience can mean different things to different buyers. Maybe a POD design is convenient because it's easy to buy on your mobile device, from anywhere in the world (like using Shopify, with say... Printful). Someone else, maybe to them, convenience is all about how easy a shirt is to buy on their desktop, such as Sun Frog, via one click Paypal. Convenience is why you'll spend $3-4 for a bag of chips at the corner store, even while knowing that you can get the same bag of the same chips at the grocery store down the block for $2.50. Whatever your buyers needs are, convenience is one area that some PODs are great with, and others are still working to improve. Cafe Press, in my opinion has one of the best selections, but isn't super convenient to order with (other buyers might disagree, and think that Cafe Press is super convenient). So remember, a POD platform can be low on some areas customers value, as long as they make it up in other areas. Merch By Amazon is great example of this. It's an amazing service within the USA, however they don't deliver their Merch BY Amazon listings outside the USA... not very convenient if you live 45 minutes north of the Canada / US border, and want to order your favorite Merch By Amazon wears, right?

Quality:

Similar to the other values covered above, quality is something that is the highest value for some buyers, and they are willing to sacrifice on time, convince and price, to obtain that high quality product that they want. It's not enough to be good for some customers, they want the best! Think there's no market this? Think of the $90 collared golf shirts, with thick lush blended weaves, and embroidered custom designed artwork on the chest? Think again, to a quality buyer, the purchase is all about the final product, and the image and prestige that it affords them after the buy. These buyers tend to seek our premium product, and are happy to pay a little more, or sometimes even a lot more, to ensure they're getting the very best, just the way they want it. Think of the diamond studded iPhones, or the gold plated supercars... Diamonds and 24K gold... are some top quality materials (yes, I realize there are no gold plated, diamond encrusted, POD products at the moment, that's not to say that it won't come sooner than you would expect - I've seen .925 silver custom cut necklaces already... gold's not far behind ;-)). You're a smart cookie, you get that to some buyers Quality is the #1 factor in buying your stuff. So be sure to always make high quality, non-copied, original designs. Even text based designs can have a premium feel to them, try using some premium commercial licensed fonts! Here's a great example of an online store that sells a lot, based on Quality and not price: how about **$395.00 for a Hoodie** from Canada Goose, link here: https://www.canadagoose.com/ca/en/ashcroft-hoody-6969M.html?cgid=shop-mens#srule=price-high-to-low&sz=123&start=1&cgid=shop-mens ... and yes, they make lots of sales, Canada Goose is a $4.6 Billion dollar market cap publicly traded company! They focus on Quality.

Exclusivity:

Quality and exclusivity tend to be good friends. Often the top quality sellers will pair their offerings with exclusivity, pushing the limits of their total market of buyers, while still delighting their core repeat buyer base. This exclusivity factor is the reason that you can easily find hundreds of T-Shirt ads on Facebook pages the world over with the words "limited time, exclusive" written in the ad copy. Exclusivity can come not only in the time available for order, but also in the places, and ways in which the items are available. Some of my items for sale are only available on limited platforms, or sometimes only on one. Being creative on how you message your buyers can also help to boost sales to certain groups, depending on what they value the most. Remember, not all buyers share all the same buying values, so cater to each group (on it's own, be specific), and you're sure to have greater success with increased sales over time. Versace is a good example. You can buy Versace online, but you can only get their full clothing lineup from very few limited retailers.

Variety:

Ever wonder why Merch By Amazon even lets us sellers partner with them to offer up our hundreds of thousands of designs on amazon.com? One reason (there are many more, I'm sure), is variety. Sure they could hire out an army of graphic designers from around the world to create their own clothing designs, but they're just as happy to let us sellers do all the heavy lifting in the area of design research and generation. It gives amazon.com an ever increasing variety of designs for buyers to choose from. The 90 day rule, as it's been come to be know by, is one way to separate the sellers from the junk. amazon.com does not want to just fill their platform with endless choices, they want the best designs around, and they want to offer a variety of designs, that appeal to their customers (Merch By Amazon, being the seller of record on what you may refer to as your listings... are actually Amazon's listings, that's why your cut is a royalty, and not a commission or just simple profit on each sale).

Another good example of variety is cold drinks in in the fridge of most convenience stores. Why have one flavour of pop (soft drink / soda), when you can also have vanilla, cherry, diet, low calorie, all natural, caffeine free... this is all about variety, and giving those buyers who crave choice, many options. Other buyers, who don't value variety, are happy to grab any version, they're just there to quench their thirst, after a morning jog, or a long bike ride... that's why the big brands also offer "energy drinks, water and juices" - VARIETY.

Customization:

The entire POD ecosystem is built to handle, and cater to this important buyer value. Customization is the difference between a buyer having a mass produced T-Shirt, just like all the other buyers who have that same design (on that same mass produced shirt); versus a buyer having the only produced copy of that design that they uploaded themselves. Some buyers who really love customization may prefer to create their own designs, and do the whole process themselves. Lucky for you and I, and all the sellers selling our things on Merch By Amazon, and the dozens of other POD platforms to choose from, there are still plenty of buyers who are content with knowing that they have the choice between Port & Co. and Bella+Canvas; or depending on the platform, maybe they love that they can choose between lightweight hoodie with zipper front vs. light weight hoodie pullover style. POD marketplaces like Zazzle exist, Zazzle takes customization to a whole other level, by allowing you to personalize any item on the entire marketplace... Even designs from Disney and Coke Cola can be personalized by adding you name, or other text and designs as you like! Amazon Custom is another good example.

Mitigating Remorse:
This is a factor that may be overlooked when choosing the select few, or many POD platforms you choose to load your designs to. Lucky for you and I, most POD services offer to accept returns, and they're usually really nice and easy to deal with if or when that happens. Merch By Amazon is a great example. If a buyer accidentally orders the wrong size, or maybe they were part of some insane weight loss completion, eating only potatoes, perhaps they weight changed while that custom order made its way to their place outside of the USA, and they need to return it and get a new size. Life happens, people return things for any reason. As sellers, it can add some security and piece of mind to our buyers to know that we'll take care of them. That they are able to return even a custom shirt if needed. Just like the other buyer values of time, cost, exclusivity, variety, etc., this is just another piece of the buying value proposition, and to some buyers it's very important, while other buyers couldn't care less. So do your best to know your buyers preferences when building custom targeted marketing campaigns, and you may just find that you see a healthy boost in sales. Another good example of this is TeeLaunch: if your customer gets a shirt and it doesn't fit TeeLaunch will send out one size up or down of the same shirt for free!

Surprise:
This is one factor that in my opinion has been gaining traction, as online systems allow for some subtle extra added value that our buyers may not expect. Adding something extra to a buyers order, that will surprise them (not too much, but a little surprise is great), and have them glowing with delight, as they tell all their friends and family about how your item delivered not only what they expected, but also went beyond and delivered a bit more.

What are some practical things you can do to add a bit of extra WOW factor to some or all of your customer's purchases. Some PODs allow you to ship or add custom branding to personalize your buyers orders. This is usually in the form of an image that they will print off and include with the order, or as a sticker on the box. Why not build in some extra value to that piece, and add a discount code for future orders, or something that your buyers would appreciate. Many of the PODs do not offer such a service, but do offer you another way to give back to your buyers, as you wish, and that's customer information - Email, address, sometimes even phone#. This allows you to delight your buyers with a thank you note email, or maybe if they did a multi-item order, you can ship them some sticker samples of your upcoming new designs, or of the same designs they bought from you. Maybe the occasional followup call to thank your clients for buying your item, or a quick message on their favorite messaging app/platform (if you know what it is and they've given you permission to do so - don't get creepy with it or anything).

Another good example of where you see this added surprise factor in buying, is with realtors. If you've bought a house, an used a realtor, the odds are fairly high that your realtor gave you a housewarming gift of some kind (in some cultures this is taboo, or not allowed), however in the USA, and Canada, it's fairly common. You might get a mirror, or a bottle of wine, or a personalized item. This is not only to delight the homebuyers, but it's a great way to build brand loyalty, and create a larger market of potential buyers. Redbubble for example includes a Redbubble sticker with every order. A new one each time.

Reputation:

Have you ever been looking for an item using Google, and found it at a place that has exactly what you are looking for, even at a reasonable rate, but since you've never heard of this "custom cut fit laser car mat manufacturer," you just click the back button, and end up buying the same thing from amazon.com ? This is the power and reach of great brand reputation. Entire books have been written about the lengths some companies will go to to ensure that their customers are happy, and that they come back to buy more in the future. Zappos (now owned by Amazon), was famous for this, and has gone to great lengths to ensure that its customers love not only the products (mostly footwear), but also the company that made it happen - Zappos. An example that's commonly known to those who have researched this phenomenally customer focused company, is where while taking an inbound phone call from a customer, the customer demanded a pizza... and Zappos delivered. Please note, Zappos is not in the pizza business... but sometimes going above and beyond is a wonderful way to build and grow your brand reputation. So how can you build your reputation within the world of merch and print on demand? One way is setting up your storefronts in a clear professional, inviting way. Many platforms, such as Shopify, cafe press, zazzle, and many others allow you to build a customized storefront within or beside their main selling platform, to drive additional traffic to your designs. As buyers come to know your company for a particular niche, or perhaps a specific design style, this repetitional customization can become a deciding factor for your buyers to come back and convert from a first time buyer, to a repeat buyer. Even Merch By Amazon allows you to identify your brand on your listings. This can be an opportunity to build your brand's reputation. If you deliver enough value to the customers who appreciate those values, then you certainly have the opportunity to leverage that advantage over your competitors.

Marketing Theory Summary:

Now that we have covered some of the basics, and gone a little deeper into the variety of mindsets, and values that your customers might be have as their priority, lets take a look at some places that you can market to them. Below you will find a wide variety of online places where your future and current customers will tend to be. Some of the ideas and methods or strategies below are paid, and many are FREE. So, like most things in the world of print on demand, there is a wide variety of options for you to choose from, and its up to you which (if any) you choose to take action on.

PRO TIP:

ACTION - this is one of the golden keys to finding ever increasing success in the world of commerce. It's not nearly enough to know how to do something, or to buy a book like this on how to do it. Or even to just read great resources on what to to. To truly unlock the full value of your new knowledge acquired throughout your seller journey, **ACTION** is needed. Implement things, set the platforms up. Make the designs. Build and launch the marketing. Target to your buyers in a way that is valuable to them. The difference between a knowledgeable seller, and a wealthy knowledgeable seller is ACTION (do the things). OR, you can just spend all your time watching YouTube, and do nothing… it's up to you. I recommend doing the things, making it happen. Get your hustle on.

Niche Research:

There are multiple ways to approach designs ideas, and how people come up with ideas for what to design. In this section, I would like to outline several approaches, as well as give some practical examples and things to consider when coming up with ideas for designs…

Before we get into some of the details, here's one thing to keep in mind whenever coming up with design ideas: People buy what they are passionate about, and tend to wear what they want to share with the world (it is a T-shirt design we're talking about).

Trending:

National or niche specific news and current events sites are a constant stream of new current and trending ideas. Social Media also gives you direct access to what's hot with what's trending on Twitter (split into News Sports Entertainment and Fun - https://twitter.com/i/moments) , Youtube (https://www.youtube.com/feed/trending), and Facebook (which splits trends into 5 categories; Top Trends, Politics, Science and Technology, Sports and Entertainment). Talk and daily shows also follow what's trending in popular culture closely. Think Ellen, The Tonight show with Jimmy Fallon, The Late Show with Stephen Colbert, Jimmy Kimmel Live, etc. There are also several sites that will search out trending topics across multiple platforms, and provide the top trends over different time periods, for example: https://all-hashtag.com/top-hashtags.php provides top hashtags used by day, week, month and all time. You can also use the same site to generate hashtags based on a word or topic you provide (which is helpful for Instagram, and other social platforms).

Current Best Sellers:

Look through Amazon to see what is ranking well (a lower BSR (Best Seller Rank) sells more than an higher BSR). Tools such as Merch Informer (https://merchinformer.com/131.html use code **MultiPODsROCK for 20% off everything**) can help you to view search and rank designs based on BSR. Chrome extensions such as DS Amazon Quick View (FREE) and Merch research Pro allow you to view Amazon BSR ranking on the search results pages, rather then needing to go into each listing to see it. (link and description above in the chrome extension area).

Seasonal:

Seasonal designs follow the time of year, think seasons like spring, summer, fall, and winter. Take it a level deeper, and think of the activities and traditions that people do, say and share during each season. Want to be specific, look at special dates on the calendar. Civic and religious holidays, awareness months, annual events (fairs, conferences, marches, protests, fundraisers). **Over 1,500+ date specific niche ideas included with the Gumroad version of this book.** Looking for a website to bookmark with special days all year long: http://www.weirdholiday.com - just select the month and day you're looking to design for, and you'll find one or more special dates for virtually every day of the year. Here is another great web-based special day finder, you may want to bookmark, for easy reference: http://www.holidayscalendar.com . See what other retailers are marketing. Most retailers from hardware stores to grocery stores and even dollar stores have a seasonal isle or section. Check out the new items in those seasonal sections to gather insights and inspiration about the things people buy in upcoming seasons (Christmas, Easter, Spring, Fall, St.Patricks Day, Valentines day, Mothers Day, Fathers Day, 4th of July, etc.).

Event Based:

Niches based on social events drive plenty of traffic, and with them, come sales. Think of non-seasonal events such as birthdays, anniversaries, graduation, retirement, new home gifts, first car, weddings, baptisms, etc. These are also generally evergreen, as they can occur throughout the year.

Big Groups:

Large groups - like events - drive traffic, and are typically passionate about their own groups. Think Hunters (duck, deer, fishing, bow, gun, lures...), Sports (hockey, baseball, football, tennis, skateboarding, skiing, soccer, ping pong ... there are loads of sports), religious designs (Christians, Jewish, Muslims, Atheists, Buddhists, etc...), Professions (any role imaginable, over 1,000+ job titles included in the Gumroad bonus files).

Causes:

From arts and culture, the environment, education, to feeding the hungry, saving the animals (endangered species, cats, dogs, wolves, livestock, etc...), caring for those in need, spreading the message (religious, political, nutrition, lifestyle, etc...), there are loads of causes that people are passionate about. Need more cause idea, check out the top 100 charities in America, as listed by Forbes here: https://www.forbes.com/top-charities/list/ There you can sort by category, and to see some of the messages they present to gather and gain support, visit any of the charities, and see the sorts of words that they use on their websites, that can give you ideas about niches to create new designs for.

Hobbies:

Beyond causes, what people do with their free time, people have hobbies. Games (board games, video games, card games, outdoor group games and communities, etc.), woodworking, sewing, knitting, quilting, makers and all things DYI (Do It Yourself). Going beyond the typical hobbies that come to mind, there are passionate communities looking for shirts among other communities of people such as people seeking adrenaline rushes - think Skydiving, bungee jumping, base jumping, hang gliding, ultralight fliers, etc. Live by the ocean lake or river? Think of all the water based activities people enjoy - scuba diving, boating, surfing, boating, swimming, waterskiing, etc. Quick **list of 50 Hobbies** people enjoy: http://www.notsoboringlife.com/popular-hobbies/

Activities:

Hobbies and activities overlap, but here are a few activities and themes to get your niche ideas flowing: yard work (lawn care, snow shovelling, maintaining a swimming pool, caring for toys and equipment at the lake house or cottage), partying (from clubbing and raves, to dance night and drinking with friends, people party and there are all kinds of niches to reach like types of dance, style of party venues, etc.), work (people do all sorts of professions and jobs and carry pride in what they do, so make some shirts people in their line of work might enjoy), school (from pre-school to post-graduate studies, people at all ages spend so much time in school and education, think of all the subjects you could make shirts for - types of maths, arts, music, philosophies and religious studies, business and entrepreneurship, professional accreditations, etc.). Here's a good list of topics people study (**over 300+ areas of study**): https://en.wikipedia.org/wiki/Outline_of_academic_disciplines

Just imagine all the people studying those things, and looking for a shirt!

Things:

Again, people are going to Merch By Amazon, and other PODs in search of designs and things they often can't find commonly, so think of all the things people enjoy, which you could design for: Animals (pets, zoo animals, endangered species, wild animals, etc.), foods (everyone eats, and they sure do buy food designs on shirts too -> BBQ, cheeses, pizzas, noodles, avocados, bananas, baking, pastries, candies, protein powders, etc.), Fantasy (unicorns, big foot, vampires, zombies, sea monsters, etc.). Just about anything that people search for, use, think about, can have an audience for your to market a design to. Some will sell better then others, so try many things, you may be surprised where you see sales coming from that you didn't expect. I've had hundreds of dollars in merch sales from seemingly monadic topics like potatoes and bananas.

Random:
This can be real hit and miss, but think of all the things that cross you mind throughout the day. Think of something clever, or that others might enjoy, **jot it down in a notebook**. Then, when it comes time to decide what to design, or send to your designers, refer back to your notes.

Final Notes on Niches:
In lower tiers on Merch By Amazon you may want to validate design ideas by checking for traffic on whichever niche you're considering a design for. I like to use Google Trends (https://trends.google.com/trends/), where I can compare search traffic for multiple words or ideas. I also use Google Trends to view the seasonality of words (for example: you may find ice fishing a hard sell in July and August, while swimming is hot). Another thing to keep in mind when considering niches is that things and topics with large audiences typically have lots of competition, while things with smaller, or more obscure audiences may have much less competition. The magic happens when you can find a medium sized audience with very little completion, you'll definitely notice these when you see sales from them.

You can use Amazon's own autosuggest as your guide. Type in the niche you're thinking of targeting, and see what Amazon suggests. this can often help you to come up with new words and related activities to your niche you may not have thought of otherwise. Also, remember the keyword section of this book, and all the tools listed there. Each one can help you expand your pool of niches, and often help with validating them as well (seeing if there is an audience for it).
Another fun experiment is running though options available in the Facebook ad manager. They have lists and lists of things people identify with, from interests, to buying habits, behaviours, locations, life events and more! See the full list of everything you can target ads via Facebook with the infographic I've linked in Chapter 5 under Facebook.

PRO TIP: When you do make a *sale* on a new design niche, consider scaling it to capture the full market. Why let others *find* your hot seller with tools like Merch Informer, or Merch Titan and dilute your design, when you can in fact upload many similar and related designs to your own seller, and keep your piece of the pie as large as possible.

MARKETING via Social Media Platforms:

facebook.com
Facebook is an online social networking and social media service. It's the biggest, and the most connected in the world. With over 1.86 billion monthly active users as of Dec 31st, 2016, Facebook is huge, it's active, and it offers you highly highly targeted marketing access.

HOW TARGETED CAN FACEBOOK GET / WHAT CAN I TARGET AN AD TO?

Here is a link to show you **ALL** of Facebook's ad targeting options in 1 Epic Infographic Made by WordStream: **http://www.wordstream.com/download/docs/Facebook-Targeting-Infographic-WordStream.pdf**

Here is a small sample of this huge infographic by Wordstream:

So, for example... If you wanted to target your Print On Demand of Merch by Amazon marketing to: Women, who work in the military, and live in a condo, who are college grads, and live in the state of Ohio, and are parents of toddlers, and are married... you can. You can go deep. You can be specific. You could even target the market above, and see if they are interested in yoga, and take cruises.

Target your paid advertising by: Interests, Demographics, Behaviors, even reach characteristics on Facebook.

FACEBOOK PIXEL

Facebook pixel is a piece of code that you can get from Facebook that you can drop into the code on your website. You can then direct people to other sites, such as Merch By Amazon. The pixel code will track that each click occurred. Then you can have Facebook find you similar buyers, like the people who clicked your ad. From there, you can make an even more targeted campaign for this new group of buyers!

You may not have realized this... but... for Facebook users who provide Facebook with their email, phone number or other personal information, you can build Facebook ads to target those users specifically! So go ahead, and use the power of Facebook to target your buyers. People who've gone to your website, email lists, phone number lists... Facebook is very very good at retargeting buyers.

Again, here is a link to show you all of Facebook's ad targeting options in 1 Epic Infographic Made by WordStream: http://www.wordstream.com/download/docs/Facebook-Targeting-Infographic-WordStream.pdf

PLEASE NOTE: Facebook is always changing so these lists can change. Plus, the list above is not the only all Facebook targeting list out there... so if you don't like the layout of it, here is another one, with a different layout: http://blog.red-website-design.co.uk/wp-content/uploads/2017/02/Stop-Wasting-Money-on-Facebook-Ads-The-Complete-Guide-to-Targeting-1.jpg From AdvertiseMint.

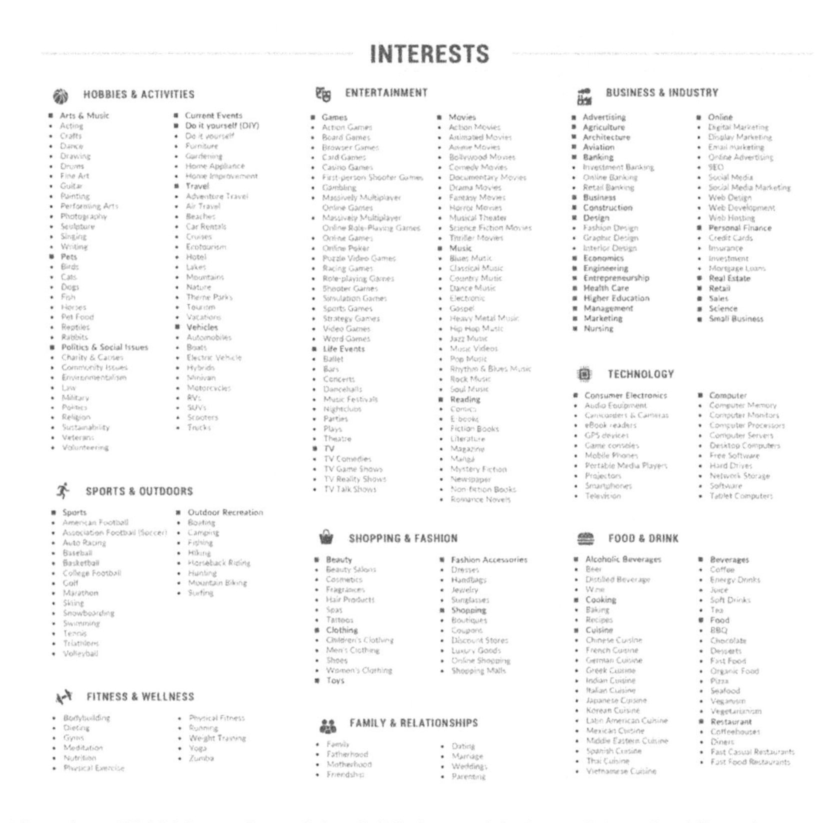

Here is a SMALL portion of the full infographic from AdvertiseMint above:
So how do I set up one of these Paid Facebook hyper marketing campaigns?
Glad you asked! There's actually **MULTIPLE** ways to setup a paid campaign on Facebook.

Facebook Ad Manager:
You could click on "Create Ads", located in the top right most down arrow you'll find on Facebook on your desktop, and be taken into the Facebook Ads Manager portal, link here: https://www.facebook.com/ads/manager/creation/creation/
Once there, you can choose your marketing objectives, and begin your marketing journey.

One tip that I can give you on using Paid Facebook ad campaigns, is to start with several simultaneous campaigns (low $ amounts like $3-$5 each). Quickly multiply the winning campaigns, and ***quickly kill those***

that are not working. Running a non-profitable ad campaign can get very expensive very fast. Multiplying a winning campaign (positive ROI), can make you a pile of profits very very fast.

So, you have to PAY MONEY to market on Facebook?
NO! You don't have to pay. There are literally a hundreds of ways you could market on Facebook both paid and FREE! However, this book is not long enough to cover them all… that's a whole book series in itself… but here's some FREE ways to market using Facebook, to get you started:

1. New Page(s) - You could create a new Facebook page (or many pages) to build an audience to market to in the future: FREE

2. New Group(s) - You could create a new Facebook group (Public, Closed or Secret), just like a page, but you can control access, and groups tend to build tight knit communities, while pages (above), tend to be more open areas… kind of like your backyard vs. the local public park.

3. Existing Group(s) - You could go to a Facebook group (even one you're not in), click on members (as long as it's not a secret group), click on admins, and BOOM, send the group admins a message to see if they're interested in partnering with you to market products in or with their group. So they have access to your potential buyers… and you have something their buyers might really enjoy… but there's a bit more to consider… like why would they let you have free marketing access to their members? What's the benefit to them? Always start with a benefit to the admin, otherwise you're likely to get a no-thanks.

PLEASE NOTE: Before contacting ANY Facebook groups admin, be SURE to consider that they work VERY HARD to build and maintain that group, and it has a HUGE COMMERCIAL VALUE… so you had better be offering them something pretty amazing, for them to consider letting you market inside their group. … Here are some things that a Facebook Admin might like:

- ***Cash*** - yes, believe it or not, but some will allow you to market to their group for $$. Some people earn their livings off managing groups on Facebook.

- ***Barter*** - some group admins will trade. Maybe access to their group, for access to your group? (this works well when the 2 groups have limited overlap in members, but interests that are common to both groups). Or maybe you have a tool or service that can help them save time or money. People generally like to save time and to save money.
- ***Exclusive content*** - you could offer their group something that is not available anywhere else. ... in this case, you'll have to be sure to not offer the exclusive content anywhere else, or else it's not exclusive, right?
- ***Recognition*** - they work hard on their group, so some kind words might help you out.
- ***A share of the pie*** - for group owners that offer their members paid products, sometimes a cut of the $ from whatever you are selling or giving away in their group, is something the admin might be interested in.
- ***Tickets, gifts, further reach, access for their members to pick your brain*** - adding value to their group.... anything that it mutually beneficial. Partnerships should never be one sided, and the more value you can offer up to an admin, the more success you may have in accessing their group :-)

4. Your Personal Page - You could post to your own Facebook personal page. You would be surprised how many people you may be connected to (Facebook allows some users to have access to thousands of friends on Facebook - 5000), and some of your friends will be happy to support you in your new venture, while others will hate that you even made the post, so use your own discretion. Another way to generate sales in your own page, would be to ask if anyone would like a custom design make, or any of the products you have access to. For example, you love coloring, would anyone like a custom calendar made, that can be colored? (Redbubble offers calendars by the way)

5. Local Group(s) / Page(s) - Post your marketing to any local (doesn't have to be local to you) buy and sell pages or groups. In my local area (around the Ottawa Valley), there are multiple Facebook pages and groups where buyers and seller offer things for sale, and buy things they want. You can find these by searching Facebook for "24 hour garage sale", "what's up insert-location-here", " location-name-here buy and sell". People in these groups LOVE to find new daily items locally, and would likely be thrilled if you offered them a Print On Demand product that "speaks to them" -meaning, something they like. Remember, a local group doesn't have to be local to YOU. It has to be local to your

BUYERS.... so if you live in Southern California, and you want to market to local buyers in say... Miami Florida... just search for the local groups there. It's like teleportation, but for marketing. Oh... and if you use Print On Demand platforms that deliver, or are located worldwide (like Sunfrog, or RedBubble, or dozens of them in the list on chapter 4), than you can market locally... WORLDWIDE!

So go for it, make a sushi shirt for say: Shiogama, Japan - the lunch sushi capital of the world! ***OR***
How about making a general store shirt and marketing it on Facebook locally to say: Braeside, Ontario Canada (where I live)- there's was only ONE general store in town, and people did everything there from local postal service, to buying gas to get to a nearby town or city like Ottawa, or maybe to check the local community board, to see when the next free community family pancake night is at the local community centre! I promise you, marketing to a small communities works!

Most people market to the biggest broadest crowds (New York, LA, Boston) ... but try marketing to a small tight knit village where everybody knows everybody's dog's name, and favorite shirt... and you would be amazed at how many multiple shirt sales you can get, and how low the competition is, and how much they love to shop online (because the closest major city is a 45-60 minute drive away).

6. Co-Branding - Big brands are looking for customized content to offer their members and followers. It builds shared values, and extends the brand's reach. You see this in TV commercials. A washing machine detergent company might show dirty kids playing in a beautiful field, only to be transformed magically into happy little angel children wearing only the cleanest, newest looking clothes after using that brand's detergent. While another ad might show people running for their lives from zombies, to build the brand for people who enjoy zombies, or horror movies (very different from a fabric detergent style commercial... except maybe around halloween...). So if your designs are well aligned with another brand, they may consider letting you post in their places of influence to build their community. Gaming, Cosplay, Knitting, Coloring groups, Quilters, Farmers, etc. Just keep in mind don't use and Trademarked or branded IP, without permission from the IP owner.

7. Rich New Content - Spoiler alert, Facebook does not show you all the posts from all your friends, all the time. I know, this can be a shocker if you are just finding this out now... What Facebook does do, is it shows you the content that it thinks you will be most likely to enjoy receiving. So... why not create some content that lots of people would enjoy, and place it around Facebook in places where buyers can find or see your content, and then connect that with the items you are looking to market on Facebook.

What kind of things does Facebook like? New original photos. Pictures of things people like. Live videos talking about things people on Facebook like. Links to things people would love to know about (but be careful with this one, because Facebook wants to keep people on Facebook)... So use that last one with caution. Also, if you can make your posts go viral, by sharing something that people just can't resist liking, and sharing... that's also a great place to market to others ... FOR FREE (or if you want faster results, PAY, like boosting a post - details on that next).

Boost:
You can write a post on your Facebook business page, and BOOST it (this shows your post to more people, in more places, increasing it's reach, and with it, more potential people to see and buy your things).

BONUS TIP:
Targeting Time based events - There are always events that happen that are time based. A festival, holidays, fairs, conferences, new movies, new TV shows, new video games, concerts, sports games, seasonal activities like skiing or swimming or ice fishing or maple syrup sap collecting! ... Find some time based things happening anywhere you want to market to on Facebook, and implement any of the items I've covered above, or any of the hundreds of more creative ways you can use Facebook to market to people.

FREE BONUS:
In the bonus section of Merch and the World of Print On Demand, in the e-book form, via Gumroad... you'll find a file with over 1,000 *time based events*, and over 1,000 job title *niches* to market to. Look to these for inspiration, if you're stuck on what to make, or who to market to :-)

FACEBOOK VIRAL MARKETING:
For more info about how use Facebook for marketing, you owe it to yourself to check out **Rachel Miller's** Facebook Page Massive Growth Strategies group here:
https://www.facebook.com/groups/pagestrategies/

In Rachel's group, you will find multiple multiple ways to grow your Facebook marketing leverage. It's a closed group, so you'll need to apply to get in, but I promise you, it's a great group on learning to leverage Facebook to grow your marketing reach and effectiveness. Rachel Miller also offers a course called the Moolah course, where you can take a journey on how to grow multiple Facebook pages or groups to new heights no matter what your starting point is, be it ZERO or 1,000,000. Link here: http://moolah.life/get_the_course?affiliate_id=684563

To see how Facebook itself uses videos within Facebook, check out its own video page, here: https://www.facebook.com/pg/facebookcanada/videos/

... Did you think it would be a YouTube link? ... nope... Facebook is targeting the online video market BIG TIME. You will notice this as time passes, more video on Facebook, more people creating and sharing videos on Facebook... a big part of the future of Facebook is video. ... and then Virtual Reality (but that's a bit off topic in a book about Merch and the World of Print On Demand).

Oh, and what if you post something on Facebook, and then realize a second later that you meant something else... or you were posting from your phone and autocorrect turn "love" into "live", or "the" into "he", or something like that... Don't worry. You can edit a Facebook post, here's how:
https://www.facebook.com/facebookcanada/videos/801235209914732/

OK, so I hope you enjoyed the section on marketing via Facebook. I hope you learned something new, like maybe how to market to your local community, or a local community that's on the other side of the world?
END OF FACEBOOK.com's Marketing section (from page 232) ;-)

instagram.com

What is it?

Instagram is the world's favorite photo centric mobile app. It enables users to connect through the world of images, and to share there photos with others, as well as have others follow their journey through photos and short videos. This may seem overly simplistic, but there's a lot you can do with photos. They say that a picture is worth thousand words, and while twitter gives you 140 characters to express yourself, Instagram enables not just plain image, but it lets you make rich, expressive images (an short videos) that convey your journey to the world. Instagram also lets you know when things are happening on the accounts of people that you're interesting in following. So, lets recap. Instagram is a way for people to follow each other, and it's mainly through photos and short videos/stories. Some people would describe Instagram as being like Twitter, but with photos.

Who cares?

The reason you want to care about Instagram, is essentially the same reason that you should care about any social media, and that is that it is HUGE, it's users are highly engaged, you can target people with paid or free marketing (just like almost all of the ways you can use Facebook above). How big is Instagram? Instagram has over 800,000,000 monthly active users. It's free to join, and it's user base tend to be skewed towards younger demographics, especially millennial and younger.
Image via Statista:

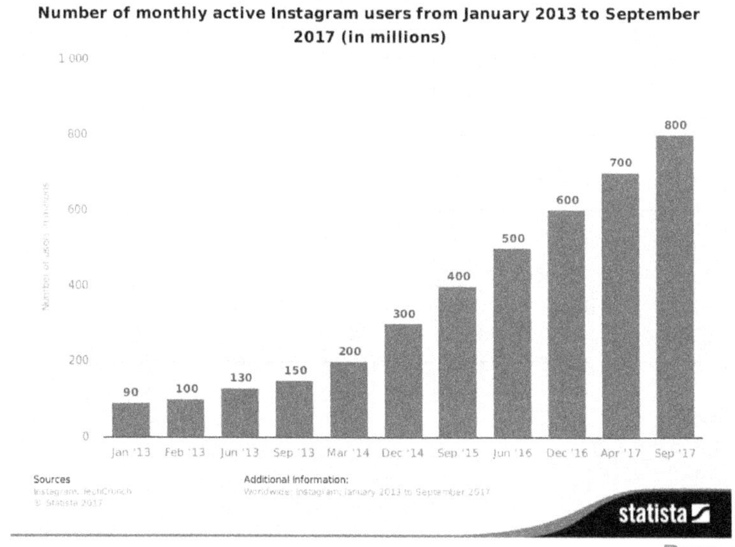

So, what do I do to market more shirts via Instagram?

Like many of the marketing methods, there are multiple ways to turn Instagram into a money marketing machine. Here are a few:

1. GENERATE FOLLOWERS:

Generate a lots of followers, over time, by posting engaging content that people are drawn to. Reflect back to the section of the book called Marketing 102, where we talked about buyer values. Build an audience with similar shopping values. combine one or more values, if you want to create some overlaps. Do this by uploading images, and content that your buyers will be drawn to. Also be sure to tag each upload with hashtags, and words that will in an honest way engage with someone who would like that image. For example, lets say you want to market a shirt with bananas on it. Find out what people who might buy that shirt are into. Maybe health and fitness. Maybe they follow a Raw food diet, or a Vegan diet, or both! Perhaps they just love things that are yellow... the key here is to know your target market, and then provide content that appeals to them. If you're not sure what a group of people likes, find another Instagram account, or Facebook page, and see what kinds of things are being posted. Create an Instagram account with similar types of things.

2. PARTNER WITH AN INFLUENCER:

How do you find an influencer on Instagram?

Here's how: anyone with a lot of followers, is an influencer on Instagram. The more followers someone has on Instagram, the more likely they are to understand the influence that they have over their followers, and how this can be leveraged to help you market to their followers. To partner with an influencer, refer to step 3 from the Facebook marketing strategies above. Except substitute the word Facebook group admin, for Instagram account holder.

Not sure if you can do that? No problem, I've got you covered. There's a service to match influencers to marketers. It's called Whalar, Link Here: https://whalar.com Whalar its a certified Instagram partner, and can connect your marketing spend with influencers on Instagram across a wide variety of niches, and categories. It assists you with the connections you need, in the ways that you need to get connected. It makes it's money by taking a cut of the deals it helps connect your marketing with. It takes a lot of the hassle factor out of partnering with influencers, and I know that it can help take your Merch/POD marketing via Instagram to the next level.

OR

You could try and do all that work yourself, but for 5% cut, it's a pretty sweet deal.

OR

For 20% cut, they manage everything for you.

OR

If you would rather not communicate with anyone, and you want to market on Instagram, use Kit (https://apps.shopify.com/kit), mentioned multiple times elsewhere throughout the book below, Kit is a marketing bot (AI), and it can run Instagram marketing campaigns of your things from multiple PODs, all conveniently connected to your Shopify account (click this link for a free 14 day trial Shopify account).

Speaking more about influencers, if you're looking for more information about which influencer you might want to partner with for Instagram, you've got to check out Websta at: https://websta.me/ here, you can use the **search** field to look for influencers in the niche you're looking to market to. Browse through the influencers provided, and select any one, to get more information about their following size, and other account details. If an Instagram influencer has DM, or shoutouts, it's a great indication that they are welcoming paid partnerships.

3. FORGET THE FORCE, USE THE LINK:

Your Instagram account allows you one very powerful tool, and that is the link on your account. You can link this link to anywhere you like, for example:

To one of your storefronts on one of the PODs you use.

To your website.

To your brand collection on Merch By Amazon.

To an individual listing that you are looking to give exposure for a set time period.

PRO TIP: Why not convert your ONE INSTAGRAM link into MANY... With LinkTree you can point your one Instagram link to linktree, and have linktree point to all the places you'd like to share about. It's FREE to use, and has a paid option that gives you even more features for only $6/ month. If you're on Instagram, I highly recommend you sign up for it right now, it's FREE: https://linktr.ee/

Free

All the basics, for as long as you like.

$0

GIVE FREE A GO

Free includes all of the basic features to get you started:

Get unlimited links on your linktree.

See how many times each link is clicked.

Pick from a selection of linktree themes.

PRO

For users who want their links to work harder.

MAKE ME A LINKTREE PRO

Includes everything in Free plus all this:

- See a day-by-day breakdown of link traffic.
- Give access to your team to manage your linktree and links.
- Complete customization of your linktree colors and button styles.
- Change the title of your linktree.
- Time your links to go live in-line with scheduled posts.
- Retarget your Linktree visitors on Facebook and Instagram by adding your Facebook Pixel ID.

4. BUY TRAFFIC:
Just like paid marketing with other social platforms, Instagram can be bought. You can use paid marketing with the Instagram for Business setting, or you can use an outside service to literally build your page for you. for $10 to $60, you can add thousands of Instagram followers to your account, organically, by partnering with a service such as Instafamous. Link Here: http://www.instafamous.pro/

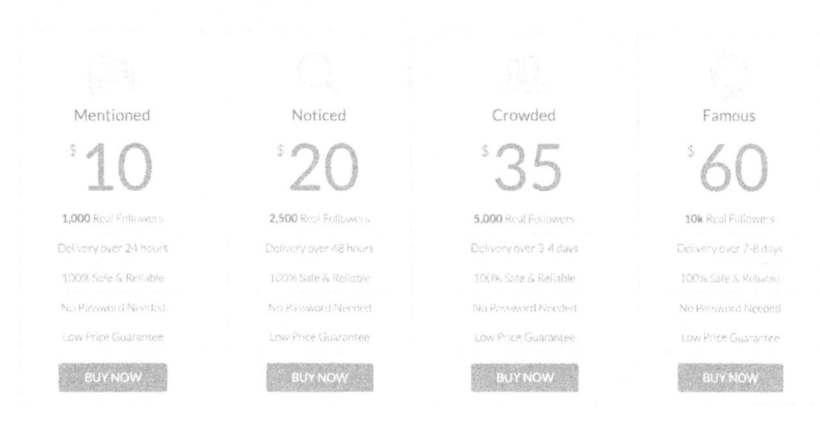

instagram.com's
Alexa's rankings:
Q1 2017
Global: 17
USA: 13
Q1 2018
Global: 15
USA: 11

HQ:
Instagram
1 Hacker Way,
Menlo Park, CA
94025, USA

pinterest.com

Pinterest is a visually focused social media platform, who's tagline is "the worlds catalog of ideas". With over 200 million monthly active users (https://www.spredfast.com/social-media-tips/social-media-demographics-current). Making it no small potato in the social media world. Of those, almost half are in the USA, so for American based marketing, Pinterest as a percentage of the population is more popular than in other countries globally. Pinterest is free to use, however it requires registration for use. Pinterest has it's own terminology. Pins are pictures, and can have content attached to them. Pinboards are collections of pins, and are useful for grouping ideas together. Pinterest is renowned for their skewed user base, which tends to attract many more women than men. For example, in 2015, about 42% of internet users used Pinterest, while only 13% of men did. Pinterest is a very strong influencer of purchases, and in 2017, according to Omnicore, 87% of Pinterest members (pinners), purchased a product because of Pinterest. For more interesting Pinterest facts, see this link here: https://www.omnicoreagency.com/pinterest-statistics/ and here: https://www.spredfast.com/social-media-tips/social-media-demographics-current

How can you use Pinterest to sell more designs? Like Instagram, or any of the social media platforms, the platform will have power users, which have many pins, or people following their content. If you can have an influential pinner pin one of your designs, or POD listings, than you will have more access to Pinterest users, and more chances to make sales to them. Pinterest also offers paid advertising (promoted pins), which provides preferential showing of your content. More info on promoted pins here: https://business.pinterest.com/en/why-pinterest-ads-work

In addition to advertising on Pinterest, and partnering with influencers, you should also consider building up your own Pinterest audience(s). You can do this yourself for free, or you can use services to do it faster. One such service is Pinblaster for $67, link here: http://pinblaster.com

In fact if you're looking to convert straight from Pinterest, you can setup buyable pins, for more info on how to do that here: https://about.pinterest.com/en/shopping-pinterest

PRO TIP: If someone influential pins your Merch listing, then that pin stays, beyond the period at which you are running a paid campaign. So, in the long term, you essentially want to market your paid advertising towards Pinterest influencers, rather that only to general Pinterest users.

Another good reason to use Pinterest paid marketing, is that there are over 50 BILLION pins on Pinterest, so it can be easy to get lost in the ocean of other content. To market to people via paid marketing, you will first sign up for Pinterest, then convert your account to a business. This will open up the options for marketing on Pinterest, giving you more targeted access to millions of new potential buyers.

Home feed
Popular
Everything
Gifts
Videos
Animals and pets
Architecture
Art
Cars and motorcycles
Celebrities
DIY and crafts
Design
Education
Entertainment
Food and drink
Gardening
Geek
Hair and beauty
Health and fitness
History
Holidays and events
Home decor
Humor
Illustrations and posters
Kids and parenting
Men's fashion
Outdoors
Photography
Products
Quotes
Science and nature
Sports
Tattoos
Technology
Travel
Weddings
Women's fashion

About · Blog · Businesses · Careers · Developers · Removals · Privacy · Terms

(Above) A listing of Pinterest's most popular Topics. Similar to Amazon's top categories.

Looking for even more info on how to use Pinterest for your POD marketing, check out this great blog post all about it from Shopify here: https://www.shopify.com/blog/18048852-social-media-marketing-pinterest-for-business-101

In terms of website traffic, Pinterest is ranked as follows:
pinterest.com's
Alexa's rankings:
Q1 2017
Global: 66
USA: 20
Q1 2018
Global: 79
USA: 28

twitter.com
Twitter is like Instagram, but it is focused on the 140 character micro-blog. Twitter is a service to provide instant customer messaging in bitesized chunks, 140 characters at a time.

Twitter in terms of marketing works very much like Instagram (above), however it has some differences. Twitter can connect to photos as well, just like Instagram has tags, to identify relevant content for the service to serve up relevant content for users. Use Twitter's trending now space, to discover current events, and identify trends as they merge. You can find this on desktop by looking at the left side of your twitter account.

NOTE: You can also set the trends based on location by country or city. On mobile: click the search symbol, and you can scroll through trends and moments. Want to know what viral phrase a presidential candidate has said, or action taken that has people talking? Check out the trending now section of twitter, and it's likely there. Trending is running 24 hours a day 7 days a week, and you can use it to find niches which are on trend, or browse through thousands of posts for inspiration for your next design.

Like other social platforms, twitter counts and measures people you follow, and people that follow you. In fact you can take a trip down the rabbit trail, and see who is following whom, and map out connections, useful for uncovering new influencers, and creating partnerships with people and brands that may be helpful in marketing your goods to the masses.

Like many of the social platforms, Twitter also offers paid marketing, and offers you access to targeted groups of people with shared shopping values (remember the marketing 201 section above), to connect buyers with your goods. Link here: https://marketing.twitter.com/na/en/solutions.html

PERISCOPE + TWITTER

For live interactive interactions with your fans or followers, or to create new markets to reach out to, connect your twitter account to a Periscope account (Periscope is owned by Twitter, link here: https://www.pscp.tv/), and speak to people live via video. Pericope is another powerful tool on it's own, but when paired with you Twitter account, you can speak to your twitter followers directly through saved/recorded periscope videos. Periscope also has a very effective finding feature which allows people to discover your live content quickly, either by popularity, or by location. You can be found by new audiences much faster on Periscope, than Facebook Live. Although, Facebook Live has it's own other benefits.

Twitter posts for business account include tracking metrics, to show you posting reach, as well as engagement and what type. Want to insert your brand into an overlapping audience of another brand that closely matched your audience, use the main weapons of the Twitter post:

Reply - allows you to directly reply to anyone's tweets (including influencers), or even your own

Retweets - Is like syndicating other people's posts onto your twitter audience. A great way to indicate to your buyers, or followers that you are associated with another person or brands messaging.

Like (the heart) - Like on twitter can us used to indicate affiliation with an idea or a brand, or an influencer. similar to likes on other social platforms, your followers can see your likes, and so can the person who's post you liked.

Message - this is a way to connect with people privately on twitter. Looking to plan a joint event, or privately discuss anything, you can message people that you follow, and who also follows you.

twitter.com's
Twitter's Alexa's rankings:
Q1 2017
Global: 16
USA: 8
Q1 2018
Global: 13
USA: 8

Other good places to market your designs:

google.com
Google Adwords, the most powerful way to get noticed when people are using Google search. Pay $, reach your audience. Simple. Learn more here: https://adwords.google.com/intl/en_ca/home/how-it-works/

Google's Alexa's rankings:
Global: 1
USA: 1

youtube.com
Build out meaningful content to reach a gigantic and growing interactive audience through video. TIP: Do a video talking about each of the new designs that you are proud to launch. Over time, YouTube rewards consistency, and you can build an audience around your brand, and your designs. Learn more here: https://www.youtube.com/yt/advertise/how-it-works/

YouTube's Alexa's rankings:
Global: 2
USA: 2

reddit.com
Known as the front page of the internet, Reddit group sources content (the more people that uproot a posting, the higher it goes, the more people that down vote a listing, the lower it goes) that its users love. More engagement = more exposure. It's a great resource to find and follow current trends. Not as hyper time sensitive as Twitter's Trending Now, but it's a great way to track trends online. You can do paid marketing via reddit here: https://ads.reddit.com

Reddit's Alexa's rankings:
Global: 21
USA: 7

Multiple ways Print On Demand can work for you:

1: **Basic POD** - make designs, list on any of the POD marketplaces (Merch By Amazon, Redbubble, Etsy, etc.), many mentioned in Chapter 4, get paid when people buy your designs on items they choose from the POD sites.

2: **Affiliate links** - not as creative? Like a design someone else made? Find a POD which offers affiliate links and join their affiliate program. Market the designs you believe will sell well. Get paid when other people's designs sell. Question: can you be an affiliate of your own designs/listings? YES! Most of the time you can earn both an artist royalty or markup, AND an affiliate commission for bringing people who buy to your own designs! Why do sites like this? Because affiliate participants are eager to make $ when sales happen, so they tend to drive traffic to your platform, AND they make more sales happen, that you may not have otherwise had. So it's a win for everyone!

3: **Run your own website** - link it to either a POD to fulfill your orders, OR another platform where people can buy your items (like Amazon), OR BOTH! Create your own custom website, OR why not use an e-commerce platform through services like Shopify, or WooCommerce. These platforms allow you to build and host your own website, plus connect loads of awesome apps or widgets, which add additional features and functionality to your website.

MORE DETAIL:
Here's an example: [**PRINTFUL -> SHOPIFY -> AMAZON (seller central side)**]
You have a website (www.yourwebsite.com), which is running on the commerce platform Shopify (shopify.com). Shopify has an app to connect your website to a POD service, Printful (printful.com/). Shopify also has an app to connect your website to Amazon (amazon.com).

You list your designs on your website. Buyers can see your designs on your website, or on amazon.com ... when a buyer buys your items (like a T-shirt for example), Printful makes the item, and delivers it to your buyer. In the case that the item is bought via amazon.com the order information is sent from amazon.com, to your website (which is tracked via all the great Shopify reporting goodness), and then through to Printful (which of course makes the item on demand, and sends it to your buyer).

Here is how to set this up. In this example, I'll use Shopify (the e-commerce platform), Amazon (The online sales marketplace) and Printful (the POD), although there's various e-commerce platforms, sales marketplaces and POD's that would also work together, but for this example, lets keep it simple and clear.

1. First you want to setup your website. Do this via the e-commerce platform Shopify. On Shopify you can connect an existing domain you own, or get a new one, your choice. JOIN SHOPIFY for 14 days FREE HERE: Shopify (for those reading the print copy: https://goo.gl/q97jbP)
2. Now you have a Shopify compatible website. You want to install the Shopify to Amazon app (link here: https://apps.shopify.com/amazon). This allows you to connect amazon.com Seller Central listings to your Shopify inventory. To connect the 2 using the app, you will also need to have a pro seller amazon.com account (which you can apply for here, if you don't already have one: https://services.amazon.com/content/sell-on-amazon.htm/ref=footer_soa?ld=AZFSSOA-dT1 the Professional seller Amazon account cost is $39.99USD/month), and be un-gated in the clothing category (this is done by requesting approval to sell in this restricted category. Info on how to do this is provided by

amazon.com here: https://sellercentral.amazon.com/gp/help/200316920).

3. Now you will want to connect your Shopify account to a POD, such as Printful Join Printful for free using this link: https://goo.gl/znYo6o. To do this, you will connect the printful app from Shopify to your Shopify account (here is the link to do that: https://apps.shopify.com/printful).

You now have all the *basic* pieces needed to have clients order products with your designs on them… **BUT**… You're not home free yet, you still need to connect all your items on all 3 spots (Amazon, Shopify and Printful). You can do this in different ways, but the recommended order is to:

First create your listings on Amazon, via your Amazon Seller Central account (link here: https://sellercentral.amazon.com). Be sure to not make the listing live until you have the Shopify and Printful is setup and ready to take the order.

NOTE: When you connect a Shopify store item to Amazon, you will need a UPC. You will need to address the elephant in the room when trying to create your listings on Amazon, and that is your UPC's for each product, including each variation for each product. Like most things, there are multiple ways to address this.

BUY UPC'S

One, is to buy UPC's, and attach a UPC you own, to each listing (there are also multiple ways to buy UPC's, the recommended source is via a registered GS1 UPC (link for that here: http://www.gs1.org//need-gs1-barcode), there are other ways, which are outside of the scope of this book, but you could Google about it [handy link here: http://bfy.tw/A64a])).

TIP: UPC EXEMPTIONS:
You could apply for a UPC exemption via Amazon, called a GTIN Exemption Request (GTIN is a Global Trade Item Number) - it is used to exempt you from needing to provide a GTIN (such as a UPC, EAN, JAN or ISBN)
You can apply for an UPC Exemption, meaning you don't need to use a UPC for each item and variation. Within Seller Central, it's called a: GTIN Exemption Request, and can be found by clicking here:

https://sellercentral.amazon.com/gp/gating/catRequestForm.html/ref=sm_xx_cont_200340230?cat=Books&requestType=upcexempt)
For more about what qualify's for the GTIN exemption, read about the policy on Amazon here:
https://sellercentral.amazon.com/gp/help/200426310 (your POD products would fall under the category of branded - Private Label).

Next, load inventory into your Shopify store and connect/sync it to Printful so that it's ready to process once you make your Amazon listing go live. More info on how to sync your printful items, and your Shopify store below.

Connecting Shopify and Amazon:

Finally, using the Shopify Amazon app, connect your Amazon listing to your inventory on Shopify.

Here is a quick 30 second video overview of how Printful links to your Shopify store, allowing you to focus on making designs and marketing, while they take care of manufacturing and fulfilment of your goods when people buy them on your Shopify site: YouTube link: https://youtu.be/SKiOES-wtml

Adding your Inventory *to* Shopify AND Amazon *from* Printful:

Here is a quick video overview of how to add products to your Printful / Shopify store, using the Printful Push generator: https://youtu.be/6TtyDs0oZd4

In case you would rather read the steps, here's a quick summary:

1. Open Printful
2. Select the add button (or Sync button, then the Add Product button - your choice).
3. Upload your image file and details (variations, shirt/item type, colors, etc.)
   NOTE: try to keep your DPI above 120, for best print results, when re-sizing your image on the product setup.
4. Choose your mockup image file type (.jpg - smaller faster loading on your site VS. .png loads a little slower, includes transparent background)
5. Add you Title / Description / Pricing info (can drill pricing down for variations)
6. Then publish product will designate if you want to show your shirt for sale now, or if you would rather save it for sale later (maybe you want to work on it more, or maybe your VA does part, and you or another VA does another part).
7. Add to one of your product collections.
8. Submit to your Shopify store.
9. Verify on your Shopify store (optional)

Keep in mind, not all designs can be done automatically with the Printful Push generator, for those that are done manually here's the basic steps:

1. Add the listing to Shopify first (click add button on your Shopify product area, add the basic product details and images)
2. Sync the listing to Printful
3. On the Printful side hit refresh (it should now appear on printful)
4. Edit the remaining details on the printful side.

IMPORTANT NOTE:
When orders are bought by buyers on amazon.com and fulfilled with a POD via Shopify , YOU need to pay for the production of each shirt via the POD. amazon.com will pay you later, on your regular payout schedule (plus time to get into your bank account). THERE CAN BE A GAP IN TIME, during which you will need to carry the cost difference... So, please be sure you have available credit or cash to carry the difference in time between your orders with the POD, and your payment from the orders via Amazon.

What happens if your POD isn't paid?
Then the Merchant Fulfilled order is stalled in la la land until you fund your POD. You can typically do this by pre-funding the POD, and carrying a balance... or by providing your credit card info, and paying off the card with the money you receive from Amazon when it gets to your account... This GAP IN TIME can be as long as 60 days... so be aware of it. It also scales, so during busy times like Q4... there might be a significant amount in the "carry trade"... the more you sell, the higher that gap can get $$... so be sure to get your credit situation in order, or have cash on hand to cover the gap!

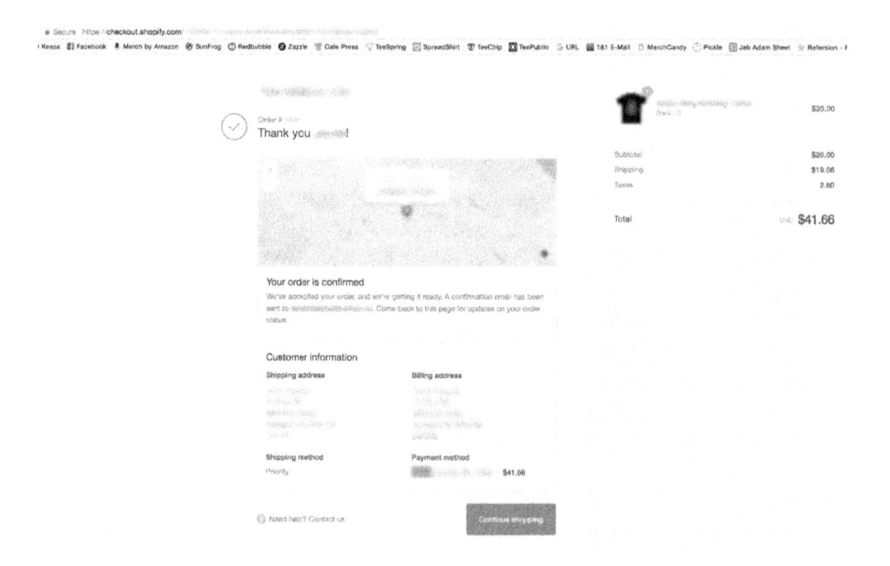

Above is an example of the confirmation screen that Customers will see when buying from your **Shopify store**. The look of this screen may be different, as Shopify includes hundreds of free themes you can set your Shopify website to look like. Don't see one you like, there are also paid themes OR you can add your own existing theme from elsewhere, OR even code your own, OR have someone else code one for you. Here's the link again for that 14 day free Shopify trial you may be wanting to start up right about now: https://goo.gl/q97jbP <—- link gets you 14 Day FREE Shopify trial.

What's the upside then?

Once the money pump starts going… you keep the difference between the POD item cost, and the after amount Amazon pays you :-) aka profit! … which you pay taxes on… ;-)

Earlier, I mentioned that there are multiple E-commerce platforms, PODs, and Sales marketplaces to connect to… let's talk about some additional options / combinations. So what are some POD services you can connect to your E-commerce based website?

PODS YOU CAN CONNECT TO MARKETPLACES LIKE SHOPIFY / AMAZON / ETSY / GUMROAD / ETC:

1 - Printful: (link here: printful.com)

One of the most popular, widest used among sellers. Great support, great quality. Expensive prices, slower delivery vs. some of the others. Unique integration tools and platform access, SUCH AS Gumroad (that's right, sell shirts to your Gumroad audience, they'll love it! More info on integrating your Gumroad account to Printful here: https://www.printful.com/landing/gumroad-print-products-fulfillment) What's Gumroad you ask? Gumroad is a place which allows you to sell digital or physical products, and build an audience while doing so. You may even have bought this book through a link to Gumroad. For more info about Gumroad, what it is, and how it works, here is a link to it: https://gumroad.com/ .

In addition to Gumroad, Printful also can sync directly with Etsy (more about that in the Chapter 4 section about Etsy), Inktale, WooCommerce, Big Cartel, Storenvy, Tictail, Bigcommerce, Ecwid, Amazon, Weebly, ShipStation, or even directly anywhere via API (more about that here: https://www.printful.com/api)

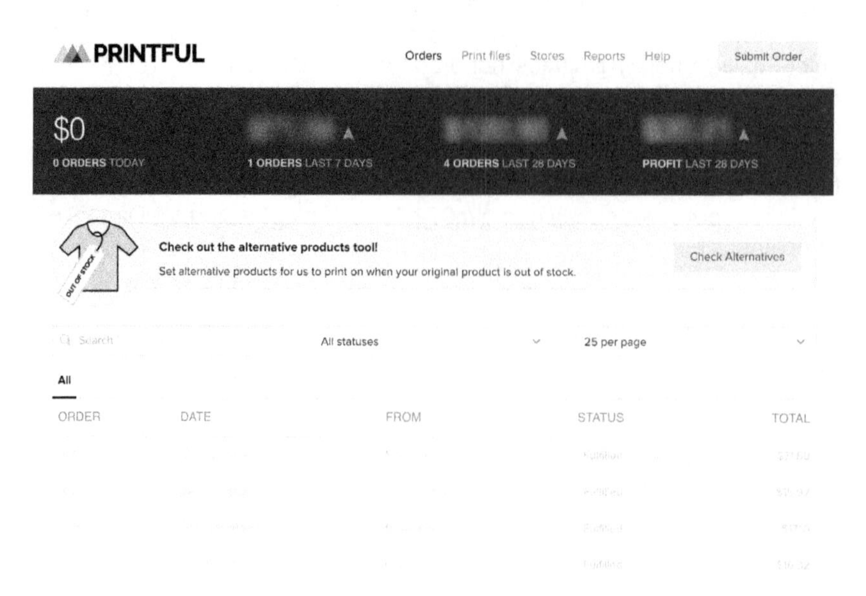

That's a LOT of integrations, and allows you to POD fulfill in a LOT of places with Printful as your back end POD provider. Here is a link to give you a nice overview of each of them : https://www.printful.com/landing/overview-print-products-fulfillment

One of these is specifically interesting, and I'll go into more detail below. It is ShipStation. What's so special about it? It gives you access to Walmart, Ebay, Jet.com, Sears, PrestaShop, Yahoo and more! More info about how to setup ShipStation to Printful here: https://www.printful.com/landing/shipstation-print-products-fulfillment

I covered most of the rest of a Printful/Shopify/Amazon in the examples above… so let's check out some others! Here is the link again to the Shopify Printful app: https://apps.shopify.com/printful

Printful has a nice dashboard where you can see your sales each day week and month, as well as all your orders as the come in, including (my favorite) how much each sale was for. Drill into these metrics for more detail.

2 - PrintAura: (link here: printaura.com)
Connect POD products to multiple e-commerce sites, including Shopify, BigCommerce, WooCommerce, Etsy, OpenCart, and more! Medium pricing on stock POD items compared with others. Global shipping, great customer service, great setup, easy to use. Standard shipping times are 3-5 business days, with Expedited processing for 48 hour turnaround available. They use Kornit DTG printers, and can process orders from 1 to 500+ per day, so never worry about large orders. :-) Here is a link to their Shopify app: https://apps.shopify.com/print-aura (more about exactly how to connect Print Aura to Etsy, in chapter 4, under Print Aura, and also under Etsy)

3 - CustomCat Fulfillment: (link here: customcat.com)
Based in Detroit Michigan, a relative newcomer to the scene, very low/aggressive pricing, when compared to other POD systems. Relatively VERY FAST turnaround times (24-48 hours), great quality. They offer on demand screen printing, on demand DTG (Direct To Garment), on demand embroidery, and over 200 different products. **I highly recommended you use this one**, if not this one AND others... YES, y**ou can connect more than one POD to your Shopify** or other E-Commerce platformed website! There is a fee of $30/month for this POD, with a 14 day free trial. This is more then other FREE POD integrations (like Printful or PrintAura above), however their prices per item are lower, so if you're selling some volume, the monthly price will easily pay for itself.
Here is the link to their Shopify app: https://apps.shopify.com/customcat-1

4 - TeeLaunch: (link here: teelaunch.com)
They offer a limited number of products compared to some of the other options above, but that's not a bad thing, they have over 35 products (here's a quick link to view them [with pricing!] here: https://teelaunch.com/collections/products). Unisex t-shirts starting at $8.50 each. They appear to prefer their Shopify integration over other E-commerce platforms, they also connect to Etsy (instructions on how to connect TeeLaunch to etsy are here: https://teelaunchhelp.zendesk.com/hc/en-us/articles/115014905408-installing-Etsy-integration). Another interesting tidbit about TeeLaunch: If your customer gets a shirt and it doesn't fit they'll send out one size up or down of the same shirt for free! (more info on that here: https://teelaunchhelp.zendesk.com/hc/en-us/articles/115003205747-Size-Exchanges)
Here is a link to their Shopify app: https://apps.shopify.com/teelaunch-1

5 - Scaleable Press: (link here: https://scalablepress.com/)
With over 5,000 businesses using this POD Fulfillment platform, it can be plugged into Shopify, WooCommerce, a customer developer API, and more. They have over 100 printing machines (40+ for screen printing, and 60+DTG), which offer screen printing, sublimation, and DTG; across over 21 products (which is a small number of products compared to others). With multiple production locations (Fremont and Fresno California, Indianapolis Indiana, and Scranton Pennsylvania), and a price match guarantee, this is one POD Fulfillment option to keep an eye on. Delivers within the USA, with SAME DAY SHIPPING on select products, up to 72 hour turnaround generally. Example pricing: **Gilden cotton T-shirt, ~ $5.57 base cost** (DTG, white, one side front…), can go as low as $2.44 for volume orders via screen printing… which is great for large events, or bulk orders!) .... just to be clear: YOU COULD SEE THESE ON AMAZON VIA SHOPIFY…
Imagine having a hot selling shirt, that you decide to offer via Amazon FBA (Fulfilled By Amazon - Prime in Q4)?? Just an idea, it's riskier, but could work.
Here is a link to their Shopify app: https://apps.shopify.com/scalablepress-t-shirt-fulfillment

6 - Teescape.com: (Link here: teescape.com)
Teescape has their POD on-point, and dialled in. Teescape only uses Kornit Avalanche printers to produce pixel sharp images. Designs printed on to your final products that won't wash out of the shirts. Know of any other well known POD who uses the top quality Israeli based Kornit's equipment… oh yes… Amazon. That's right! Teescape uses some of the exact same equipment that Merch By Amazon uses… but miraculously, they produce their shirts for you for less… and I know that you're a seller, you know what happens when more than one company is selling something for less price than another, right? WRONG. Amazon is a behemoth, and Teescape is tiny. So leverage the power of Teescape, bypass your tier ups and your upload throttling, and your 1 item, in 5 variations, AND list these on amazon.com, with full access to Custom ASIN listing, and PPC, and all the other things that your own Private Label ASIN on amazon.com gives you! Break free from single marketplace myopia, and use more PODS, and sell MORE SHIRTS… and other things!

More details about Teescape's products and pricing here: http://teescape.com/ts/tsf-garments TeeScape T-shirts starting at $7.50 each.

teescape.com's Alexa ranking: it's irrelevant! You hook it up to Shopify, and list your ODPL (On Demand Private Label) goods on amazon.com … AND cross list all of them to EBAY also! (more on that later).

7 - Shipstation.com: (http://mbsy.co/lBZPS Register for free, Monthly plans start at $9/month)
Shipstation itself is not a POD, but it allows you to connect PODs (like Printful) to multiple marketplaces, such as Shopify, Etsy, Ebay, Jet, Walmart,Yahoo, Prestashop, Storenvy, and several others! It acts as a middle connection, to take orders from the Marketplaces, and send them the PODs.
Example:
WALMART -> SHIPSTATION -> PRINTFUL
Buyers shop for your items on WALMART. When they buy them on WALMART, your order is sent to your order processor SHIPSTATION, which then passes the order for fulfillment to your Print On Demand Platform PRINTFUL. Printful makes the item, and mails it your WALMART customer :-)

More info from Shipstation here: https://www.shipstation.com/partners/walmart/
Join Walmart's Marketplace using your ship station integration here: https://info.shipstation.com/walmart
NOTE: in order to enter the WALMART Marketplace, be sure to have your registered **D-U-N-S number**. If you don't have one, you can buy one in the USA here: http://www.dnb.com or from Canada here: http://www.dnb.com/ca-en/

8 - GearLaunch: (link here: gearlaunch.com/)
Relatively new, and with big ambitions, this back end POD service was one of the featured speakers at the 10X Merch Conference fall of 2017 in New Jersey. The GearLaunch founder and CEO is Thatcher Spring. It can be connected to Shopify. You select items to sell, they do the rest. GearLaunch helps clients create online storefronts, and handles back-office and logistic tasks. They offer an assortment of items which you can fulfill via your Shopify store (done by application here: http://info.gearlaunch.com/gearlaunch-shopify-app), or your own storefront on your own domain.

Some things that set GearLaunch apart from other POD services (such as Printful, PrintAura, TeeLaunch, etc.), are that they offer PERSONALIZED CUSTOMER SERVICE. That's right, when buyers call for customer service, they are greeted by YOUR BRAND, not GearLaunches. From a buyer's perspective the banding is 100% yours. GearLaunch provides full access to purchaser emails, allowing you to build out personalized email campaigns, and know who is buying. They also have one page product creation, which speeds up loading your listings, and they offer Flags! ***Not too many other PODs have flags ;-)***

GearLaunch offers tiered pricing for volume sellers. Tier pricing starts with the first unit sold, and the top volume tier is 20,000+ units. T-shirts can start as low as $6.15 to $8.95, depending on sales volume. Here's their full catalog with pricing: https://www.gearlaunch.com/product-catalog To see all of their current product offerings visually, click here: https://www.gearlaunch.com/products
Refer to the info on Gearlaunch in chapter 4.

9 - ViralStyle: (link here: viralstyle.com/)
ViralStyle offers both a back end POD service (integrates with e-commerce solutions such as Shopify ViralStyle Shopify app link here: https://apps.shopify.com/viralstyle-fulfillment) and an online marketplace of it's own where people can buy you items. Full product pricing available here: https://viralstyle.zendesk.com/hc/en-us/articles/115000686090-Product-Pricing-Shipping-Costs

They also have a great Seller Academy to help you learn ways to sell more. It contains multiple full video courses, case studies, and weekly webinars on how to drive more sales. All FREE! Located here: http://sellers.viralstyle.com

ViralStyle ships over 1,000,000 printed items per year, and is well known as a trusted POD partner. They have a wide variety of items that can be POD fulfilled including Kozies, Dog Tags, flip flops, and of course all the T-shirts you would expect - from brands such as Anvil, Bella + Canvas, Gildan, Hanes, LAT and Next Level and more!

They print DTG, and All-over dye sublimation, so you can get your repeating patters, and full image shirts made easily, with this fully automated fulfilment option.

DEMO: If you would like to see a quick example of the product loading procedure into your Shopify store, from a POD integration, here is a quick video by Justin Cener showing integrations into 3 popular POD platforms (GearLaunch, ViralStyle and TeeLaunch): https://youtu.be/oiP611jpuLk

10 - TeeZily Plus: (link here: https://plus.teezily.com)
TeeZily has both a marketplace (TeeZily), and a back end POD fulfillment side called Teezily Plus (connect it to Shopify for example with their Shopify app, here: https://apps.shopify.com/teezily-plus) One thing that makes this appealing is their low base pricing, both in Europe, and the USA. In addition to pricing and shipping worldwide, they also have production facilities in both the USA and Europe. Having production near buyers saves in both shipping time and costs. T-Shirts starting at $9 (or as low as $6 each with volume).

Here's a short video showing you exactly how to add it to your Shopify store, and add products: https://youtu.be/mTMvWaMG7Fs
More information and pictures about TeeZily in Chapter 4, under TeeZily.com

Which Other Sales Platforms could you POD list on?

amazon.com - Via Merch By Amazon, Printful, Shopify, Gearbubble, and more
amazon.ca - via Printful
amazon.mx - via Printful
amazon.co.uk - via Printful
amazon.de - via Printful
amazon.es - via Printful
amazon.fr - via Printful
amazon.it - via Printful
facebook.com - via Shopify, via Facebook WHAAT? You can sell via Facebook?!?!? YES! You can!! It's crazy!!
ebay.com - via shipstation, teeSpring and Joelister
ebay.ca - via Joelister
ebay.uk - via Joelister
Wait... you can list POD via a Shopify integration beyond just the USA? HECK YA YOU CAN! I show you how later in THIS BOOK!
walmart.com - via ship station and TeeSpring
wish.com - via TeeSpring
jd.com - via TeeSpring (announced, coming soon)
rakutan.com - via TeeSpring (announced, coming soon)
tmall.com - via teeSpring (announced, coming soon)

The TeeSpring Boosted Network, your qualifying TeeSpring designs can be cross listed to 4 large platforms (Amazon, Ebay, Walmart and Wish). For more specific details on this program directly from TeeSpring go here: https://community.teespring.com/training-center/teesprings-boosted-network/ and more details in Chapter 4 under TeeSpring Boosted network.

3 Thing to be Eligible for TeeSpring's Boosted Network:

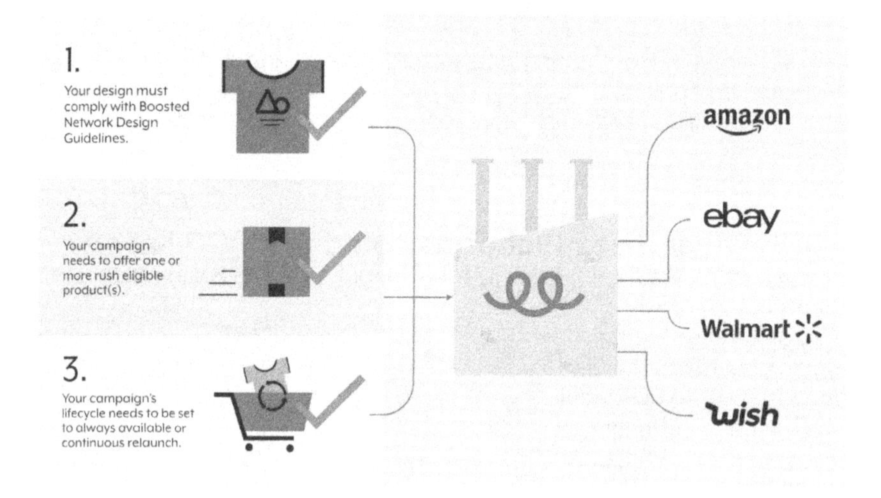

NOTE: you'll also need a 4th criteria for the Boosted network, which is to opt into it, which can be done in your account settings on TeeSpring (more details about this in Chapter 4, under TeeSpring).

And what are some good E-Commerce platforms to use?

shopify.com (this one is my favorite, and the best... in my opinion)
woocommerce.com
bigcommerce.com
bigcartel.com

Websites which you could connect POD fulfillment to or on:
wix.com
squarespace.com
godaddy.com
wordpess.com
joomla.com

END OF CHAPTER 5

CHAPTER 6 - COMMUNITY RESOURCES

Things you can use to do research, get ideas, and more!

Keyword Optimization tools/services/ strategies:

Helium 10 (Manny Coates):

Cost: Some free trial to start, multiple plan costs from $0 to $297/month (details below)
Link here: http://www.helium10.com/
Software designed for Amazon listings, and keywords. Want to know what Amazon sees and wants for your Merch By Amazon listings? Consider this awesome suite of tools, built right into your browser! How to think of these tools in the context of a POD->Shopify->Amazon (Seller Central) maneuver... think of that play, as a Private Listing (PL), and like any other private listing, Helium 10 is specifically designed and used by sellers who want to both maximize their Amazon private label listing, and minimize any issues or problems, or problem competing listings... This is a great tool! There's a great overview of it further right on their front website page. Designed and built by Manny Coates and his team, it is used to provide great success quickly with Keyboarding as it's central proposition. Highly recommend this tool for any Private label listing, including your POD manufactured Apparel inventory!

Here's a quick look at all the parts of this amazing online tool Helium 10:
There is a detailed description of each one here: https://www.helium10.com/tools/

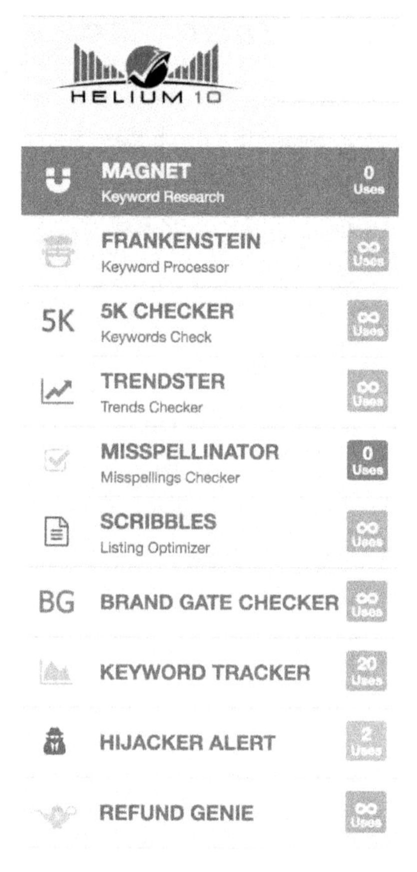

	FREE PLAN	GOLD PLUS PLAN	PLATINUM PLUS PLAN	DIAMOND PLAN
	$0	$97	$197	$297
	Monthly	Monthly	Monthly	Monthly
Magnet	0 uses	25 uses	75 uses	150 uses
5K Checker	0 uses	25 uses	75 uses	150 uses
Misspellinator	0 uses	100 uses	300 uses	600 uses
Frankenstein	-	Unlimited	Unlimited	Unlimited
Scribbles	-	Unlimited	Unlimited	Unlimited
Trendster	-	Unlimited	Unlimited	Unlimited
Brand Gate Checker	Unlimited	Unlimited	Unlimited	Unlimited
Keyword Tracker	Up to 20 keywords	Up to 300 keywords	Up to 900 keywords	Up to 1800 keywords
Hijacker Alert	Up to 2 ASINS	Up to 50 ASINS	Up to 150 ASINS	Up to 300 ASINS
Refund Genie	-	Unlimited	Unlimited	Unlimited
Inventory Protector	Unlimited	Unlimited	Unlimited	Unlimited
Cerebro	2 uses/day	10 uses/day	25 uses/day	50 uses/day
Black Box	20 uses/day	50 uses/day	125 uses/day	300 uses/day

The above pricing plan is for the ongoing cost of the Helium 10 suite of browser based: Keyword tools, and Amazon Listing software. Initial free use of parts of the tool are included when you create a free account with them, at no cost to you.

KeyWordShitter:

Cost: FREE
Link here: http://keywordshitter.com/
OK guys… I know, this looks like it's not real, but trust me it's really real. This is a keyword site that pardon the language… "shits out keywords"… literally. It's a machine! Looking to turn one niche into 1,000? Just click the link, in the big white box, type in the word you want to keyword expand… and then start. The site will "shit out keywords", until you stop it. … then use the download button to download a .txt file, with a huge list of the keywords! It's really fast, and it has a really hilarious, and slightly offensive name, but if you want to generate keywords for a niche, or listing description, or for whatever, it's great!
It comes in a PRO version as well!

PRO TIP: There WAS a PRO version! The PRO version of keyword shitter, has way more options, is also free, and it looks pretty!

~~Keyword Shitter Pro: NO LONGER AVAILABLE :-(~~

~~http://keywordshitterpro.com/~~
~~Keyword Shitter Pro is just like the site above, except it takes long tail keyword generation to the next level! Choose country of preference, keyword for SEO by platform, by language, and more! Also, just like the Pro would indicate, instead of just a .txt in keyword shitter… keyword shitter pro gives you a .csv file! Maybe because the .csv file format is like the pro version of a .txt file format, lol!~~
~~So, if you ever want to see what keywords can be made using, or related to your idea keywords, this is like an idea generator on steroids! Enjoy!~~

~~Link to a full review of the pro tool: https://www.youtube.com/watch?v=lznl7hvwFlk~~

~~Still don't think it's real, and scared to click the links? Relax. I've been to every link in this book… they're all good. They're all safe too.~~

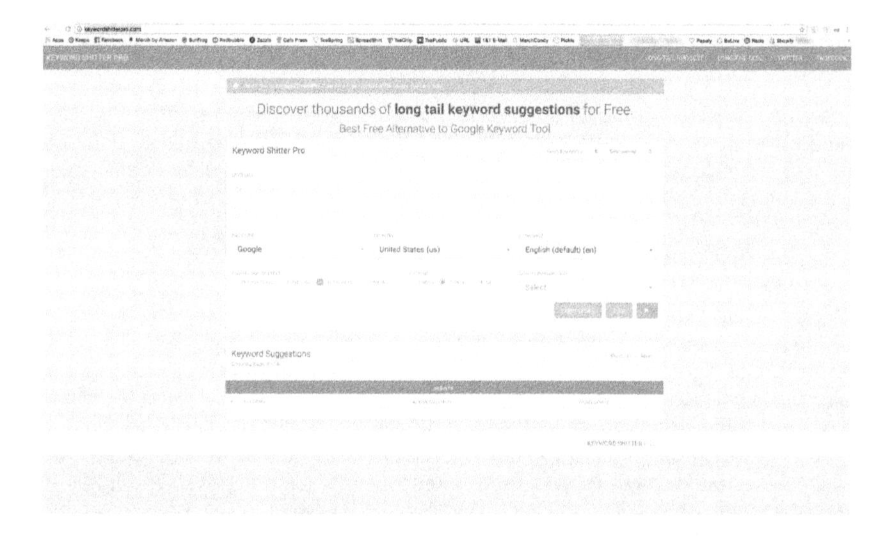

~~Here's a pic of the keywordshitterpro.com page:~~

Keyword Tool:
Keyword Tool does not use the Google Keyword Planner to generate keyword ideas. It finds keywords that people search for on Google using a different source - Google Autocomplete. On their site, without a subscription, you can try a keyword, and it will show you related keywords. Subscribe to their service with one of 3 monthly or annual plans, and see additional information about your results.

Cost:
Trial: NO FREE TRIAL
Pro Lite - $48/Month
Pro Basic - $68/Month
Pro Plus - $88/Month
30-Day Money Back Guarantee
Link here: keywordtool.io/

Subscribe To Keyword Tool Pro Right Now

Monthly Subscription | Annual Subscription (Save up to $211)

Features	Pro Plus (MOST POPULAR!)	Pro Basic	Pro Lite
Search Volume	✓	✓	✗
2x More Keywords	✓	✓	✓
CPC on AdWords	✓	✗	✗
Competition on AdWords	✓	✗	✗
Export All Data to Excel or CSV	✓	✓	✓
Price in USD	**$88 / month**	**$68 / month**	**$48 / month**
Choose Plan	Subscribe Now	Subscribe Now	Subscribe Now

30-Day Money Back Guarantee

We provide 30-day money back guarantee. It means that you can safely subscribe and try Keyword Tool Pro for a month. If you realize that it is not for you, you can email us within 30 days to get a full refund.

Merch Informer:
Cost: $9.99/mo to $59.99/mo depending on which play you select (see graphic below)
Link here: https://merchinformer.com/131.html (affiliate link)

USE CODE: MultiPODsROCK for 20% off any order from Merch Informer

Currently the most popular overall tool available today for Merch By Amazon Research. Merch informer helps in many many ways. Click the link and check it out now. Including: Merch By Amazon specific keyword search, and analysis. Clothing TOP CATEGORY rankings (yes, don't worry about that amazon.com Merch Informer brings back the joy and happiness in your life, and gives you pure Merch By Amazon rankings). It also helps with trademark searches (now, and in the future - it tracks up to 100 items on an ongoing basis - in case something you have becomes trademarked in the future! it's amazing. Everybody needs to use this tool. Here are some videos showing how Merch informer works, and what it does:
https://www.youtube.com/channel/UCMJ3AVdhDiVQs6DuPl2qGGg/search?query=overview

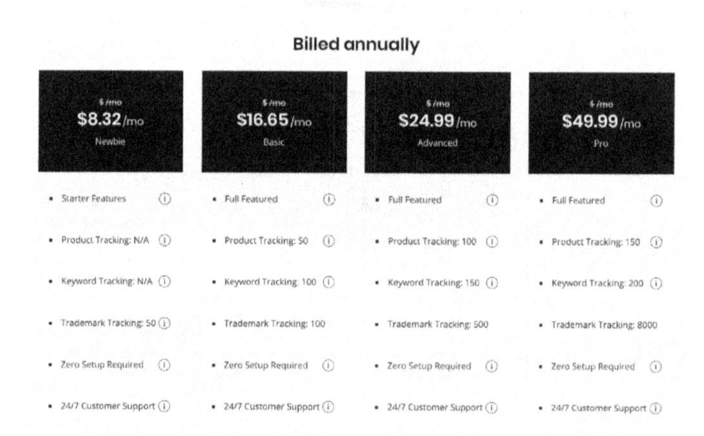

Monthly Yearly

Billed annually

$8.32/mo Newbie	$16.65/mo Basic	$24.99/mo Advanced	$49.99/mo Pro
Starter Features	Full Featured	Full Featured	Full Featured
Product Tracking: N/A	Product Tracking: 50	Product Tracking: 100	Product Tracking: 150
Keyword Tracking: N/A	Keyword Tracking: 100	Keyword Tracking: 150	Keyword Tracking: 200
Trademark Tracking: 50	Trademark Tracking: 100	Trademark Tracking: 500	Trademark Tracking: 8000
Zero Setup Required	Zero Setup Required	Zero Setup Required	Zero Setup Required
24/7 Customer Support	24/7 Customer Support	24/7 Customer Support	24/7 Customer Support

Merch Titans:

Cost: $7.49 to $9.99 monthly, depending on length of monthly plan selected (1-6-12 months)

Link Here: https://merchtitans.com/?r=18 (affiliate link)

Merch Titans is quite similar to Merch Informer, however this newer platform has rapidly been adding new features, and is starting to offer a more unique experience vs. Merch Informer. For example, in addition to product and brand search it also offers a Vault (showing historical ASINs), a Product SEO analyzer, and Trademark alerts. It also has an image search function, to help you find new design inspirations. Merch Titans has 24/7 live support, and detailed videos showing you all their features step by step. You can also set your search to search Merch By Amazon for T-Shirts, Hoodies, or soon - Mugs (if they're released).

Here is an example of a product search result:

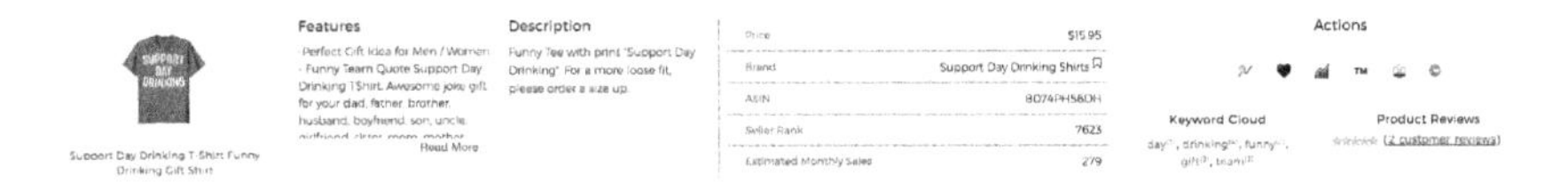

Google Keyword Planner:

Cost: Free

Link here: adwords.google.com/KeywordPlanner

This is a hidden little gem of the google keyword ecosystem. You should certainly check out all the insane scope and data that the Google Keyword PLANNER gives you. So go ahead, make some keyword plans with Google… they like it when people find what they're looking for, and as a seller, remembering marketing 101 in chapter 5 above, you'll remember that it's what you want also. Connect your buyers with your products. Take some action, make your sales happen!

Google Chrome browser extensions:

About Chrome extensions:
Chrome extensions extend the capabilities of your Chrome browser, so that it can do more things. From adding more abilities to the right click of your mouse, to completely re-writing websites as you browse! Chrome extensions are a fast and powerful way to take your Merch business to the next level.

If you're new to chrome extensions, don't worry, they're still catching on in many areas, and Merch By Amazon, and other PODs are no exception. Find loads of helpful Chrome extensions here:
https://chrome.google.com/webstore/category/extensions

Some are free and some are paid. Some are useful, and some less useful. I expect to see many more of these time savers in the coming days and months (hint, hint) ;-)

What about Safari, or Firefox or Internet Explorer?
YES! They all have extensions, but Chrome is basically the king of the Merch By Amazon extensions jungle at the moment.

Here are some Google Chrome extensions that I highly recommend:

DS Amazon Quick View
Price: **FREE**
Available here: https://chrome.google.com/webstore/detail/ds-amazon-quick-view/jkompbllimaoekaogchhkmkdogpkhojg?hl=en
this allows you to see BSR ranks on the search results page on Amazon, so that you don't have to go into each merch listing to see each BSR. This saves a lot of time, if you're browsing Amazon looking for low ranked BSR's.

Merch Research (by Chris Green):
Price: Variable, 3 levels from Free to $9.99 to $29.99/month
Available here: chrome.google.com/webstore/detail/merch-research-pro-merch/agalombefbplceanlmojdjdlainefijc
Save time finding design inspirational ideas to create for multiple POD's, report copycats on Merch by Amazon, check for trademarks by listing title, search across multiple Social Media channels for any printed text in your browser, download top Merch by Amazon ASIN's and info about each listing like price, title, etc.
Quick explanation video here: youtu.be/GD8M2OJPAgg

Merch Lister Pro (By: Jonny King) <— newly updated in 2018!
Price: $34.97 one time fee
Available here: https://gumroad.com/a/442315891
Merch Lister Pro allows you to create a profile for each design grouping that will save your Brand Name, Title, Price, Bullet Points and Description AND Color Selections. Once saved via .csv, you can easily fill out each Merch By Amazon listing with the click of a button (or keyboard shortcut). Here's an in depth video showing exactly how it works: https://youtu.be/1i3XEE8uAOU
This can save time on every listing - you or your VA's time! Super great tool for anyone who needs to get lots of designs uploaded daily to Merch By Amazon.

Merch Lister Data Machine (By Johnny King)
Price $10
Available Here: https://gumroad.com/l/merchldm
Save even more time by combining Merch Lister Pro, with Johnny King's Merch Lister Data Machine. This tool helps you to create suitable listings based on core keywords. Works great for listing across multiple Merch By Amazon products (t-shirt, premium t-shirt, hoodie, long sleeve, sweatshirt…). For a full demo of Merch Lister Data Machine go here: https://www.youtube.com/watch?v=wubwBgobQpw Create hundreds of shirt listings quickly!

Amazon Merch Tools - Merch Batch Uploader (By. Rick Blyth)
Price: $24.99
Available here: https://gumroad.com/a/424326259/zAGIW
USE CODE "jacob" or "marchmerch" to **get $5 off** (limited to first 100 people)
As described by Rick: **Merch Batch Uploader** streamlines your listing process on Merch by Amazon. Based around listing in batches and utilizing the power of excel/CSV files you can create 100s of listings in excel in seconds. You can then navigate through the upload data and it will auto-populate the relevant fields during the listing process.
Merch Batch Uploader has the following features:
- Display the design you're uploading and record X of Y in the upload batch.
- Auto select the colors/price/brand, title, bullets and description text boxes.
- 100% written and maintained by the author - Rick Blyth of Amazon Merch Tools.
- 100% client side chrome extension.
- No transmission of ANY listing data or design details to any 3rd party servers.

This extension will save you or your Virtual Assistant (VA) hours of listing time. It is possible to list shirts in under 20 seconds using this extension. I can list over 100 shirts per hour using the extension. This extension is ideal for designs that are based around variants or scaled/boilerplate designs.
Video Tutorial of how it works here:
https://www.youtube.com/watch?v=g_BVoOSFUYE

Amazon Merch Tools - Merch Batch Editor (By. Rick Blyth)
Available here: Price: $14.99
https://gumroad.com/a/424326259/MulJI
USE CODE "jacob" or "marchmerch" to **get $2 off** (limited to first 100 people)
As described by Rick: **Amazon Merch Batch Editor** allows you to edit batches of Amazon Merch products quickly and painlessly. The manage page on MBA only allows you to edit each design one at a time.
This chrome extension allows you to edit as many designs as you want in bulk. You simply add the designs to the batch to edit and click on the "Open Tabs" button to open all the edit pages for the designs in the batch. You can simply open up a batch of edits or optionally apply a blanket price update or consolidate shirts to come under one brand.
This extension has been well tested and is used by many well respected Merch teams to streamline their pricing updates and brand consolidation.

Video tutorial of how it works here: https://www.youtube.com/watch?v=QjS1WO7aYVI

RiteTag (by RiteKit):
Price: FREE
Available here: chrome.google.com/webstore/detail/ritetag/hclhpnhohpmlbadmeieecaandnglfodm

Rite Tag is a service delivered via their website AND/OR Chrome extension which allows you to get instant feedback on you hashtag choices as you type. Set alerts to see new hashtags related to your niche, instant color coded feedback about hashtags you wish to use. Mouseover tags to get instant feedback and trend analysis, and more. Works with Twitter, Facebook, and other social media platforms.
Quick explanation video here: youtu.be/sje0NiLkd5g
For more info, link to their website here: ritetag.com/

Merch Check (by Jacob Bates):
$12.49 on time fee
Link Here: https://gumroad.com/a/387789939

An easy and fast way to check for IP violations like trademarks and copyrights, without leaving the page you're on. Use this Chrome extension from any webpage, no need to be anywhere specific. Users will enjoy saving time and taking care of business. At the time of writing (Q1 2017), this plugin is in version 2.0 (released in early March 2017). One time fee (no monthly payments), and updates forever (at no extra cost), and no data collected (so use knowing that nobody is collecting all your data for use elsewhere) this is a quick plugin you'll love for IP. Plus, it shows you the Merch specific designs with every search… so it's kind of like using the big green button on merchresearch.com … except it works from any page you're on, saving you even more time!
Quick Explanation video here: https://youtu.be/XMV23elx_0Y

NOTE: Watch for more interesting and innovative products, and possible services from Jacob Bates, and Monte Werle… Because this pair of guys are tight, and you'll want to see what they come up with next…

Example of a great Safari Extension for Merch By Amazon:

Keepa (by Keepa):

Link Here:https://safari-extensions.apple.com/details/?id=com.amptra.keepa-63N6CG26VL

That's right, Google Chrome is the gorilla in the room, but it's not the only pony ride. This Keepa extension for Safari (Apple's desktop browser, built into all Apple computers), is great for seeing pricing changes of Merch By Amazon listings, as well as seeing how long the design has been tracked by Keepa.

NOTE: Keepa does not follow ***ALL*** Merch By Amazon designs... but it does follow some of them, and when it does, you can be sure that at one point or another that design was selling like hotcakes. ... not sure when that was? Check the Keepa timeline, and see the time rage of possible high selling periods. Anything under a year, and you can eliminate a number of variables in your search for the worlds greatest keywords and designs.

Searching For Merch Designs On Amazon:

When Merch By Amazon was being created, it used a code term called ORCA. This ORCA can be used to locate Merch By Amazon listings (separate from all Amazon results). Here is a quick search tool called *Merch Research* used to isolate Merch shirts for any search performed. To see them all, just click the green button, and run a blank search:

Merch Research

(FREE)

Link Here: https://merchinformer.com/merch-amazon-listings/

This is literally the #1 FREE top used tool across literally every seller on Merch By Amazon I have ever talked to. Originally it was located at merchresearch.com, Merch Research by Chris Green brought hope to sifting through amazon.com listings to locate Merch By Amazon specific listings. It is seen by everyone used by everyone - THE GREEN BUTTON:

Originally it looked like this:

Now it looks like this:

All Merch By Amazon Listings

Enter keyword or search term

Search T-shirts | Search Hoodies | Search Sweatshirts | Search Long sleeve shirts

If this is a new tool to you, or you have never used this magical green button, located on https://merchinformer.com/merch-amazon-listings/ than stop reading right here, go to the site, and hit that green button. The book will be here for you when you get back.

You don't even have to type anything in the search field! Just hit the green button! You will now be looking at a new browser tab, containing only Merch By Amazon listings. This is amazing, fast, convenient, and works not only on your desktop, but on your smartphone as well! Want to see if some words are used on a Merch By Amazon listing? Enter them into the search field, and then hit the green button. Want multiple windows open, with just Merch By Amazon listings? Just go back, and click that green button again! There was way more on the site than just the green button on the front page, most of these resources and links have now migrated to the resources menu of https://merchinformer.com/merch-amazon-listings/ . Check it out. Connect with Chris Green, and thank him for giving you free access to one of the single greatest free online Merch By Amazon tools - the green button. There are some additional online tools that do some other things, but that green button can help you retire if you use it correctly. Also, check out Chris Green's live events surrounding river-bank.com which will teach you multiple ways to earn money with Amazon, and it's group of companies and services, it's great.

The Merchinator of Merch Empire
by Anthony Busciglio & Kevin Levonas
$9.99/mo to $49.99/mo depending on which plan is chosen
Link Here:https://merchinator.com/ or if you prefer: https://goo.gl/7YpmBG

The Merchinator is a design variation tool created to multiply your existing design base, by applying filters. Cut your cost of design creation by quickly turning each existing design into many. Anthony explains what the

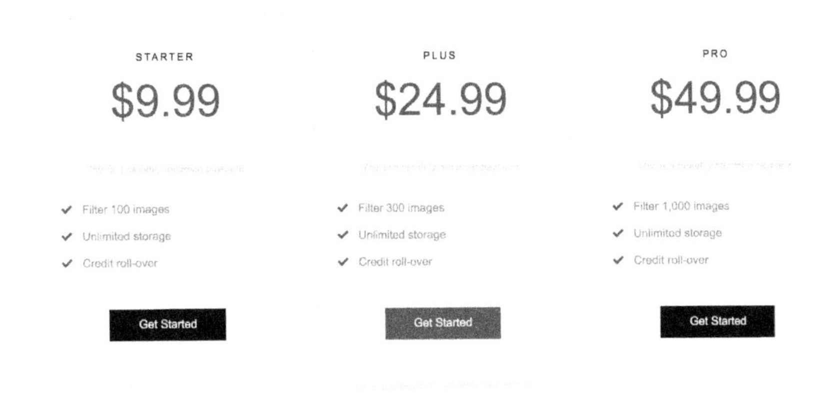

Merchinator is in this quick video: https://v.arxius.io/cc17c569
Amazon sellers. Enjoy!

MERCH BLOGS:

Second Half Dreams (by Diana Poisson):

Link here: www.secondhalfdreams.com/merch-by-amazon/
Diana is working towards a full time income selling on Amazon. What's even more exciting is that she's also on Merch By Amazon, in addition to selling on Amazon! With multiple Merch specific blog posts, as well as a condensed resources/ tools page, see what Diana is up to next!

Micheal Essek's Blog (by Micheal Essek):

Link Here: https://www.michaelessek.com/
Michael is one of Merch By Amazon's top sellers. This is his blog, and it is a powerhouse of information on Merch By Amazon, and even some POD things as well. Not only does he go through his own progress, but he has fresh content up regularly, a great newsletter with even more info beyond his blog, and an e-book "How to Sell More Shirts". Michael is based in the UK, and went from around $50/month, to around $13,000/ month, in

about 3 years. As a designer, he also has a great eye for design. Definitely a blog you want to check out.

Merch Pursuits (by Danny):

Link Here: http://merchpursuits.com/

A great Merch centric blog by Danny, including things that he's learning along his Merch by Amazon journey, including Monthly income reports (a great way to see how a seller's income has progressed selling via Merch By Amazon - **NOTE:** every seller will have unique results, so don't worry if your results are more or less than other seller's) :-)

Merch Informer (by Neil Lassen):

Link here: https://merchinformer.com/blog/

This is a great blog covering both Merch by Amazon, as well as additional POD options. A great resource (literally one of the best merch blogs ever - well done Neil) from the makers of Merch Informer the software (which is great for Merch searching, key wording, brainstorming, tracking trademarks on your own designs, and more link to the software here: https://merchinformer.com/131.html). Great timely topics all the time, from marketing on social media, to case study of his girlfriends account growth, and more!

Bandzoogle:

Link here: https://bandzoogle.com/blog/the-ultimate-guide-to-selling-band-merch-online

This Merch blog is geared around band merchandise options. It covers both online and offline (in real life, aka not online), and is a great resource both for general Merch ideas, as well as band specific ideas, tips and tricks. In a band, definitely check this out.

Geek Husttle (by Yong Jae Chong):

Link Here: http://www.geekhustle.com/

Online since June 2016, this is one of the newer BLOGs in the group. Yong Jae Chong's (aka the Retro Aficionado) blog is a treasure trove of both new and accumulated information, across multiple online selling platforms, it spans Ebay, Amazon FBA, Merch By Amazon, even Craigslist! Young himself has been in the business of business from a young age, working in his family, to selling online across multiple platforms. Learn from this seasoned seller, as he shares with you the secrets he learns along the way. It even features a rich resources section which covers things from creative design software, through to finances, and so much in between.

HustlaGirl Tees - Making Money with Merch by Amazon:
Link Here: https://marcymo.com/
Newly launched in 2017, Marcy Mo should be no stranger to anyone following the Merch By Amazon communities. Marcy has rocketed up the Merch By Amazon tiers, from Tier 25 a year ago, to T6000 today (Q1 2018). Like Yong (see above), Marcy is not only killing it on the Merch By Amazon sales per listings ratio game, but she is also an accomplished Ebay titanium Powerseller, and active on the Amazon FBA scene as well. The HustlaGirl blog goes beyond the comfort zone of anonymity, and proudly showcases the amazing Merch By Amazon designs that is quickly making Marcy Mo a household name not only in race to get tiered up (;-)), but also in the world of top selling designer brand designs!

Redbubble's Blog:
Link Here: http://blog..com/home/
Here's a tip, to multiply the number of places you can find new and current information about your favorite POD platform: Almost all of them have their own blog's. This is where PODs will post all of the most cutting edge content that they have, for their most die-hard artists, and fans. Redbubble's blog is no exception, it offers fresh content on a regular basis. Things to help their seller sell more products, and make Redbubble more likely to be their favorite place to list your next design! Tips on designing, resources for artists, hottest trends in POD, featured artists, step by step how too's (such as how to create pixel art), and MORE! Want to sell more shirts on Merch By Amazon? Why not learn better keyboarding, or how to make better designs, or the latest trends in the industry … at the Redbubble blog!

POD Podcasts:

Merch Minds (with Glen Zubia - Texas and Yong Jae Chong - California)
Link Here: https://itunes.apple.com/us/podcast/merch-minds-podcast-glen-yong/id1153199733?mt=2
Glen and Yong host a weekly conversation about all things Merch by Amazon, including sharing their own experience and numbers. Follow their journey from the beginning with over 70+ episodes. I've been on the podcast multiple times, check out Episode 51.

The 45/54 Podcast (with Nick Eden)
Link Here: https://soundcloud.com/4554podcast
The 45/54 Podcast is a weekly show dedicated to educating content creators. Focusing on new sellers to the Merch By Amazon platform (tier 10-25-100-500), it also covers and discusses things among other print on demand platforms as well. Typically Nick also shares his progress, as well as his wife's account. Easy listening, great audio quality. Also be sure to check out Nick's new Merch In A Minute series on youtube here: https://www.youtube.com/user/Stepchylde/videos

Merch Entrepreneur (with Elaine Heney - Ireland)
Link Here: https://itunes.apple.com/ca/podcast/merch-entrepreneur-sell-t/id1171930091?mt=2
I've got to tell you, I'm a huge fan of the podcast. Worth watching from episode 001 all the way to whatever is coming out next (60+). Elaine Heney not only covers the current Merch By Amazon, and Print On Demand issues of the day, but she also manages to edit these podcasts into impact filled, yet interesting capsules of golden knowledge. After hearing the amazing content you find here, you're also going to want to visit her website merchentrepreneur.com and maybe even take her Masterclass, hint hint ;-) I had the pleasure of joining Elaine Heney on Episode 36 here: https://itunes.apple.com/ca/podcast/36-jacob-talks-expanding-past-merch-how-he-used-secret/id1171930091?i=1000384459429&mt=2

Merch Mates (formerly Merch Nerds) (Luke Kelly - Australia)
Link Here: https://www.merch-nerds.com/podcast/
One of the newest Merch podcasts on the web today, Luke Kelly gives an honest look at some of the struggles that Merch By Amazon sellers face, as well as tips and advice on how to improve your Merch By Amazon sales. Luke himself also works full time, and is working within Merch By Amazon to replace the 9-5, and earn some full time online income. Helpful links to additional tools are sprinkled around and within both the blog, and the podcast. A great resource for people looking on tips to improve upon their existing Merch business. Currently with several episodes at the time of this book's release. Be sure also to check out Luke's Etsy Masterclass located here: http://www.etsyprintfulmasterclass.com ($197) - OR, use this link and **SAVE $100USD**: **https://lukekelly.clickfunnels.com/epmcourse?affiliate_id=1010565 ($97)**

The Print On Demand (POD) Podcast (Alf Brand)
Link Here: http://thepodpodcast.com/
Talking about all things related to Merch By Amazon, this is a relatively newer podcast as well, which began July 14, 2017. It's got some great info, and discussion all around Merch By Amazon, and surrounding topics. Paired with the podcast is the website, and the Facebook group: https://www.facebook.com/groups/PODPodcast

MORE:

The Official Merch By Amazon Forums:
Link Here: https://forums.developer.amazon.com/spaces/80/index.html
Where better to talk about Merch By Amazon, than the official Merch By Amazon forums? Did you know there were Merch By Amazon Forums? ... yup, there are! With over 745 people following, it's also a hard core and growing community of Merch By

Merch / POD YouTube Channels:

Merch Informer (Neil Lassen):
Link here: https://www.youtube.com/channel/UCMJ3AVdhDiVQs6DuPl2qGGg
This is a great how to resource about the operational logistics of the Merch By Amazon business. It focuses on using the tool Merch Informer, as well as effective strategies on how to accelerate your Merch BY Amazon business.

Merch Empire - Jersey Edition (Anthony Busciglio and Kevin Levonas):
Link here: https://www.youtube.com/channel/UCLqVUrwhl5l6TxPO93YGyjA
Daily videos discussing all things Merch By Amazon. Additional videos showing quick tips, as well as behind the scenes footage of their business and team. Focus on scaling, optimization, business process. Quickly building a community of engagement, this channel is both fresh, fun, and entertaining. **NOTE:** Language alert, lots of f-bombs.

UGR (Daniel Martinez):
Link here: https://www.youtube.com/playlist?list=PLnr7HLkt0Yd1cObWH4LpLsUy5IRD082hy
A very authentic personal journey with Merch By Amazon, includes lessons learned along the way, processed, tools used and more. Canadian (Toronto area).

Mitch On Merch (Mitch Fairchild):
Link here: https://www.youtube.com/channel/UCtntEDyTqzYML-mtyaYpVvQ
Mitch offers reporting on current Merch By Amazon events, as well as commentary and advice on how to improve your designs and your design business. Mitch teaches at a local College, so he has some unique insights not found in other places.

Essetino Artists (Jewel Tolentino and Auret Esselen and crew):
Link here:
https://www.youtube.com/playlist?list=PL50W2jUB3jud7NN4JJO_Unt-dtsr0dsVx
In this sequential update style playlist about Merch By Amazon, Jewel provides direct insights into their Merch By Amazon experience, including sales updates, tools used, and more. With over 40+ update videos and counting, this is a great way to follow a fellow Merch seller's journey, including the successes and failures they've had along the way. Canadians (Vancouver Area).

Charley Pangus:
Link here: https://www.youtube.com/user/charmediagroup/videos
While not directly related to Merch By Amazon specifically, Charley Pangs is a talented digital artist, and on his channel, he shares how his process for making T-shirt designs, and digital art creation in general. By explaining how he creates each design, you can learn principles which you can apply, should you be creating your own designs, or which you may want to share with your designers, if you see something neat that you would like them to try on future designs. Easy to follow, with tips on digital workflow and design creation a YouTube channel for nights from a designer. California.

Katie Patton:
Link here: https://www.youtube.com/user/katiemariepatton
Katie walks sellers through her journey of selling on Merch By Amazon, as well as several tips and tricks on how to do Merch better. She outlines here actual sales, so if you're curious about how much people make on Merch By Amazon, this gives you a peak.
NOTE: Her channel also covers other topics, often related to selling online, and on Amazon and Ebay, so you might need to search for other topics to find the Merch videos, but they are there, and they enjoyable.

Texas Gal Treasures:
Link here:
https://www.youtube.com/channel/UC5Ud_GtWebRSJQeNgSQJ6tg
Channel features Merch By Amazon as a major feature, among several others such as Ebay, Etsy, and yard sales. Live sessions often feature regular guests including Joe Clay (Merch University), and Mike Peterson (Treasure Gnome) and others. Texas.

Treasure Gnome (Mike Peterson):
Link here: https://www.youtube.com/channel/UCzknM7jRIVusl9jjcsvEtQQ
Mike offers insights into tools and tips that he uses for his Merch By Amazon business, including demos, interviews, and more. One of the hidden Merch By Amazon youtube channels you should really subscribe to asap.

Thrift Shop Hustler (Chris Avalos):
Link Here: https://www.youtube.com/watch?v=KmhJmt1U9T0&list=PL0OU3uMkbEuoxVqRCt0zUYA7P1TtLE60-
Chris covers multiple online sales marketplaces including Merch By Amazon, Ebay and others. with years of experience selling online, this is a great channel to check out on youtube. For even more, be sure to check him out on SteemIt as well! Link here: https://steemit.com/@reseller

Merch / POD Facebook groups:

Merch By Amazon (by Chris Green)
Link Here: facebook.com/groups/MerchLife/
By far the largest and most popular of all things Merch By Amazon on all of Facebook, this undisputed apex Facebook group is the definitive place for all things Merch By Amazon on Facebook. With over 58,000 members (up from 29,000 members a year ago), it's clearly one place you cannot miss. Essentially this is the heartbeat of the Merch By Amazon community.

Merch Minds (by Glen Zubia and Yong Jae Chong)
Link Here: facebook.com/groups/1824530797822546/
Connecting the FB community to the Merch Minds podcast this is one very active and engaged Merch By Amazon, and Print On Demand group. With 8,143+ members, you're sure to see some familiar faces, and bridge the worlds of podcasts (Merch minds podcast), blogs (Yong's blog), and YouTube coverage (Glen's Hustler hacks). This is a great place to find a mix of online seller, with a focus on Merch By Amazon, you'll occasionally find posts on topics ranging additional online seller market places from time to time.

Merch By Amazon Top Sellers for Newbies and Pros
(by Jacob Topping)
https://www.facebook.com/groups/merchtopsellers/
There's no better opportunity than right here for me to shamelessly self promote... so this one is totally biased... This is Jacob Topping's FB Merch and POD group...

BEST MERCH FACEBOOK GROUP EVER!

With over 3,300+ members and growing quickly, **Merch By Amazon Top Sellers for Newbies and Pros** is just that, a place for top sellers to join together, and share the best tips and techniques for maximizing your Merch game. This group bridges beyond Merch By Amazon a much further than other groups, evidence of this is the giant list of additional PODs, including Merch By Amazon.

Need a break?
There's a lot more pages of premium content coming up in this book... so take a breather, and stand up, stretch your legs, move around little... join my Facebook group link here: https://www.facebook.com/groups/merchtopsellers/. Great, now continue, and enjoy the rest of the book, there's a LOT more!

Merch University (by Joe Clay & Margaret Collier):
https://www.facebook.com/groups/MerchUniversity/
Merch University with 4,829 members, is a great community based group focusing on helping new sellers tier up and sell more. There appears to be some overlap with the Merch Minds Facebook group. *Joe Clay* provides great engagement with the group, and has been known to offer up creative collaborations, challenges, and good information regarding design based information.

Merch Empire Jersey Edition (by Anthony Busciglio and Kevin Levonas)
https://www.facebook.com/groups/merchempire/
This active and vocal community of 3,521 members of Merch By Amazon sellers is focused on uncovering the secrets of optimizing and growing your Merch By Amazon business. A theme within the group is 10X-ing everything, and steps you can take to grow your business quickly. The group has live videos Mondays to Wednesdays, and the language can be quite colorful (lots of f-bombs). Thursdays it also has weekly paid podcasts, where they interview merch sellers, called shakedowns. In addition to Merch By Amazon, the group sometimes also covers Amazon FBA, sports (especially football), and crypto currencies (occasionally). Also see the **Resources** section of this book, for their tool the ***Merchinator*** - a photo filter tool that helps you to scale designs, by quickly modifying existing designs (see the tools section for more info on it): https://merchinator.com/ - OR 3 FREE Dredits with signup here: https://goo.gl/7YpmBG

Merch Elite (by Manny Coats and Guillermo Puyol)
facebook.com/groups/MerchElite/
Two of the dark horses in the Merch By Amazon world, Manny Coats, and Guillermo - known for their AMAZING Private Label journey via Amazon FBA, are creating a well informed, and energetic following on the Merch By Amazon side of the fence. Check out Merch Elite and its 3,197 members for hard hitting, philosophically engaging questions about Merch By Amazon. This is one fresh group, with new and different content, often not seen elsewhere.

Amazon Merch and Beyond (by Travis Renn):
facebook.com/groups/teeshirtdomination/
This Facebook group tends to focus on the tools and products which Travis creates, mainly merchlab.io (keyword research) and designcandy.io (merch design service). It incorporates interaction beyond only Merch By Amazon, to include other Print On Demand platforms. Currently around 2,100 members.

Merch Success (Merch by Amazon) (by Daniel Caudill, Dave Espino)
https://www.facebook.com/groups/MerchByAmazonSuccess/members/
Lead by one of if not the all time highest sellers on the Merch By Amazon platform Daniel Caudill, this is a great place to learn from the other sellers with plenty of sales success. 6,623 Members

Merch Momentum - Merch By Amazon (by Michael Essany):
https://www.facebook.com/groups/MerchByAmazonMomentum/
Michael has built up a great group of over 7,700+ members by providing fantastic commentary on Merch By Amazon. Michael is also the author of a very popular weekly strategy guide, which delivers insights to and about multiple niches weekly. I highly recommend you ***check it out here: https://gumroad.com/a/1063433331 for $10 a month***, you'll have a fresh stream of insights on 100-200 fresh keyword/niche leads (separated by t-shirts and long sleeves), as well as weekly updates on trends, and other things happening within Merch By Amazon.
Merch by Amazon Mastermind - (by Rj Martinez, Matt Sheeran, and 9 both admins)
https://www.facebook.com/groups/MerchByAmazonMM/
Sharing knowledge with the 9,300+ members to help scale their Merch by Amazon POD business. One of the most popular regular events they have is regular lifestream interviews with other Merch By Amazon seller, called Real Talk with RJ and Matt, found here: https://www.youtube.com/channel/UCgUAPPjwz--1MRiEojS1QPw/videos

Merch Services (by Chris Green): https://www.facebook.com/groups/MerchServices/ 1,079 members

Books on Merch:

What others have written on Merch...

Merch and the World of Print On Demand (by: Jacob Topping)

This is the book. You're reading it right now.
Here's a link to share with your friends: **https://gum.co/LzoyC**

Merch and the World of Print On Demand is an expansive guide to all things Merch and the World of Print On Demand (POD), including selling via Merch By Amazon and many other popular top POD sites.

Step by step instructions (beyond just what to do, but - how to do it as well), glossary, a list of 50+ POD platforms (with metrics about each one! Tips for settings, tips to boost conversions of existing designs), technical specifications, plus additional tools and resources to help you improve your sales.
Full disclosure, I am the author of this book, and this review of my own content is totally biased, that being said... I love this book, and it really is the best multi-POD resource around.

Merch Life: An Introduction to Using Merch By Amazon to Design Shirts and Make Money (by: Chris Green)

Link here: https://www.amazon.com/Merch-Life-Introduction-Amazon-Design/dp/1517795990
Merch Life is a great little book, which provides you insights to many of the aspects of Merch By Amazon, in addition to the content about Merch By Amazon in his book, it also includes links to 12 password protected videos walking you through the Merch by Amazon platform, and 7 videos which will teach you basic Photoshop. It's a great resource for anyone *getting started* into Merch By Amazon, and the photoshop videos are a great resource for anyone looking to learn photoshop, especially for Merch design! Often referred to as the Godfather of Amazon, Chris Green is knowledgeable in things related to Amazon, and I highly recommend you seek out his books, courses, and other materials, they're great.

Etsy Printful Success - Launch Your T-Shirt Business Today (by: Monte Werle, Jacob Bates and Jason Huesgen)

Link Here: https://gumroad.com/a/982168691
This book walks you through Etsy+Printful, down to **how to** write your titles, pricing structures, tips, tricks, and **video lessons** brought to you by Jason Huesgen.
They have stuffed the book full of information to help you become more successful on Etsy. This book includes video lessons, and access to their secret Etsy POD Mastermind Facebook group.

NOTE: This is a good book to pick up after you've set-up Etsy and Printful, using the instructions provided in Chapter 4 of this book, under Etsy, and Printful.

Courses on Merch:

Courses are great ways to learn more about the topic in a methodical fashion...

Quick FREE 90 minute course on how to Outsource, and Automate your business further (by: Kevin and Anthony Busciglio):
http://jerseymerch.com/merch-automation/
In this training video you will learn how to: Hire A Virtual Assistant To Run Your Business,
Get High Quality T-Shirt Designs Made For low cost, Free Tools To Communicate With Your Virtual Team, Compliance "Musts" So You Don't Get Terminated. These are keys to a productive and efficient Virtual Assistant workflow.

Merch Dojo $497 (by: Chris Green)
Recently announced, but not yet released at the time of this book's publishing, you will be able to access this course March 28th, 2018 or later using this link:
https://goo.gl/bqxRw6

Merch by Amazon - How to Research & Market T-Shirts (by: Michael Peterson - aka the Treasure Gnome):
Link Here: https://www.udemy.com/merch-by-amazon-how-to-research-market-t-shirts/
According to Udemy's description: This Merch by Amazon course will show you how to research & market shirts that will sell using social media. Michael Peterson is an amazing person, and has quality content on a regular basis. If you're not familiar with him already, take some time to seek him out. He's friendly, approachable, and is a great example of what a great community of sellers exists within the Merch By Amazon, and POD ecosystem. I haven't taken his course yet, but I definitely plan to soon. I've heard great things about it, and I wouldn't expect anything less from the Treasure Gnome himself.

Merch by Amazon - How to Start Your Own T-Shirt Business (by: Dan Vega):

Link Here: https://www.udemy.com/merch-by-amazon/

According to Udemy's description: In this course Dan will show you what Merch is, how to sign up and then how to be successful. He will show you that Merch is not only made for designers but for creative entrepreneurs as well.

Dan will give you the guidelines you need to submit designs but it is important to note that this is not a graphic design course. He will show you some of the programs you can use like Adobe Photoshop and Illustrator but he will also introduce you to some other programs that don't have a steep learning curve. Finally Dan will give you all the tips and tricks he has learned to help you along your Merch journey.

Merch Autopilot (by Phillip Stone)

Price: £59.50 (British Pounds)

Link here: **https://gumroad.com/l/tSzE/Jacob** <—15%OFF with this link

This extensive video course will show you exactly how to outsource specifically for Merch By Amazon. Info is provided, such as:

- Where to find your virtual assistant (VA)
- How to find a top quality loyal VA
- How to keep your account safe
- How much to pay them and how
- How to find a graphics designer
- How to find a researcher (My epic secret)
- Training videos are provided for your potential VA
- Many awesome tools to make the process much efficient, faster and cheaper
- A special tool that hides your personal information from your employee

Merch Input (By Phillip Stone)

Price: $51

Link here: https://gumroad.com/l/tzWPw/Jacob

This video course will educate not only on the basics but also in-depth advanced info of the 2018 Merch By Amazon business model and put you on the right path to making a semi-passive live-able income

Sections on: What is Merch By Amazon?, Proof of sales, Quick Start tutorial - How to create a merch listing for free, The criteria for sales, Multiple methods of research - Amazon/Pinterest/Google, How to find profitable niches using the Merch Informer software, How to keep your account safe from trademarks & infringement, How to navigate around the dashboard, How to make a design, New products on Amazon, what you need to do, How to create an optimized listing that is ready for sale, Pricing Strategies Explained (Important), How to stay organized, Quantity VS quality, How the tier system works (Important), Understanding the art of patience, Researched vs bulk scalable designs, Outsourcing resource, Don't know how to make designs?, Facebook support, tools, and resources

LIVE VIDEO / SCREEN SHARING TOOLS

BeLive.tv

- host a live 2 person video stream, leverage the power of Facebook Live

zoom.com

- host a meeting with multiple people, free up to 40 minutes

hangouts.google.com

- connected to YouTube live - find out more

join.me

A great tool for training a VA, or hare your screen shared with someone FAST, free, and easily. Paid options are also available, with additional features and functionality.

END OF CHAPTER 6

Chapter 7: OUTSOURCING

The secret weapon to compress time, save money, automate processes and get more done…

What Is Outsourcing?

Outsourcing is essentially a way of assigning tasks to people or companies to complete, separate from your own efforts or your own company's permanent staff. One benefit of outsourcing is that while you are working at the things that you and your internal staff are the best at, or enjoy, or want to do, or are the most valuable parts of your workflow; those whom you have chosen for outsourcing can be working on the other parts.

This distributed workflow is not bound by location, and can often be done concurrently, allowing you to "time stack" your workflow. The result of this being that you are able to produce MORE, FASTER (and often at LOWER COST as well). You may already be more familiar with the world of outsourcing than you might imagine. Some people pay other people to cut their lawn in the summertime, or depending on where you live, may shovel the snow off your driveway in the winter time. These are services which can be done for you, while you focus on other things, like reading a book, or making supper.

Other common outsourcing that people may use that they don't even realize include hiring a house cleaner, using a taxi or Uber to transport you from place to place. People even outsource their utilities (heat, water, mobile phone service)… imagine you had to generate your own power to heat your home, or setup your own satellite network to receive phone calls… people outsource all the time! Now that you know a bit about what outsourcing is, what are some areas that can be, or are often outsourced?

Things you can outsource in your Merch / POD workflow include (but are not limited to) the following:

- **Niche/design Research** (Example: VA Rentals)
- **Design Creation** (Example: Design Pickle or Penji)
- **Managing design requests made & received from your design teams** (Example: custom VA)
- **Uploading designs across POD's** (Example: VA Rental, or Custom VA)
- **Marketing of your listings** (Example: Kit, or a marketing service)

Outsourcing can be done by literally anyone that you can **trust.** Your family members (kids, wife, husband, parents, cousins, nieces, nephews, grandparents, etc.), your friends (partner with friends and share in the results, or pay them, and provide them with extra reliable income, while you taken the risk of marketing and selling your designs online), existing staff (imagine how many things your babysitter, or house cleaner might be able to do, if you trust them, and they want to pickup some extra work on the side), Paid staff (run a warehouse? maybe your staff would like some workplace variety, and upload designs while they take a break from packing boxes for FBA?).

Virtual Assistance (VA's, can do work for you while you do other things. They can be local or in remote geographies, depending on the tasks), VA services (don't know how, or don't have time to train a VA, why not hire a fully trained VA, or use a service to deliver digitally any component you want to outsource!

Here are some VA services that you can use, with links and details about some of their services:

Niche/Design Research:

Do you ever wish that you didn't have to come up with new ideas and niches that are both new, and yet will also have good sales results? Wouldn't it be nice if you could just outsource that whole process, and have well researched, good selling ideas and niches sent to you daily? You Can! Outsource it!

VA Rentals:

Website Link Here: http://www.eliteproductsource.com/merch-by-amazon.html
All Available Products Link Here: https://gumroad.com/a/891630707
(hover over each image for a description of each service)

Your designs are safe with Elite Product Sourcing and it's employees and/ or subcontractors agree to keep the designs, emails, and customer's personal information private.

Our Research & Design Process

- Researched design leads, including trademark check
- Completed t-shirt designs ready for immediate upload to Merch by Amazon (PNG Files)
- Unlimited revision requests for each design
- Designs and leads that are only used once and go to only one client
- 100% Confidentiality
- Full ownership rights to the designs
- Optional: Keyword optimization for the title & key product features can be added on for an extra fee

VA Rentals offers multiple Merch / POD services, and packages, at multiple price points. With per image prices averaging between $4/image to $5/image for design only, OR you could pay only for niche research and keyboarding, without the design, OR you could pay for only keyword optimization, OR, combine all of the above for $14/design such as the following package:

Package Example – 10 fully researched, designed & optimized T-Shirts ready for Upload to Merch = $120 https://gumroad.com/a/891630707

- Research Is Not Niche Specific
- Keyword Optimization Includes The Title And 2 Bullet Points
- PNG Files Are Provided

Here is how the process with VA Rentals works:

1. Download the appropriate spreadsheet you will use.
2. Fill in the spreadsheet column indicating whether your design will be plain text or include a graphic.
3. Provide a link to a shirt or graphic in the appropriate column on the spreadsheet.
4. Under the modifications column, indicate how you'd like the design modified or altered. If there is a font preference, indicate the font name.
5. Add any additional notes you'd like the designer to be aware of.
6. Fill in the fields beneath the upload including name, number of requested designs and the PayPal/email address you are using.
7. Upload the saved spreadsheet under "upload files". This will then redirect you to the payment page.
8. Get draft designs within 72 hours, though VA Rentals strives to have them available within 24 hours.

- You will be provided with a dropbox link to a draft PNG for your review.
- VA Rentals offer unlimited revisions.
- Your final PNG will be suitable for you to upload for your Merch shirt.

SEE ALL PACKAGES HERE: https://gumroad.com/a/891630707

Outsourcing Design Creation Services:

Design Pickle:

Link Here: **http://share.designpickle.com/hGtgt**
The above link gives you access to their 14 Day Risk Free Guarantee!

Design Pickle provides you: unlimited revisions, you receive multiple files per design delivered including: .png, .jpg, .pdf, AND ORIGINAL ADOBE FORMATS! .psd and/or .ai. Depending on what was used to create the design. Design pickle will make your original designs by request on *weekdays*. A dedicated designer, and their team, is assigned to your account, and the more they get to know what you're looking for, the better and easier it becomes to request and receive back finished original designs.

Available as a monthly service, design pickle typically costs $370/month. On rare occasions, this pricing is offered with a small discount, with longer timeline signups (such as a year).

I joined for a year, and I love it! I use them every weekday, and I absolutely am thrilled by both their quality, and the volume they are able to produce. People often ask what the cost per design is, and that number will be a factor of how many designs your Design Pickle designer provides to you, and how long each request takes.

At the moment, my designer is cranking out 10-30 finished images per weekday. Some important things to know about Design Pickle are:

1. They don't do logos (and they have some other limitations, all listed on their site here: http://share.designpickle.com/hGtgt)
2. They do your requests in order they are received, and can accommodate for rush or prioritized designs if needed.
3. They are extremely customer satisfaction focused, and offer a phone call, as well as other online resources on their site to help you make the most of their service. This includes unlimited revisions to your designs, if ever the need arises.
4. Your designer is assigned to your account, so you will be dealing with a real person, and the same real person, so it's to your advantage to communicate what you're looking for with each design clearly, and to maintain a great relationship with your designer.
5. Design Pickle wins when you do, so they offer you a **2 Week 100% Risk Free Guarantee (14 DAYS)**. This is a way for you to know with confidence if their service is a great fit for your business. If for whatever reason you find it's not what you're looking for, then let them

know, and they'll try help in any way they can. If it's still not working out, then you're free to part ways within the terms of the agreement, and there's no hard feeling, for you or them. They do have a few rules in place which must be met for a full refund (things such as you must have used them at some point, and they get a chance to make things right). Details are clearly laid out on their site, as well as on the on boarding videos that are part of the new account setup process. More details about Design Pickle are on their website, here: http://share.designpickle.com/hGtgt

NOTE: Typically they give you 2 requests per day. You can maximize the effectiveness of these designs by requesting that your designer creates 2-3 versions of each design, and includes variations for light background, dark background, and both color, and black and white. One of the great benefits of using multiple PODs, is that you can cross test your design variations, and see what kind of designs your buyers respond to, then adjust to generate an even better buyer experience.

Affiliate Link Here: **http://share.designpickle.com/hGtgt** Design Pickle offers every member a share of new users, when you help them bring in new thrilled customers. By default you can earn a little $ with every referral that stays for 2 months.

Daily I am so thankful that someone shared Design Pickle with me, using their affiliate link, as this service has created loads of value beyond it's monthly cost, and saved me literally days and months of time, while also generating fresh custom designs by request, week after week. — After my first FULL YEAR using them, I pre-paid for another FULL YEAR. This is not something I would have done if I wasn't getting great value from the service! —

Penji (by: Johnathan Grzybowski)
Link Here: **https://penji.co**
$349 or $978 per month
Penji similar to Design Pickle is a full service subscription design service. Designs are available in the file format of your choice, anything from .psd to .ai, .pdf, .png etc. They offer real time communications with your designer, and typically produce 10 to 35 unique designs per month at the $349 level, meaning if you scaled say 4 variations per design, your costs would be around $2.50 per design. They are US based, located in Camdon, New Jersey and are dedicated to offering employment to the people in that area, so you know that by using Penji, you're helping build America. Penji also offers uses a unique custom SAAS back end system,

which makes revisions, or changes to an existing design quick and easy. Penji is also working towards a 7 days a week service, at the moment they are typically available 5 or 6 days a week. Current pricing here: https://penji.co/pricing/

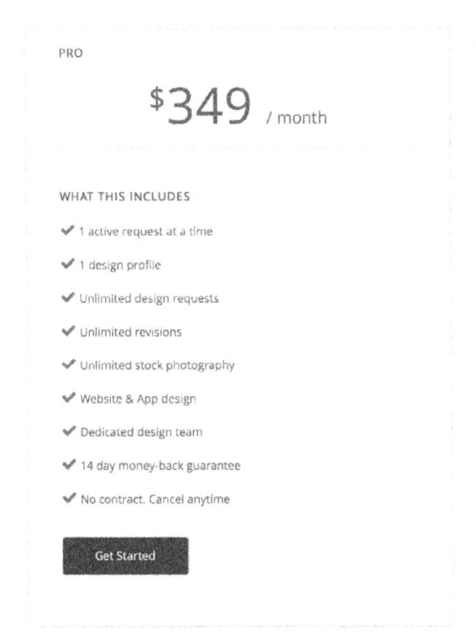

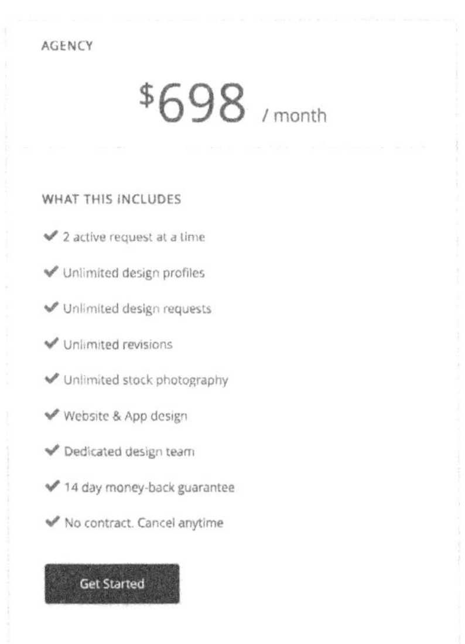

Flocksy:
Link Here: **https://flocksy.com/**
$349/mo, $549/mo or $749/mo

US based Unlimited design service. Like Design Pickle they give you the multiple file formats, including the source files. In addition to image designs, they offer copyrighting and e-mail template designs as well. Where Design pickle give you a 14 Day Risk Free trial period, Flocksy gives you a 7 day money back guarantee. Flocks also offers website and LOGO development/design as well, including Shopify and Wordpress. They offer 3 plans, the main difference being # of active designs per day at ONE ($349), TWO ($549), or THREE ($749) - monthly prices.
For more on each plan, and their pricing go here: https://flocksy.com/pricing/

Brand Strong:
Link Here: **http://brandstrong.co/**
Designers based in the UK, Philippines and Australia. Brand strong is a 4th unlimited design service option. unlike Flocksy above, Brand Strong DOES NOT DO website, email templates, coding or copywriting. However unlike Design Pickle above, Brand Strong DOES DO logos. It again has a different pricing model, and different price points, starting from $199(1 design per day - at a time) to $349(1 design a day-at a time- , with fewer limits on what can be made) to $599 (5 live job submissions at a time), all charged monthly. Designs have a 3 day turnaround window, and can be back quicker, depending on the designs. For more info on what each package includes, and specifics around pricing go here: http://brandstrong.co/pricing/

Merch Candy (by: Travis Renn)
DesignCandy.io
$19.99/mo subscription (or save by going annual $199/yr)
Join Here: https://goo.gl/uHnWza USE CODE: FP50NEW for 50% OFF COUPON
Design Candy (Formerly Merch Candy! [formerly 10x10 design]), provides custom high quality designs for POD's for only $10 each! You can join Merch Candy which allows you to choose from a wide collection of professionally crafted designs for use on Merch By Amazon AND/OR other additional POD sites. Once purchased, you obtain full rights to use the image as you like. Designs are only $10, so often just 1 or 2 sales will cover the cost, and everything else is gravy! PLUS, new this year they have implemented a buyer discount where every 10th design bought is FREE, so over many designs, the cost averages $9 per design. Sometimes they also offer up sales of designs for $5 each or $2 each which are open to all members. There is a monthly membership fee of $19.99USD per month, and this is designed as a deterrent to copycats, and tire kickers. Additional services include custom design requests, and key wording done for you. Check out the site for current pricing, and additional services. I have used Merch Candy, and had multiple sales on designs that I have bought from them. They're great for anyone starting out into the world of design outsourcing, and are a fantastic bridge between designing yourself, and fully outsourcing to an unlimited design service, or a low cost full time VA designer (which can often take some time and effort to find and figure out). Merch Candy makes design easy, and they have an ever growing roster of designs to choose from, so check them out. For everyone who bought this book, an **exclusive 50% OFF Coupon** has been negotiated when you use the code: **FP50NEW** and link provided: **https://goo.gl/uHnWza** , so check it out!

BONUS TIP: Travis also runs Merchlab.io, which is a handy search tool that allows you to do some deep research on Merch BY Amazon listings, as well as come up with new keywording, and do trademark checking, and more. Join Merchlab.io here: **https://goo.gl/L8cwGY**

Pre-Made Designs For You Merch Graphics Services:

2017 saw the rise of Merch specific design services. Here are a few that have been highly successful and have proven to deliver:

Mayo Designs (By Shawn Mayo)

Price: Packages vary from $29 to $229
Link Here: https://gumroad.com/shawnmayo
These designs are great, and they're pre-researched for hot selling niches. Looking for ready to load to Merch Designs, these are perfect. Packages typically include: The original (.psd or .ai) file, .png file (4500x5400 - to Merch specs), mock-up .jpg, .jpg file so you have everything ready to load immediately.

MerchReady Designs (By:Brendon Sullivan & Nate Mcallister)

Link Here: https://merchready.com/
Prices: Vary
Bulk Designs are available with or without Keywords, and Individual designs are available with keywords. Designs go live to the public every Wednesday, at 1pm EST and 10pm EST. Each design (both bulk or individual) will be available to ONE consumer. Once you purchase, your 4500×5400 pngs and keywords will be available for immediate download.

Merch Design Factory (By: Matt Carlett & Kyle Wright & Lesley Rich)

Price: $6-15/design, packages at multiple prices
Link here: https://merchdesignfactory.com/
Both Scaled and Individual designs are available, as well as holiday packages, with and without keywords. Individual designs also come in SuperPaks. Custom designs and Auto deliveries are also available upon request.

Merch Juice (By Jacob Bates)

Price: Packages and subscriptions at various prices
Link here: https://goo.gl/xk4Q5c

Designs are available in both Design packages, which have several designs, and prices range from around $130 to $250, depending on how many are included in the package. Monthly subscriptions simply take convenience to the next level, and send designs to your email monthly. Packages range from $350 to $950 per month, depending on what you would like in your package. Several options to choose from.

Merch Complete (by Phillip Stone)
Price: Various packages
Link here: https://goo.gl/PPh8Lk <— Use this link for 20% off
One of the newest Merch design services, Phillip is an experiences seller and graphics designer, so you get the advantage of both side with Merch Complete. Another unique feature of this service is that you get a free sample. This way, you have a good idea of how the service works, as well as the design style/level that you may be getting.

Managing design requests & received from your design teams:

Now that we have covered how to outsource your niches, key wording listings and design creating; you are ready upload your new custom designs to whichever POD platforms you are on. This process is simply to take the designs, and metadata associated with your designs (the titles, descriptions, keywords / tags, category, etc.), and upload them to the platforms you are using. Like any other part of the outsourcing ecosystem, you could do this yourself, but why not outsource this stage as well?

For this stage, I would recommend training your own VA team (Virtual Assistant team). While you could hire this out as well, the task is not difficult to train, and the skill level to upload existing images and metadata is not difficult to train or to do.

So how would you train your own VA?

1. **Find a VA to train:**
   There are many sites and places to find people who are willing to work at specific tasks for you.

One popular site is https://www.onlinejobs.ph (link to a detailed explanation of their process here: https://www.onlinejobs.ph/how/employer).
Another is upward.com (link to explain their process here: https://www.upwork.com/i/how-it-works/client/). There are even many others such as https://freeeup.com/ which gives you access to pre-trained VA's, which saves you the time of sourcing your VA, and gives you access to pre-interviewed, pre-qualified remote workers.

2. **Train your VA to upload to the POD's you are on:**
   You can do this either by recording some screen captures of you uploading to the PODs they will be using.

   Apple computers (Mac's) have quicktime built in (and FREE), which can be used to record your screen as you do anything on your computer. Here is a quick 4 minute video on how to find and use Quicktime to capture a video screen capture: https://youtu.be/m4s7YF7OEBY .

   Windows 10 has a secret video screen capture tool built in (for FREE), here's how to locate and use it on Windows: http://winsupersite.com/windows-10/how-use-windows-10s-screen-recording-utility

3. **Have your VA upload all your content, to all your PODs:**
   Now that you have trained your VA, take the plunge, and have them get started uploading your designs. Be sure to verify their work from time to time, as well as to treat them kindly, and ***pay them well***. A well trained VA is one of the keys to accelerating your business growth, and saving you time and energy doing activities you can outsource. The better you treat your remote workers (VA's), the happier they will be, and happy staff produce the best work for you over the long run.

Outsourcing - Marketing of your listings:

There are so many companies that have built their whole business around marketing other people's businesses. Many of them are terrific, and many of them are not (there are so many). You could also train your own VA to do marketing for you, or you could use a VA service like VA Rentals to provide you with a trained VA for marketing. You could even use a curated expert list, such as the one provided by Shopify, to locate connect and hire and outsource your marketing (Link Here: https://experts.shopify.com/search?q=marketing)

However, there is one employee that has blown me away, and I encourage everyone to use this one employee (yes, this employee is that good, and yes, everybody can hire this one same employee, it works 24/7 for everyone, all the time, and it's FREE).
Who is it? ... wrong question... the question is more of what is this employee...

KIT CRM (AI to do all your marketing for you!)
Link Here: https://apps.shopify.com/kit
It's Kit, by KitCRM. Kit is now free with a Shopify account (previously this service was up to $25 per month) and can connect directly into part of your business. Kit is a marketing bot. A computer. Like AI (Artificial Intelligence). Kit can analyze your inventory, and make recommendations on whom and where and what to market. Kit can also build your ads for you. Rich, engaging ads, on multiple platforms, including Facebook, Instagram and E-mail. Kit give you options. Kit runs reports for you on your marketing campaigns. Kit is fast, easy, and I have used Kit multiple times. Kit will send your clients followup e-mails, thank you emails, post updates to your business Facebook page for you. Kit is a certified Facebook manager, and you can talk to Kit via either SMS (text message), OR Facebook Messenger! WHAAATTTTT??? You can talk to a computer that does your marketing for you, on Facebook messenger? YES!

Oh... and one more game changer (maybe), Kit's not the only virtual assistant on Shopify (http://1.shopifytrack.com/aff_c?offer_id=2&aff_id=18920)... check out these gems on the Shopify app store, link here: https://apps.shopify.com/search/query?utf8=%E2%9C%93&q=virtual+assistants

PS: Chloe adds full voice assistant to your Shopify store... it's pretty insane.

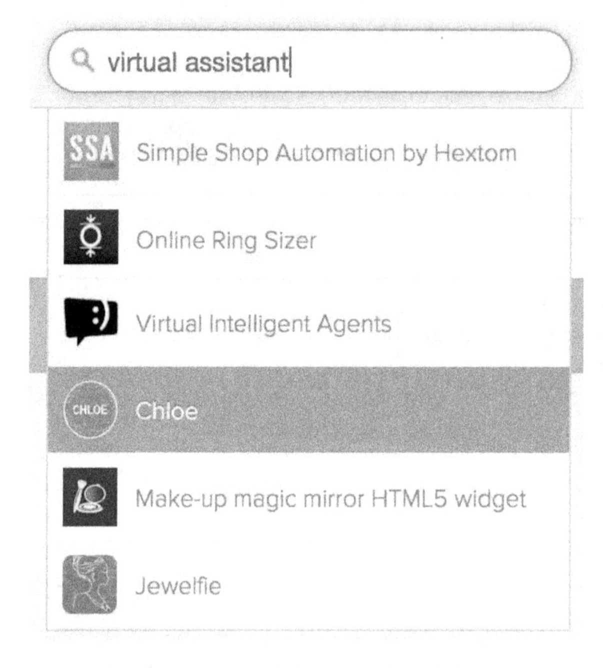

MORE INFO ON KIT:
Kit is an official Facebook Marketing Partner for small businesses. Kit is a fast and productive employee to add to your Shopify enabled website/ store. Kit is available 24 hours a day, 7 days a week. I'm using Kit currently, and Kit is AWESOME, best new hire ever! Remember, Kit is artificial intelligence (a computer, a bot)... so it does everything for you, when you want it, fully automated.

Kit once asked me if I wanted to run an ad campaign, I said yes (1), Kit asked me where (Facebook, email or Instagram), I said Facebook (1). Kit asked me about what I wanted to market, and for how much ad spend... I let Kit know...

Then **Kit BUILT AND PUBLISHED THE AD MARKETING CAMPAIGN ON FACEBOOK**!!!! OMG!!! It did this itself! It made up inviting copy, it grabbed the images, it built the ad, it found a market to push it to, it ran the ad marketing 100% by itself (no call, no email, no type what you want the ad to say, no load pictures, NOTHING ELSE....). Kits can simultaneously market multiple products for you across multiple channels, and it's fully automated. It's mind altering!!! Kit can even do multi-photo carousel ads, and video ads!

Even More about kit:
Lol... you thought that was everything about Kit... LOL... haha... nope! Kit can also do Facebook re-targeting, e-mail personalized customer

thank you notes, post to your Facebook business page, post updates about your store. Kit Pro can also plug into additional services for your store, like SEO, products discount campaigns, holiday promotions, retargeting abandoned carts, integrate customer reviews, and much much more!!!
Link for more kit Skills here: https://kitcrm.com/skills

Oh, and I made sales within 8 hours of Kit setting up my marketing on Facebook… awesome!!

1. Market products
2. Run business report
3. Update fans
4. Adjust Kit settings
5. Set a new goal

1

What would you like me to do, Jacob?
1. Run an ad on Facebook
2. Run an email marketing campaign
3. Run an ad on Instagram

1

What would you like me to market?
1. Priority products
2. New products
3. Recent best sellers
4. Slowest moving inventory
5. Showcase my store

1

Which of our priority products would you like me to advertise?
1. Easter Baby Birthday T Shirt

1

Easter Baby Birthday T-Shirt it is! How much marketing budget do I have to advertise this product on Facebook?
1. $10
2. $20
3. $30
4. $40
5. $50

2

Here's a preview of the ad www.kitcrm.com/a/a8lBRv0A. Can we publish this?
1. Yes
2. No

1

Great! The ad will be live on Facebook in a few minutes and will run for 2 days. I will keep you updated on how it performs. Can I do anything else for you?
1. Market products
2. Run business report
3. Update fans
4. Adjust Kit settings

	KIT BASIC	KIT PRO
Thank you emails to new customers	✓	✓
Thank you emails to repeat customers	✓	✓
Business reports	✓	✓
Facebook Ads	✓	✓
Multi-product Facebook ads (5 products)	✓	✓
Instagram Ads		✓
Instagram video ads		✓
Facebook posts	✓	✓
Email marketing campaigns	✓	✓
Premium email marketing templates		✓
Connect to other apps		✓

Straight from the kitcrm.com website:

- Kit will write the ad message, build the ad, choose the right audience, and recommend a budget for your Facebook ads.
- Kit will help keep your fans in the know by proposing Facebook updates for you to approve.
- Kit can market your store on Instagram with photo or video ads.
- Kit can build Facebook Dynamic Product Ads to retarget your store visitors.
- Kit will send personalized thank you emails to new customers. Turn new customers into repeat customers!
- Kit can send email marketing campaigns to your customers and showcase your newest or best selling products.
- Kit will help keep your fans in the know by proposing Facebook updates for you to approve.

END OF CHAPTER 7

Chapter 8: FAQ

Frequently Asked Questions: public questions and things your wonder yourself...

I've sold past my Tier level, When will I tier up?

Nobody knows. Based on when people report being tiered up, it appears that the tier ups come in waves (groups of people). So if you find someone that tiers up in the group before you do, then as you are qualified to tier up (you've made the qualifying number of sales for your current tier to tier up), you can sometimes know that you will tier up shortly after they do.
There is also a lot of chatter online about an 80% rule that essentially says that you must have at least 80% of your total maximum tier slots filled, before you qualify to move to the next tier. This has definitively been disproved for tiers 10-25-100. For tiers 500 and higher, it remains unknown, but may be possible. For example you may need 400+ live listings in Tier 500, before Merch By Amazon would tier you up to the 1000 tier level.

I've applied to Merch By Amazon, when will I be accepted?

Like the tier up question, there is no way to know, but since changes were made to the Merch By Amazon application process, the common timeline is somewhere between a few days and a few weeks. Previously it was roughly 3-6 months, and you may or may not receive an e-mail notification once you're accepted into the program. I recommend checking to login to Merch By Amazon once a week.

How big is this type of thing?

It's HUGE. For example, one company: Cafe Press, is a publicly traded on the NASDAQ (NASDAQ:PRSS), and currently has a market capitalization of around $31Million dollars. This is just one of the many Print On Demand companies. Redbubble has annual revenue sales of over $140 Million per year. Spreadshirt has annual revenue sales of over $100 Million per year, Zazzle has annual revenue sales of over $100+ Million per year. Etsy has even more! Between those 4 PODS (4 among more than 50+ out there), that's over $500,000,000 in sales EACH YEAR!

What about each item, how much can it make?

Well... it depends on how many sell... but to give you an example, the women's march that happened in Q1 2017, had one shirt for sale, on one website, which sold over $500,000 worth... from ONE SHIRT! Of course this is not typical, but it's true. A design that makes no sales makes $0, and many don't sell at all. However, many will sell, and it's not too uncommon to have a shirt sell 5-20 units a month (one one design),

multiply this by the royalties you earn on that design, say $5 (the amount varies, it could be more or less), and you have $25-$100 per month, for a single design! That's $300 - $1,200 a year... for ONE DESIGN. ... I'll go into more details about how things can start to add up...
Imagine 50 - 100 designs that are selling...
or 500...
or 5,000...
you see where this is going... ?

If you missed it, here's the math: 5,000 designs X 5 sales a month X12 months a year X $5 a sale =

<u>$1,500,000 PER YEAR</u> in sales!

SO MANY QUESTIONS!

How much does it cost to have access to all these millions of dollars of production equipment, thousands of products, warehousing, staff, and more? (hint: free. it's all free, it's insane).

- **What kind of stuff can I sell?**
- **I don't live in the USA, can I still sell?**
- **How much does the stuff cost to buyers?**
- **How do I tell people where to buy my stuff?**
- **How do I get paid?**
- **When do I get paid?**
- **What's the best place to sell on?**
- **Who else is doing this?**
- **Why haven't I heard about this before?**
- **Why isn't everyone doing this?**
- **Is this real? (hint: yes)**
- **What should I do?**
- **What should I not do?**
- **How do I connect with other people doing this?**
- **How much money do I make when someone buys my stuff?**
- **How much money can I make?**
- **How much money are other people making doing this?**
- **Wait... can you repeat that last one again... are you for real, really?**
- **Where are the people that do this?**
- **How long will it take to start making the money?**
- **Who can do this?**
- **Who can't do this?**

and more...

You now know places where you can upload your artwork to, and where people can buy your things (chapter 4), you've got lots of questions. Below I've created some questions that you may be thinking (WITH ANSWERS!).

SO MANY MORE QUESTIONS! AGAIN!

How much does it cost to have access to all these millions of dollars of production equipment, thousands of products, warehousing, staff, and more?

There's no $ cost to you. It's free and the great news is there's:
- No sign-up fee.
- No monthly fee.
- No out of pocket expense to you when people order your products.
- No annual fees.
- No surprise costs that pop up.

It's amazing!

What kind of stuff can I sell?

Depending on the POD Sites you choose, just about anything which can be printed upon. T-shirts, hoodies, mugs, pillows, clocks, phone cases, leggings, etc... The biggest market tends to be T-shirts, but here's a bigger list to give you some ideas, and help you know what you have access to, when people ask you if you can make them a XYZ.

T-Shirts:

Kinds: You have access to not just one kind, but ***SO MANY KINDS*** of T-shirts:

Sizes: Men, Ladies, Youth (that's kids shirts), Infants, etc. Each site has different variation in kinds and sizes. Most cover S,M,L,XL,2XL. Some sites also carry up to 3XL,4XL,5XL, even 6XL sizes!

Colors: Merch by Amazon (the largest marketplace by organic shopper volume, and likely sales) has 21 colors, which are:
Kelly Green, Asphalt, Black, Navy, Royal Blue, Cranberry, Slate, Lemon, Baby Blue, Silver, White, Brown, Red, Grass, Brown, Olive, Pink, Orange, Heather Blue, Heather Grey, Dark Heather.

Other sites have more or less Colors, such as tan, plum, maroon, hot pink, forest green... the list goes on and on.

NOTE: Some sites offer different colors depending on the type of shirt, or mens or women's. Some even let you set your own color by Web colors (actually called Hex values), from #000000 (BLACK), to #FFFFFF (WHITE), and everything in between!

Link to color selector value tool: http://www.w3schools.com/colors/colors_picker.asp

Types: Merch by Amazon currently offers 2 T-shirt types: Port & Co. and Bella+Canvas. Other sites offer even more types of T-Shirts: Hanes Tagless Tees, Premium Tees, American Apparel, Fruit of the Loom Tees, Relaxed Fit, Next Level, Royal Apparel, LA Apparel, Alternative, the list goes on and on!

Cuts: Some t-shirts are thicker, some are thinner. Regular cut, V-neck cut, long sleeve, sleeveless, you get the picture, there's a load of T-Shirt options.

TAKE SOME ACTION:

To get a better understanding of what each site offers in terms of products, and choices on it's products, I recommend checking out the ones you would like to sell on, and seeing what they offer, and the choices they each provide. https://www.alexa.com/siteinfo offers a website research tool that lets you see a website's ranking worldwide, and in top trafficked countries. I use it to see which sites have the most traffic. Traffic = buyers. The more buyers a site has, the more I want my designs loaded on it. Anything in the top 5,000 worldwide, is very very popular!

I don't live in the USA, can I still sell?

Yes, in most cases Print On Demand platforms will have various ways you can receive payments. From Paypal and Payoneer to direct deposit into your bank accounts. One common question is for how to receive payments from Merch By Amazon from countries where they do not offer direct deposit. Here is a simple service that allows you to have a bank account which is currently acceptable to Amazon: Payoneer

Payoneer

Link Here: https://goo.gl/qe5vj8 (affiliate link - gets you $100 FREE cash)
Using the link above, you will receive $100USD FREE MONEY from Payoneer, once you've setup you account, and received your first $1000USD in payment processing.

Payoneer has:
NO sign-up fee
NO monthly fees
NO annual fees

Payoneer can be used as a US domiciled bank account, for receiving payments for international seller on platforms like Shopify and Merch BY Amazon. Payoneer can also be used to make payments, and transfer funds to many sites and sources (excellent to pay or receive payments to or as a VA). Several PODs allow you to receive your payments to your Payoneer account (vs. Paypal). Another advantage of Payoneer is excellent international currency exchange rates. Often less than other methods. If you're doing high volumes of sales in other currencies, or want to convert back to your currency, Payoneer is a great choice. I have a payoneer account, and once it's set-up, it's easy to use. **Think of it like a no monthly fee US bank account.**

Trusted as a payments processor by many large, international companies, Payoneer is really worth taking a close look at to solve your international payments and exchange needs. For example, if you also get a payoneer card, you can withdraw funds from ATM's in countries and currencies worldwide, or transfer funds to your local bank account if that's what you prefer. Payoneer converts to over 150 currencies, in over 200+ countries. They have over 4 million users. There's no monthly fee, or sign

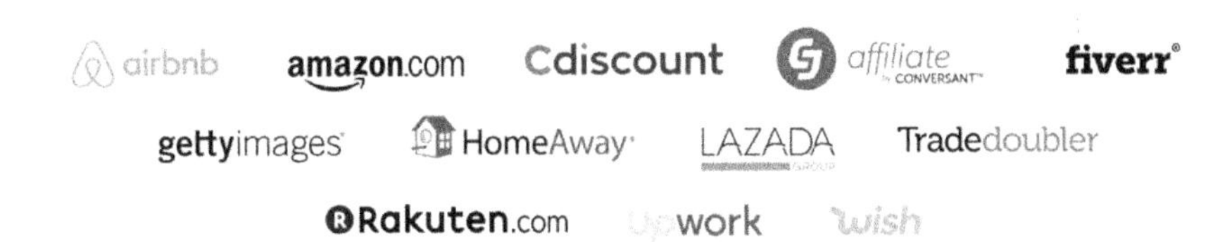

up fee. They only make money when you use the account, and their fees are very reasonable (better then many other banks, or other services).
"Do you need to pay your contractors, suppliers or service providers?
Use Payoneer's 'Make a Payment' service it's quick and completely FREE.
If you transfer $1,000 they receive $1,000 – simple as that!" ... great solution for paying your VA's (cheaper than Paypal, and they get 100% of what you send them, with no cost for the transfer to either of you!)

Join **Payoneer** for **FREE** here today: https://goo.gl/qe5vj8 - Not only is it free, but you'll receive $100 from them, once they've processed your first $1000, that's AMAZING value!

(THEY GIVE YOU FREE MONEY WHEN YOU USE THAT LINK!)

Payments with Payoneer:

RECEIVE PAYMENTS WITH PAYONEER

FROM ANOTHER PAYONEER CUSTOMER

Using our Make a Payment service, receiving payments from other Payoneer customers is always free.

USD | EUR | GBP | JPY

FREE

VIA RECEIVING ACCOUNTS

Using our Global Payment Service you will be given local receiving accounts in USD, EUR, GBP, JPY, CAD, AUD & CNY* - It's just like having local bank accounts in US, UK, Europe, Japan, Canada, Australia & China.

EUR | GBP | JPY | AUD | CAD| CNY*	USD
FREE	1%

DIRECTLY FROM YOUR CUSTOMERS

Using our Billing Service you can request a payment from My Account and get paid directly.

Credit Card (all currencies)	eCheck (USD)
3%	1%

VIA MARKETPLACES & NETWORKS

Receive funds from Wish, Fiverr, Upwork, Airbnb or any of the thousands of companies that pay via Payoneer.

Fees set by each marketplace or network may vary.
Please check their website for precise rates.

Note: Additional fees may be charged by your bank. Bank processing fees, landing fees, or intermediary fees may be deducted from the received amount by your bank or any other payment provider not directly associated with Payoneer.

Withdrawing funds is also super simple, and affordable with Payoneer:

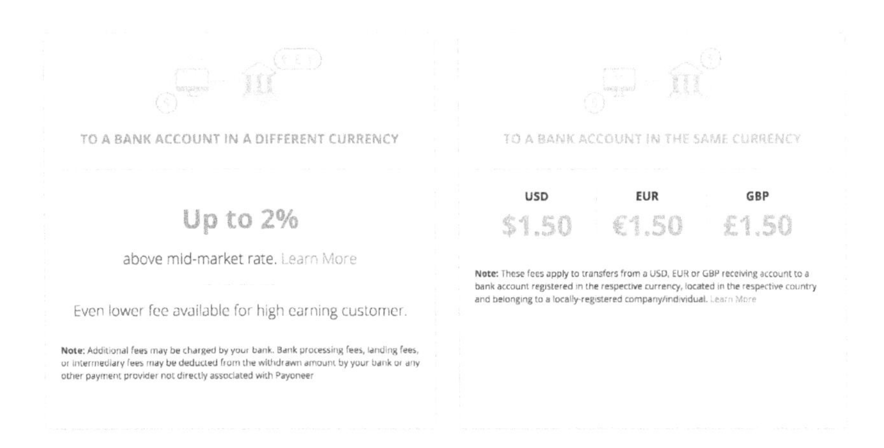

WITHDRAW FUNDS FROM YOUR PAYONEER ACCOUNT
With Payoneer you can easily withdraw funds to your local bank account in local currency at excellent rates, giving you more local currency for your hard work!
TO A BANK ACCOUNT IN A DIFFERENT CURRENCY
Up to 2%
above mid-market rate. Learn More
Even lower fee available for high earning customer.
Note: Additional fees may be charged by your bank. Bank processing fees, landing fees, or intermediary fees may be deducted from the withdrawn amount by your bank or any other payment provider not directly associated with Payoneer
TO A BANK ACCOUNT IN THE SAME CURRENCY
USD
$1.50
EUR
€1.50
GBP
£1.50
Note: These fees apply to transfers from a USD, EUR or GBP receiving account to a bank account registered in the respective currency, located in the respective country and belonging to a locally-registered company/individual. Learn More

What about buying things online with Payoneer?

Want to use your Payoneer account for online purchases? You can! They have a master card option as well! You can even use it to withdraw cash at ATM's, or via bank teller. It's a really neat tool to have if you like saving $, and want to reduce your payments fees, and get a great rate on exchange. Perfect for people living internationally, using Merch By Amazon, or any of the number of PODs and other Marketplaces.

Full Payoneer Fees outlines here: https://www.payoneer.com/fees/

Join for FREE here: https://goo.gl/qe5vj8

How much does the stuff cost to buyers?

As you might imagine, the prices are different for each POD site. Some include shipping, some do not. Some have fixed pricing (like Teepublic's $14 and $20 T-shirts), most let you set the price for your buyers, with a threshold minimum price, so that they always cover their cost of production and fulfillment. Generally speaking, in the US, the items will cost around the same as typical retail prices, often lower, sometimes higher, depending on what you're comparing them to (as retail pricing is also all over every price range). The lowest I've seen retail is $6 T-shirts, from you guessed it sixdollartshirts.com.

When buyers are shopping for graphic design shirts, I believe the order of importance is: Keywords (this helps them see what they're looking for, generally), then Design (they browse through the designs that come up from their shirt, and choose what they like. THEN price. Price is the last factor when buying shirts online. One exception is if a design is in a heavily saturated market, in which case pricing can play a larger factor.

How do I tell people where to buy my stuff?

This can happen so many ways. If you are wanting to share a specific shirt, you can go to the design you want to sell, on the site you want to sell, copy the URL, and send it to the person, or group. Some of the sites allow you to group your products, or to build full storefronts (Zazzle, Cafe Press, SunFrog, and many more). This can be helpful when you want to direct people to groups of related designs. OR direct different groups of people to different sets of designs.
NOTE: When sending SunFrog URL's, be sure it has your 4 digit ?XXXX code at the end of the URL. This is how you earn the affiliate portion of your sale.

You can also market your designs in a number of ways (see chapter 5), and you can get plenty of organic traffic from search engines (google, Yahoo, Bing, Duck Duck Go, etc.), as they index the words you use, and they will appear in search engine results (for more info, learn more about SEO - search engine optimization).

How do I get paid?

Like Many of the answers here, the answer is "it depends". Most of the sites will allow you to link your Paypal or Payoneer account email address (some need it to be verified first, others don't care). Some sites also allow you to get paid by direct deposit to your bank account, or by check in the mail. The payment setup will be in your account settings on almost every site. Payments becomes more important after you have sales, and those can take a while (or they could be the day you load your designs, you never can tell how they'll take off).

When do I get paid?
Again, it depends, but here's the most common ways of payments, and is different from POD to POD:

- On a fixed schedule, usually monthly
- On demand (aka when you request it)
- Once sales reach a certain amount (this is often tied to monthly payments, the payment is given once you cross a threshold, say $50 or $100).

What's the best place to sell on?
There's no best answer here, each POD service targets a different audience. Some are focused on youth, some on artistic design, some by price point, some focus on fast delivery... with one exception, you guessed it: AMAZON. Because Amazon is so huge, and they SEO so well, and have so many buyers, and they have so few Merch by Amazon sellers compared to buyers, you'll likely notice that your sales are highest there.

Prices are pretty low comparatively (even though you set the price), but... you can set the price as low as $12.88 (was $10.96) (this is great for ordering it to yourself, or people you know). Some sites are checked by people (Amazon, Spreadshirt, Designed By Humans), others are fully automated. TeeZily for example you can have shirts starting at $9, or even as low as $6 with volume.

Who else is doing this?
There are hundreds of thousands of other sellers across all the POD platforms. Of those, most are not on more than 3-4 platforms, and most are not very very active. There's a LOT of casual sellers. There are some hardcore full time sellers though - some sellers have paid designers, Virtual Assistants (VA's) for uploading, even software that helps them target likely to sell keywords, and niches! There's no true best way to tell how many designs the biggest sellers have online, or where they sell them the most, but I do know there are certainly several people in the 10,000+ Tier on Merch By Amazon, and a few have 18,000+ designs loaded! Some sites, like Redbubble have over 600,000 designers, 1/3 of them are actively selling. So there's plenty of people doing this. Just remember many do it part time, or as a hobby. Some people start, then later lose interest or move to other focuses, so don't be intimidated by the large numbers of other sellers. You can compete with them, and the market is not saturated, and continues to grow across multiple PODs. Let me repeat that THE MARKET FOR POD IS NOT SATURATED (it can seem that way with many sellers targeting specific niches, but one way to overcome this flooded situation, is to target less flooded niches).

Why haven't I heard about this before?

Well, in retail sales, there are all kinds of things that people don't know about. There are professional thrifters, coupon clippers, yard sale fans, auction addicts, wholesalers, retailers, distributors, liquidators, e-commerce empires of all kinds and sorts. The POD crowd of sellers is large and growing, but still relatively small, and not yet mature. This means you can expect many more sellers to come onto the internet each day, and more services trying to get a piece of the pie. For example, Merch By Amazon only started allowing 3rd party POD selling to non-app developers in September 30, 2015 (just over 2.5 years ago)... so the whole industry is changing, and quickly. Cafe Press, Redbubble and Zazzle have been around for a while. Printful is quickly growing with integrations into multiple other online platforms (like Shopify, or WooCommerce for example). Think of POD as one of the best kept secrets that people mostly haven't heard about yet.

Why isn't everyone doing this?

Similar to the answer above, lots of people have never heard about it. They don't know it's possible, or they've never looked into it. There are other reasons as well, some people try a few designs (1-10 for example), and when they don't see sales happening, they give up and quit. There's also people that grow the business huge, and sell their companies, and invest the proceeds elsewhere, such as real estate, for example.

Is this real?

YES! ITS REAL!

It's totally real, and legal, and happening. You've got multiple POD accounts setup already, right? if not, you should! With designs on them ready to be bought. It's really real. People really buy things online. The things really get made and delivered to real buyers. The best part, you really get money put into your account / mailbox or PayPal or even better your Payoneer account (mentioned above). In my first 3 months selling t-shirts, I made around $1,000USD. My wife was shocked, and wondered where all these sales were coming from! I just let her know that I put up things people liked, and when they bought them, I got paid. She said: "Think of all the people right now walking around wearing the shirts you made!"... True, it's amazing.

What should I do?

DO: upload lots of your designs. Making sales is generally a volume game. The more designs you have available, the more chances you have for someone to see your work, and buy your things.

DO: make quality designs / art. People browsing online will either be stumbling across your work, or they will be searching for it, or you will be marketing it to them... so make sure you put your best and greatest designs where people can find them.

What if you want to make more $?

DO: Invest some time into keyword research when you list a design. What is keyword research? Well, when someone searched for a shirt/pillow/whatever, they usually will either go to a site they like (like Amazon, or one of the POD sites they used before), or they might Google it, or ask a friend, who might give them some advice on where to find things. ... so make sure your listing keywords are helpful in those buyers to finding YOUR listings - among all the listing out there.

You can research what people are looking for in many ways, but here are a few: open up **Google Trends** (https://trends.google.com/trends/), and type in the things you want to compare, separated by a comma (this , that). Google Trends will show you a graph of relative search volume of one thing versus another, or a group of things.

Slowly type in what you think people will look for into the Google/Yahoo/Bing search bar. They all have suggestive ideas on what you are looking for, based on what other people are looking for, and your own search history. Amazon also has this predictive search, so take advantage of what Amazon suggests, and use those words also.

DO: Check if the words associated with your art or design or keywords or title or description or anything related to the listing are **trademarked**. You can check this by checking the words with the trademark office (USPTO link here: https://www.uspto.gov/). I use this site: http://www.trademarkia.com it's great. Avoid anything that had a registered trademark in the clothing category. Especially if it's registered in the item you're thinking of selling (like clothing, T-shirts, etc.).

For more info on IP, feel free to read the ***Digital Millennium Copyright Act*** ("DMCA" for short) located here: https://www.copyright.gov/legislation/dmca.pdf

If listing a design on multiple platforms (and you should!):
DO: Keep track of where your things are listed. I use a spreadsheet, some people keep a journal, some people have a database made or bought to track their designs... Whatever you use, *know where your listings are and what you have listed.*

DO: Keep track of payments and costs. You're hopefully making profit, so there will be taxes. Make a lot of profit, you get a lot of taxes. Knowing what you have spent, and what you have earned will be quite important come tax time.

DO: Read and understand the rules/regulations/agreements of whatever platform you are on. You don't want to break any rules.

What should I NOT do?

DO NOT: **I REPEAT, DO NOT EVER COPY other people's designs.** This can get you kicked off platforms, and have your accounts shut down. Beyond that, it can be illegal!

DO NOT: Try to keyword stuff a listing (like adding too many keywords for something, or that are way too general).

Keyword stuffing Example: "The best greatest bestest T-shirt for your mom dad grandfather son husband father brother niece nephew family member cousin's aunt uncle second cousin gift present idea design tshirt TShirt shirt T-Shirt".

You can use a few variations sprinkled throughout your title, listing, description, tags, etc... but don't go crazy with it. The sites will spot this, the search engines will see this, buyers will see this, and it will hurt you in the end.

DO NOT: Break the rules of whatever platform you use.

How do I connect with other people doing this?

Facebook is a great place. Type into the search bar Merch, or POD, or Print on Demand. There are plenty of great groups of people doing the same thing, and they're often willing to help, and bounce ideas off each other. Join the Facebook group I made for Merch by Amazon sellers, so ask questions, read the posts, and interact as much as you like there: facebook.com/groups/merchtopsellers/ . There's also conferences and trade shows. You can find these by searching online, or by seeing them as they come up in the Facebook groups. One group that is one of the biggest Merch by Amazon groups is called... wait for it... "Merch By Amazon", and it is lead by Ken Reil and Chris Green, who is an online marketing, and Amazon pro. The group is over 50,000 people. (SEE CHAPTER 6 for many additional resources for connecting with other POD sellers)

How much money do I make when someone buys my stuff?

This depends on how much you price your items for, and the platform they're listed on, and sometimes even how many you sell (some sites give you extra if you sell high volume of shirts). For Merch By Amazon: ***for a $19.99 listing, you'll make $5.38 royalty*** (previously $7.68, and before that it was once $9.89). That's currently a 26.9% royalty at the $19.99 price point. In the past it was 38.4%, and before that even higher.

Since each site is different. It's worth your time to find out how each pays you when a sale happens. There are no similar cases, it's best to check where you are listing.

Example: Sun Frog: you start at 5% artist commission, and 40% affiliate reward if you directed the traffic using your code, so you start off with the ability to make 45% if you make the listing, and bring in the traffic with your affiliate link. However even this can change... if you sell enough volume, the percentage's can go up! Neat right?

How much money could I make?

So much!

POD sites make $ when your things sell, so they want your items to sell as much as possible. Plus, since their expenses are covered with each sale, there's no limit to how much you could potentially make (except if they run out of stock). The more items you have, the more buyers could buy, and often do. When Amazon lets you in, and as you make more sales, they give you more room to upload more designs, called tiers. When you start the tiers will be: 10, 25, 100, 500,1000, 2000, 4000, 6000, 8000, and higher. Sometimes Merch By Amazon is frozen... When there is so much demand, they're having a hard time keeping up with it (they ran out of shirts in Q4 2016 and 2017, and they have only a limited number of machines to make so many shirts per day). However... they keep scaling up! More machines, bigger shirt orders, more sellers, more listing.... it's in GROWTH MODE. Here's how the tier ups normally work: as you sell the # of your tier, you move to the next tier. So sell 10 shirts, and you unlock tier 25. Sell 25, and you unlock tier 100. Sell 100, and you unlock tier 500, and so on. Some sellers have over 10,000 sales, and over 8,000 live designs!

I've not heard of any of the other platforms limiting the number of designs, or having tiers, so load as many as you like elsewhere.

How much money are other people making doing this?
I have talked to some On Demand sellers making over $100,000USD per month, after less than 5 years. Many sellers are making over $5,000/ month from just Merch By Amazon alone. Outside of Amazon, there are many full time businesses making and loading designs. I'm confident that several people make over $1,000,000in combined sales a year selling designs online, from multiple PODs.

The industry is HUGE, multi-BILLIONS huge!

The biggest limits to how much you can make are:
1: How many designs you can upload (that's when some people pay VA's to do their uploading full time, every day all day).

2: Making designs (to upload all these designs, you need to make the artwork/designs)... again, that's why people will outsource their design making to one or more designers.

3: Uploading things people like/want. Volume alone won't do it all... someone somewhere needs to want your things, and be able to find them.

Wait... can you repeat that last one again... are you for real, really?
Yes! Many many people make over $5,000/month selling Print On Demand, and some have had months of over $100,000USD. It's pretty crazy!

Where are the people that do this?
ALL OVER THE WORLD! Since the PODs that offer this are worldwide, and since payments can be sent via Payoneer, PayPal, or direct deposit, there are sellers worldwide. Most sellers are in the USA, the UK and elsewhere. Some sellers make so much $, that once their regular expenses and needs are easily paid for, they go "location independent", meaning they move to the beach somewhere they like. Popular places include Thailand and Central America.

How long will it take to start making the money?
It depends on how many things you upload for sale, how many people buy your things, and how you get your clients. It's very possible to get sales starting the same day you upload a design, but as a rule I think it's fair to give every design around 60 days before starting to wonder if it will sell. Some designs are seasonal (Halloween, Christmas, Holidays, etc.). Some are "evergreen" (birthdays, anniversaries, sports, job related, etc.).

It can seem like forever to make your first sale, but when you do, let me know. It'll be a GREAT feeling, and it's repeatable. Q4 (October-November-December) is BY FAR when most sales happen generally. Christmas shopping, Holiday shopping, etc. Some designs never sell, so if you have something that never makes any sales, don't let it get you down, it's normal. You are likely to get 80% of your sales from 20% or less of your designs.

Who can do this?
Just about anyone! Most of the sites will have an age limit in their terms of service, or agreements details, like must be age of majority, or must be able to enter the contract (16+)... it depends on the sites.

Who can't do this?
People that are not old enough to meet the terms of service for the platform they are on. Basically if you're over 18, you're mostly safe to start selling on most platforms. DON'T get your account terminated... that's how you can stop selling. DON'T follow the rules, you'll eventually get kicked off the site. As long as you play within the platform rules, load things you own, don't upload forbidden content, etc. you're safe.

People who will fail at doing this:
Anyone who does not take action will likely fail at this. Action is the great separator of this who do well in this business, and those who fail.

Technical details:

KINDS OF PRINT ON DEMAND PRINTING:

Sublimation:

This is where the design covers the entire item. Sublimation can also be applied in layers, to multiple materials, such as shirts, leggings, even mugs!

Heat Press:

Where the design is bonded to the material using heat and pressure. This is often done with Vinyl cutouts on t-shirts (vinyl heat press).

Digital / Direct To Garment (DTG):

The design is printed directly into/on the material. Special inks are used through special ink heads. These inks are designed to be absorbed into the t-shirt material, and can be setup as a continuous feed to the POD's DTG printers... meaning they can run continuously for long periods of time.

Digital Screen:

A base white is printed onto the material, then the rest of the design is printed onto that. Similar to DTG mentioned above.

Screen Printing / Silk Screening:

A design, is converted to a film, and the film is transferred through a screen. The film layer (emulsion) can be pre-done, or it can be made by the Screen printer as needed. typically these films, or dye's are cured via UV light, and once set, can be re-used or keep on file for later use. Here's a good video to show you one way to do it: https://www.youtube.com/watch?v=MDDE8VvViFo

Embroidery:

Thread is stitched through the garment/apparel. It creates a great feeling design, and it can add additional strength to those portions of the garment, since it is additional threads. Here's a quick video to see how this is done by machine (it can be done by hand, but as far as I know ZERO of the PODs do their embroidery by hand, LOL!): https://www.youtube.com/watch?v=9LUPCimY5rk The industrial machines used at several PODs can stitch over 700 stitches per minute! WOW!

FILES ACCEPTED:

Most sites will require designs with a transparent background, or capable of a transparent background, so .png is the industry standard file type, accepted everywhere.

In terms of file size and shapes, this varies from site to site, Merch By Amazon for example wants 4500px X 5400px 300DPI .png image file, under 25MB in size. More info from Merch By Amazon here: **https://merch.amazon.com/resource/201849250**

Other sites will ask for a range, like minimum 1000px X 1000px. Some offer a minimum DPI of 150 dpi. DPI is Dots Per Inch. Really each site is different, so check with each, or just try uploading... if your file doesn't meet the guidelines, then you'll usually get a message pop-up, or it won't upload.

Things you CAN control with POD:

- *Pricing* (usually)
- *Design Quality*
- *Volume* (how many and how often you add products, sometimes Amazon limits volume)
- *Traffic...* sort of... YOU CAN market traffic to your designs and listings on the POD sites you list with.
- Which POD site you wish to use, and which you chose to not use. Some you'll find are easier than others to use. Some of them may bring you more organic sales, while others bring you less organic sales. Each has and serves different markets, so choose what you want to focus on and what you want to avoid.

Things you have LESS CONTROL over with POD:

- *Base costs* on each site are usually set by the service
- *Types of products offered on a per site basis* (Merch By Amazon for example currently only offer T-Shirts, Hoodies, long Sleeve T-shirts, and sweatshirts, nothing else directly)
- *Quality of each site's work...* Each POD site will offer different quality (types of materials and technology used). If you want, you can always order you own things, to see what's being delivered to your clients.
- *Inventory levels.* Although rare, sometimes a POD will run out of inventory (they literally will use all their black large mens T-shirts, for example). Lucky for you, you can list on multiple POD site :-)

WHAT ARE SOME ALTERNATIVES TO POD?
(AND PROS AND CONS TO POD)

1: You can order finished shirts/other items, and hope to sell them.
PRO: The cost per unit can be less than POD.
CON: If they don't sell, you just poured a lot of money into finished products. Inventory can eat up your profits, and storage / warehousing costs can get expensive. Not recommended unless you have something with regular, constant sales.

2: You can do your own POD.
Buy the machines, space, etc, and make your own shirts.
PRO: Ongoing costs are super low! Blank T-shirts for example can be $2 or less, they can be very very inexpensive. You control the types of materials used, and you can control every aspect from timing to quality, location, and more.
CON: Can be very expensive to startup, or setup. Complicated: there are many things that would need to be done, which almost definitely means hiring staff, or working a LOT. Equipment can range from tens of thousands, to millions per machine. Although the per unit cost of the materials is lower, you need to have some of everything you plan to sell available, which can get very expensive; especially initially.

3: POD - Print On Demand
PRO: You can print as little as 1 unit, and you get to use the POD's equipment, staff, systems, website, warehousing, fulfillment services, shipping and manufacturing relationships products and more FOR FREE! Since the cost of the order is covered by each order, so there's no inventory to keep track of. You never run out (hopefully), you can control your profit margins with pricing (often). It runs while you do other things (like sleeping... YOU LITERALLY MAKE SALES IN YOUR SLEEP!!). Lets you focus on making great art and designs people will love.
CONS: You play within the rules of the POD sites you use. Costs to the buyer can be more than the alternatives. Some offer little organic traffic, so you may need to market your stuff so people know it's there.

Action Item:

Create and account at sunfrog.com and redbubble.com . They're both free, there's no monthly cost or anything, and it should take you just a few minutes to create those 2 accounts. Take action, get results. OR Take no action, get poor results. OR Pick from any of over 40+ PODs mentioned in Chapter 4.

Printful custom DESIGN services: (this is new in the last year)
Link Here: https://www.printful.com/design-services
Sign up for Printful here:
https://goo.gl/znYo6o (affiliate link)
Printful offers custom design services to assist you as needed. Not as cost effective as a monthly design service subscription, but it's a great way to get small jobs done in a hurry.

Word Counter:

Link Here: https://wordcounter.net/
With some of the POD platforms (like Sun Frog for example) having limited space allowed for either the description, or the tags, or other spots. I recommend bookmarking an online word counter.

When I load across multiple POD's I keep the word counter off to the side, and use it as and when needed. It's fast, accurate, and available online!

The Jacob Topping POD to EBAY maneuver...

POD -> Shopify - > amazon.com -> Joelister -> Ebay

Choose any POD that connects to Shopify.
Connect Shopify to Amazon using the shopify Amazon app
Once listed on Amazon (FBM), connect Joelister to Amazon
Push Amazon listings over to ebay.com, ebay.ca, ebay.uk

Link Here: https://www.joelister.com/
For a more info, also see this video example here: https://youtu.be/VT_FbchiAGo
Tiered plans starting at 2 listings for FREE! Paid plans range from $29/mo to $499/mo
How to designate Joelister to connect to your seller fulfilled (Merchant Fulfilled [MF]) Amazon listings: https://joelister.zendesk.com/hc/en-us/articles/205390927-Can-I-use-JoeLister-to-sell-my-MFN-Merchant-Fulfilled-aka-Seller-Fulfilled-items-

NOTE: Alternatively, you could also connect to Ebay from **Printful -> Shipstation -> Ebay** for as little at $9/mo (see sections on Shipstation in chapters 4 and 5).

Text only vs. Graphics on shirts?

One question that is asked all the time, as a new seller, which sells better, "text only designs", or graphic designs with images/pictures? To be honest, I believe that there is no set right answer here. You will find that both sell well. Most designs on most platforms are chalked full of text based designs, so there are certainly more of them. As far as selling ratio of text based designs to graphics based designs, there is no consistent winner in my opinion. Although, text based designs can often be made faster and more cheaply. That being said, I do subscribe to the belief that a design which combines both text and design will be more protected agains both copycats, as well as competitors. For some reason the added graphic adds a sense of added value, where as pure text only designs can be seen as "low hanging fruit" by those looking to re-make similar designs, which are not exactly pixel for pixel copies, but might as well be.

Regarding Copying:

DONT COPY! MAKE ORIGINAL DESIGNS! USE ORIGINAL IDEAS. The market rewards great content.

Can you setup PPC through the Amazon Marketplace via an ASIN connected to a POD?
YES!!!!!! I've done this, and it's great!!! Via Seller Central!

Can I add PPC to Merch By Amazon Listing?
... yes... through Vendor Central/Vendor express... also called Sponsored Listings, you can pay to have any ASIN on amazon.com boosted/marketed. You must be a vendor to Amazon to gain access to this madness. Sponsored Listings are managed via ams.amazon.com
NOTE: Amazon has announced it will be shutting down Vendor Central, and is no longer accepting new applicants into the program (March 21 2018).

PRICING STRATEGIES: (6+ strategies / approaches)

There are multiple theories on pricing strategies.

A few people have been asking me about POD and Merch by Amazon Pricing strategies... here are some things to ponder...

1: PRICE LOW

Price very low and move up incrementally... until you find a sweet spot you are comfortable with. **NOTE:** Starting with the low prices can put your listings at risk, as many buyers are not comfortable buying listings that are far below the average... it sends buyer red flags on quality among other things.

2: PRICE SPLIT

Price between the highest and lowest sellers of similar designs (split the avg.). Works well for Listings with a few competitors on the main niche terms.

3: MAXIMUM PROFIT

Price in a manner that maximizes your profit, without compromising sales. This will vary per listing, and must be evaluated on a regular basis, depending on competitors. Can be time consuming, but it's great for profitability when done right.

4: PRICE HIGH, THEN LOWER

Price high, and lower the price, as it will get you alerted on price drop sites, and can drive more traffic to your listings. This is a little risky depending on your starting price, however the deal finder site traffic can make up for it long term... the bigger the drops, the more external exposure you might get.

5: PRICE MUCH HIGHER
Price much higher than you would expect, and get picked up by bloggers, and Amazon affiliate sellers... this can make you a lot of $ if/when it gets picked up, and gets external traffic driven to your listings. Can stall some sales, and there's no guarantee that an external blogger, or affiliate marketer will pick up the listings... however, if you want to see insane $$ roll in on a single ASIN, this can work really well in Q4, when shoppers are looking to blogs and outside advice on what to buy. Get picked up by a big influencer, and you're about to make bank on that listing ;-)

6: PRICE BY NICHE
Price on a niche by niche basis, offering a price which is competitive in your niche. This allows you to maximize exposure among similar designs. This can be a bit time consuming at the start, but as you do it more, it gets easier. This is used by several Top Volume Sellers. Works best in higher tiers via Merch By Amazon.

7: PRICE LADDERING
List several similar designs in a focused niche at many incremental price points. For example: $12.99, $14.99, $16.99, $18.99, $19.99, $21.99. Wait to see what sells best, and adjust as you go. This will not only offer multiple price points which might appeal to different buyers, it is also a good way to list multiple designs in a niche, potentially giving you more opportunities for multiple keywords in each listing, and more ways of getting found when buyers are searching for this niche.

8: MORE
Other - This is Amazon folks... there's many ways to test, many ways to rationalize any pricing strategy. Many buyers, with multiple buying motivations, some are price sensitive, some are not. There's no 100% correct method on pricing that is always the best one. If there was, then everyone would be doing it, and it would quickly become the method for everyone, which would quickly make it become not the best method... Did I miss a pricing strategy? Guaranteed. Sellers are constantly testing new methods and techniques. I encourage everyone to always be running some side tests, and share the results. It's a great way to grow. For more pricing strategies, look around (I recommend this cool new website called Google, it lets you search for some things…), pricing has been a topic for thousands of years.

Say whatever you want about the above strategies. You may totally disagree. No problem. Everyone is welcome to their own pricing theories, or strategies.

I sincerely hope that everyone finds what pricing strategy makes them happy, and also makes them lots of sales :-)

SALE PRICING / COUPONS ON MERCH BY AMAZON? :

You *CAN* offer your shirts with any price (from $12.88 to $80.00, formerly $10.96-$49.99), and create a custom sale/special offer price using this setting on Merch By Amazon (use the "Sample - Direct link only" option near the end of the listing screens). The only catch is you need to send the buyers the link... Or put the special link anywhere you want online, and drive special pricing traffic to the listing.

Select availability of your t-shirt

Draft - Save progress

Sample - Direct link only

A product page will be created on Amazon.com. We'll send you the URL so you can purchase a sample. Anyone with this link will be able to purchase.

Sell - Public on Amazon

HOW DO YOU KNOW IF YOU'VE UPLOADED ENOUGH DESIGNS FOR A DAY?

The golden signal to look for that you've maxed out on the daily uploads:

products live and have reached the submission limit for the day.

HOW DO I KNOW WHEN MERCH BY AMAZON MAKES MAJOR CHANGES?

Merch By Amazon makes most of their major changes known via their *Messages* section on your Merch By Amazon dashboard. Here's an example post they made recently:

Messages

3/15

Due to the changing costs of printing, fulfillment, transportation, and customer service, we will be adjusting the Amazon costs of Merch by Amazon t-shirts from $9.31 to $9.80. To give you time to plan for these fee updates, starting April 17, 2017 we will begin updating costs on a rolling basis. Shirt pricing will be automatically updated to have at least a one cent royalty. To find out more please visit our royalty calculation page. Thank you for your continued support of Merch by Amazon.

I recommend always following any links they put in that *Messages* box. Merch By Amazon puts them there for us to read and follow.

What about Taxes?

PAY YOUR TAXES OWING!

Tax advice should be sought by your trusted tax professional, such as a CPA. Tax rules and regulations change (sometimes often), and are quite different from region to region, so any info regarding taxes is for general purposes only, and should not be considered in any way tax advice.

In the USA, you're likely going to want to file a form 1099. Depending on how much you sold, and which platform you sold it on, where to find it can be quite different.

Example: if you are receiving payments via Paypal, they will normally issue a Form 1099 if you're total sales volume is above $20,000, or 200 payments for goods or services. Refer to Paypal on how to access it here: https://www.paypal.com/us/selfhelp/article/How-do-I-find-my-1099-tax-statement-in-my-PayPal-account-FAQ919

TAX FORMS IN MERCH BY AMAZON

Form 1099 can be found by going to the section "My Account", then selecting Tax Information, then clicking "Update Tax Information", then in the section "Year-end tax forms (Formed 1099-k, 1099-MISC, 1042-S)" select the button "Find Forms". From there, you'll find your 1099, 1099-k, or 1042-S. In Canada for example, the 1042-S is used to claim the 30% withholding tax they've been keeping all year long ;-) You also have a few options on declaring this tax status when your are initially taking the Tax Survey on Merch By Amazon.

VAT Taxes on Print On Demand:
VAT Taxes or Value Added Tax is something you should be aware of. In Europe, they can seem quite complex. Essentially, countries within the European Union pay VAT taxes on all goods and services that are bought and manufactured there. Printful has made a wonderful video to help understand VAT better. I highly recommend you watch it here: https://youtu.be/uFEHGAgeqRE

More info on VAT Tax rates:
https://europa.eu/youreurope/business/vat-customs/buy-sell/vat-rates/index_en.htm

More info on VAT thresholds as of April 2017:
https://ec.europa.eu/taxation_customs/sites/taxation/files/resources/documents/taxation/vat/traders/vat_community/vat_in_ec_annexi.pdf

END OF CHAPTER 8

CHAPTER 9 - Conclusion

You're almost through the book reading part!

Well done for reading so much, it's a lot, I know, took over 1,000+ hours to put everything together.

Thank you, thank you, thank you! You are almost through the book, and I wanted to thank you for covering this much information. You've now got what you need to get started, take action, and increase your existing business to even greater success!

Now it's your turn to take some action!
Open some new POD accounts, load your designs and content to them, and bring new customers to YOUR original art and designs. Once they are available on all kinds of things (skateboards, hoodies, pillows, T-Shirts, etc.) in all kinds of places (over 50+ platforms listed in Chapter 4 & 5), the choices and combinations are AMAZING!!
Good luck with everything, and let me know how it's all coming along. I'm interested to know. Really! My actual contact info is listed next!!

CONTACT INFO:

If you have any questions in the meantime, shoot me an email at **podbook@themelonink.com** I can't guarantee a quick response, but I will read through them all as I can.

You can also call or text me at **613-883-0353** (it's a Canadian #, but it works worldwide)

OR

You can reach me on Facebook:
Merch By Amazon Top Sellers, For Newbies and Pros:
https://www.facebook.com/groups/merchtopsellers/
If you're a huge fan, you're also welcome to mail me things to my US Address:

The Melon Ink Multimedia Corp.
C/O Jacob Topping
Unit 28030
808 Commerce Park Drive
Ogdensburg, NY, 13669-2208
USA

END OF CHAPTER 9

CHAPTER 10 - Extras

COMING SOON: VERY SOON

MULTIPLE MULTI-POD Uploaders:

#1: The big secret Multi-POD uploader - That a handful of people are using now. In late March, or early April, we will be seeing the release of the first of ***MULTIPLE*** Multi-POD automated Bulk up-loaders. You may have heard about this one from a few select Influencers, as it is currently in operation.

I have seen this uploader live, at the time the uploader had listed over 20,000+ designs across 4 PODs. Since it hasn't yet been officially released, lets just say it will be one of the first of a few coming, and it just may start a race to MASS uploading. So get lots of designs made ASAP (I recommend Design Pickle, for more reasons than you may thing, more about this coming in future days). Once it is released, I'll share all the details with you guys.

*#2: **SURPRISE! There's a SECOND confirmed BULK Multi-POD uploader***

Singleupload.com

Single Upload is designed to be the one place you upload all of your designs so they can be distributed across multiple PODs. It's much faster and more efficient then uploading designs to each POD individually.

Created by the owner of Rapid Creator, (an invitation only Amazon POD integration that's been running for 3 years already) and a former VP from Cafepress. They know how inefficient and time consuming it can be to upload designs to each platform one at a time, so they built a solution to solve it.

By working directly with each platform, they've created official integrations. Meaning, your accounts are never put at risk using their system. Currently Single Upload is in beta testing in Q1 2018, its anticipated to launch in April 2018.

Initially it will include Etsy, Cafepress and Spreadshirt integrations and the goal is to add many more POD platforms, ensuring that each platform has significant additional traffic.

Some Unique Features of the System

1: USPTO database integration. When you upload your designs, they are cross checked against all USPTO records, and the system provides you with any potential matches before you confirm you want to upload the design. Plus the system will check your existing designs against any new Trademark applications daily, and alert you. So you'll have an opportunity to protest new applications before they get approved by the USPTO!
2: All designs are reviewed by Single Upload, prior to being uploaded to the platforms. The review process is built into the cost for the service. Because they have great knowledge of what is allowed on each platform, it helps keep your account safe,.by catching issues before designs are uploaded.
3: Bulk upload features with predefined default settings. Designs don't need to be uploaded one by one.
4: Create templated designs, with many variations in seconds and automatically they are uploaded everywhere. Imagine creating a design for 100 different dog breeds at once and they're automatically uploaded to multiple platforms on thousands of products.
5: Future improvements and additional platforms will be available to your existing package without additional cost.
6: Rapid Creator is the only platform that guarantees shipping times within Amazon's timeframes, and has the experience of doing this for the last 3 Christmas seasons. The same assurance will be provided for any platforms they are doing POD production for through Single Upload, starting with Etsy. Most products are printed at their facility in Elizabethtown, Kentucky.

NOTE: If you intend to upload any objectionable content, or want to bend the rules of intellectual property rights, they're not the platform for you, as your account will be banned. They don't want to waste time dealing with sellers that don't follow IP rules.

Join Single Upload through their Indiegogo campaign (Link to be pushed up when available, here:). There's a video there that explains the whole system, including a quick demonstration of some of the features. You can check it out at link here: . If you read this after their campaign has finished, you can still use the same link to join their waitlist. As soon as an opening becomes available they will get you in, first come first served. So, you should get on the waitlist ASAP.

I've been in talks with the developers of this one for a while, and I think it will be AMAZING! Once it's released, I'll also be able to share more specifics with you guys!

#3: Changes to Merch By Amazon: Coming soon, can't say what they are or when, but I've heard several of the plans, and they're awesome! Stay tuned for more!

#4: TeeSping's adding Asian mega sites [jd.com](jd.com), tmall.com , rakuten.com to the Boosted network. This has technically been teased, but it's not yet fully released. It's coming soon, and will open up your designs to HUNDREDS OF MILLIONS MORE BUYERS (once rolled out, this will reach more online buyers then ALL OF MERCH BY AMAZON, in fact, more online customers than all of the USA internet users combined). You may or may not have heard of these 3 sites, but they sell tens of BILLIONS of $USD worth of goods QUARTERLY across China and Japan.

#5: ** **** LAUNCH:*** (sorry guys, i'm not authorized to say it's name yet) This is a collaborative group of Merch and POD sellers that work together to learn and share. You can join ***** **** once it is launched (coming soon), and enjoy its content across multiple platforms: Youtube, Facebook, Instagram, Snapchat, Twitter, Periscope, Website, Blog, Pinterest and more. You're going to LOVE IT!

#6: Fully Automated Printful to Etsy lister (name not yet announced): Just like the name suggests, this will allow you to fully automate bulk listings into Printful, for use in Etsy. I've also seen this in live operation, and WOW, it's FAST! Can't wait to share the full details with everyone!

#7: TOP SECRET: Some NDA's are worded so well I can't mention this one, but THERE'S MORE to come, and you're going to LOVE it!!!!!!!!

Place It:
Place your design on a lifestyle image or VIDEO! Choose from over 2500+ images! Choose from: male, female, groups, multiple settings, and situations. Sports, countryside, city, gym, you name it they just might have it. Great for use on social media ads!

Place it plans run monthly, for as little as $29/month for 9 images/month, to as much as $199/month for unlimited videos (a great deal for those who plan on marketing a lot, as high quality videos like these could run you more than that price for each professional shoot, with models, editing, lighting, etc. Videos are silent, so consider pairing them with sound if you plan on marketing on YouTube, or silent if you'd prefer them as a passive motion eye catcher. Your choice!

Affiliate link: https://placeit.refersion.com/c/9074f
(available through their affiliate program, upon special approval process to select providers)

Example: You choose the image, and custom shirt color, with your design on it!

Place It Plan pricing (below)
Some of the Place It tags and objects/types (above/left side)

PlaceIt's Plans:

AFFILIATE LINKS:

How to Pay for the cost of this book, and earn money by helping promote it to others:

Enjoyed this book? Let others know, and when you use your affiliate link, you can earn a commission on every sale, just for helping promote the book. :-)

For more info on how to become an affiliate of this book,
contact me, Jacob Topping by E-mail at: podbook@themeloninlk.com of by **Facebook Messenger at Jacob Topping**.

How does an affiliate link work?

An affiliate link is a way for people to connect others, with great content that they use and love. When an affiliate shares their link with others, any sales from buyers clicking that link are attributed to the affiliate. In this way, when people buy the products that the affiliate uses and loves, the affiliate makes a % of the amounts paid for the item. **This does increase the price for people who bought the item**, and sometimes it even gives them some extra time to try out a product or service, before they committed to their purchase. In fact CODES and affiliate links can also sometimes SAVE buyers $$, by offering the products at a discounted price for people that receive the affiliate link. It's a TRIPLE WIN.

TRIPLE WIN BREAKDOWN:

WIN ONE: The Buyer of the end product **WINS** by getting access to something they will love. Plus sometimes at an even lower price than may be available elsewhere.
WIN TWO: The Affiliate WINS by building trust with the people they know by offering only items that they themselves enjoy. They also **WIN** by earning a small income, for simply connecting the people they know, to the things those people will love.
WIN THREE: The Creator of the product or service **WINS** as it allows them to reach more people with the product or service they have worked very hard to make.

Is being an affiliate hard? Does it take hours of training and courses?

No, it's easy. Becoming an affiliate does not take any special skills, or training. If you have a Print On Demand account with SunFrog for example, then you're already an affiliate with Sun Frog, it's built into their account, and it allows you to earn an extra 40%+ in affiliate commission, just for marketing your designs (or other even people's designs). Shoppers benefit from learning about great products on SunFrog they wouldn't have otherwise known about. Affiliate (you), earn 40% of the revenue from the transaction, when a buyer buys the item on SunFrog that you sent them to with your affiliate link. The Artist (you or someone else) wins by earning extra $ from buyers that would not have otherwise seen their listings! It's a WIN WIN WIN. Everybody wins!

To show your support this book, and help fund updates and future books like this, please feel free to click and use the affiliate links found throughout this book.
Thank YOU! I love you long time! - Jacob Topping (author)

END OF CHAPTER 10

CHAPTER 11 - GLOSSARY

What does that mean, whaaa?

A

AI: Artificial intelligence - a computer uses reasoning to make decisions about things. Kit is a good example, and can be used to run your marketing. See Chapter 8.

Affiliate / Affiliate link: An affiliate link is a way for people to connect the people they know, with great content that they use and love. When an affiliate shares their link with the people they know, any sales from buyers clicking that link are attributed to the affiliate. In this way, when people buy the products that the affiliate uses and loves, the affiliate makes a % of the amounts paid for the item. This does not change the price for people who bought the item, and sometimes it even gives them some extra time to try out a product or service, before they committed to their purchase. It's a TRIPLE WIN. For Example: the Sun Frog Print On Demand platform provides every artist with a 4 digit affiliate code, which will be preceded with a '?' (?XXXX). If you sell on SunFrog, you're already an affiliate! See Chapter 10.

ASIN: Amazon **S**tandard **I**dentification Number - this number is normally 10 characters long and made up of either letters or numbers (alphanumeric). It is a way to uniquely identify products associated with Amazon, and partner organizations.

All Over Print: Also known as sublimation, or dye sublimation, is an all over print which allows for edge to edge printing, as opposed to just a small rectangle portion on the front or back of the shirt. These types of shirts are a little bit more rare in the world of POD, and this could be a good thing, if you can offer such interesting and unique designs!

B

C

D

DTG: Direct **T**o **G**arment - this is when a specialized inkjet printhead is used to print designs and images onto garments/ apparel directly. Specialized inks used for DTG are designed to be absorbed into the garment. DTG offers manufacturers high quality, quick and accurate setup, and continuous operations, due to the ink medium used. DTG can use used at various resolutions, and is the preferred method for manufacturing designs containing detailed images, such as pictures. For other images with less colors, other technologies may be preferred, such as screening, or vinyl heat press, or other methods. Some DTG machine manufacturers have interchangeable parts, while others use proprietary machine parts. Merch By Amazon is known to use Kornit DTG printers, and has increased their order volume to this Israeli company (aka, Amazon is buying LOTS MORE PRINTERS - YAY!). This is especially interesting, as Kornit brand DTG printers, are capable of printing on ***more than just clothes***. They can be setup to Print On Demand to multiple materials. More info about Kornit is available on their website, link here: http://www.kornit.com/

Deboss: Debossing uses a metal-engraved die along with pressure, temperature, and time to stamp into fabric a design mark that will not fade or wash away. It is an extremely rich look on fabrics and a nice alternative to traditional decorating techniques. It works well on cotton, polyester, leather, pleather, fleece, and polar fleece fabrics. Here's a quick video showing how it works: https://youtu.be/M1x4oVOijeY

E

Embroidery: Embroidery is when a needle and thread is used to create the design on a shirt (as opposed to printed on, soaked, heat press, silk screened, or other processes of applying the design to the garment). Because thread is being added to the garment, it has texture you can feel, and creates a unique, and durable look. Embroidery is generally viewed as a more premium technique, compared to other methods. Often seen on things like hats or caps, embroidery could be applied to any material which a needle and thread could penetrate. If you have never seen or felt something made with embroidery, you should check it out. Offered by some, but not all POD's, for example CustomCat, Printful and Zazzle all offer embroidery.

F

G

H

HXD: HXD is an apparel decoration technique which allows you to choose from multiple types of finishes (including metallic effects like silver, gold, brushed metal, carbon fiber, chrome, metal plate, etc), as well as multiple colors, and an assortment of 3D heights. Here's a quick video that show you more about the process, and options: https://www.youtube.com/watch?v=eu9tbwpJXmk

I

J

K

Keywords: Keywords are words that people use to find your products. *Example:* if you're looking for a T-shirt for your Mom, who loves cats, when you search for that shirt on Google, or Amazon, or elsewhere, you might type into the search fields something like: "Cat T-shirt for Mom". The search algorithm of the platform you've used to search for the t-shirt will then attempt to provide you with relevant results. It will match your search with content it thinks match what you are looking for. As a seller, you'll want to be sure that your listings contain words that will match your items with keywords that people might use to find your item. In this example, your listing might be shown to the potential buyer, if you had the words: cat, T-shirt, and Mom in your listing, or some or parts of those.

L

Laser/Laser Etching: Laser etching is a decorating process that burns a pattern into the top layer of fabric, giving it a subtle tone-on-tone appearance. The image the etching creates has an upscale look that is usually the same color but several shades darker than the original fabric's color. It works well with both big or small logos.

M

MF - Merchant Fulfilled: This term is usually associated with Amazon listing. Also known as FBM (Fulfilled By Merchant), it means that when the buyer buys the item on Amazon, the seller (also called the Merchant), will fulfil the order (aka, the seller ships the item to the buyer). This is opposed to FBA (Fulfilled By Amazon), in which Amazon will fulfill the order (aka, the item is in Amazon's warehouse, and they will pick it off the shelf, pack it, and send it to the buyer).

MBA - Merch By Amazon

N

O

P

POD - Print On Demand: The term used to describe things that are made at the time of order. In other words, blank products are available and waiting, until a customer places an order for that item, with a specific design. At that time, the design is applied or "printed" on the product, and the service or platform which does this usually will deliver the newly made product to the customer who ordered it.

Q

R

S

Sublimation: Also known as an all-over-shirt, sublimation allows for edge to edge printing, as opposed to just a small rectangle portion on the front or back of the shirt. Closely related to Cut-And-Sew, which uses sublimation to apply designs to the fabric directly, which is then cut to the pattern of the shirt shape, and sewn together to make the shirt. Sublimation is considered to be a more premium method than DTG or Screening. Cut-And Sew is another level up from there - super-premium.

T

Tryptychs: Three images which together form a single larger image, or set of images. Available on Zazzle, and elsewhere. AWESOME!

Thermal Mugs: These are color changing mugs, which start out black when cold, then the black fades as the mug is heated, revealing the beautiful design underneath, against a hot white background. Also referred to as a Color Changing Mug. Available via Gearbubble, Zazzle and several other PODs.

U

V

VA: Virtual Assistant - Someone that you can hire to do work for you remotely. For example, they could do keyword research, make designs, or even upload designs to multiple platforms. They are remote, and can work while you do other things, this allows you to multiply how much you can do in the same period of time. Since their work is location independent of where you are, many people will hire Virtual Assistants in areas where labour costs may be lower then their local area, for example popular locations for VA's are - the Philippines, Bangladesh, Eastern Europe. Virtual Assistants should be treated just like your local staff - very well! They're often as skilled or more skilled than you are - another great bonus!

W

X

Y

Z

About The Author:

Jacob Topping is a husband to Tara Topping and father of 3 young kids (Jono, Oliver and Alexis). Jacob lives in a small countryside village about an hour west of Ottawa, Ontario (Canada's capital city).

At the time of publication, Jacob recently worked as a private contractor for the Canadian Federal Government doing the secret things, as well as part time on many other projects ranging from this book, selling via Merch by Amazon, multiple other POD platforms online (20+), Amazon FBA (.com AND .ca), custom software development of mobile apps for smartphones and tablets, as well as web.

Jacob's prior activities include: financial planner, financial advisor (including stock broker), licensed mortgage broker, licensed insurance agent, licensed travel agent, English teacher, and more! Jacob loves travel, and has enjoyed either travel to, or living at the following: Across Canada (every province coast to coast, even up north in the Yukon and North West Territories) and the United States of America (most states, including Alaska, Hawaii, east coast and west coast), South Korea, Japan, China, Hong Kong, India, even Mexico.

A big believer in continuous education, Jacob holds a 4yr BA Degree in Economics, and a Minor in Business from Carleton University, and has achieved several professional designations including the following: CSC, PFPC, CFP1, Senior Advisor, LLqP, ACTRA, OSSAD, and others.

Jacob enjoys the outdoors, including camping, cycling, walks in park forests and beaches, swimming, baking, lego, and gardening.

If you spot Jacob at an event or conference, be sure to strike up a conversation, as there's lots of interesting things about Jacob to discover beyond everything here.

About the Editors:
A wide group of people helped in the editing of this book, and without their hard efforts, guidance and support, the book would not be what it is today. I wanted to especially thank my Wife Tara Topping, and Stephen Harrison, who ***each*** put in over 60+ hours reviewing and providing feedback, and adjustments. There will likely be some additional tweaks and changes rollout out shortly, as we prepare the printed copy of this book. I really appreciate all the feedback we have received so far, and hope to make adjustments to the book asap.

Here's a picture of the editors working at a feverish pace for over 12 hours (at the initial launch of the book in March 6 2017), to push out a better quality book (version 1 of 5) for everyone to enjoy! THANKS GUYS!

CPSIA information can be obtained
at www.ICGtesting.com
Printed in the USA
LVHW102353161218
600699LV00010B/824/P

9 781986 702614